Eastern Band Cherokee Women

To Roxanne,
with much gratitude.
for all you're doing here.'

Jenny

Eastern Band Cherokee Women

Cultural Persistence in Their Letters and Speeches

Virginia Moore Carney

The University of Tennessee Press / Knoxville

A version of chapter 1, "Mothers of Men," was published in a collection edited by Barbara Mann entitled *Native American Speakers of the Eastern Woodlands* (Westport, CT: Greenwood, 2001).

Library of Congress Cataloging-in-Publication Data

Carney, Virginia Moore, 1941–
    Eastern Band Cherokee women : cultural persistence in their
    letters and speeches / Virginia Moore Carney.— 1st ed.
        p. cm.
    Includes bibliographical references and index.
    ISBN 1-57233-332-4 (hardcover : alk. paper)
    1. Cherokee women—Correspondence.
    2. Cherokee women—History.
    3. Speeches, addresses, etc., Cherokee.
    4. Eastern Band of Cherokee Indians—History.
    I. Title.
    E99.C5C224 2005
    305.48'897557075695—dc22   2004024529

Contents

Illustrations

Tribal Council House, Cherokee, North
Carolina. Photo by the author.

Preface

My interest in this project began several years ago when I read a letter that had been written by a Cherokee schoolgirl in 1838. If Jane Bushyhead's letter had survived, I reasoned, the letters of other nineteenth-century Cherokees must exist also. Eagerly, I searched through Cherokee history books, hoping to learn Indian perspectives on the history of the southeastern United States. Eventually, I did find several letters, speeches, and newspaper articles written by Cherokee leaders—all of them *male*. As a child, I had heard stories from my aunts about Cherokee women who had such a need to write that they penciled poetry on weathered kitchen walls, kept diaries on scraps of paper hidden away in the family Bible, or stitched "little stories" together and stashed them away in trunks and attics—silently waiting to be discovered. What would those words tell us, I wondered, of the world in which my ancestors lived?

Aurora Morales has written that "tracing absences can balance a picture, even when you are unable to fill in the blanks. Lack of evidence doesn't mean you can't name and describe what is missing" (7). Scholarly works, however, demand evidence. This study is the result of my "tracing absences" of Eastern Band Cherokee females in the written history of the United States and attempting to fill in some of the blanks of that record. The completed "blanks," in this case, are the words of Cherokee women, long neglected and silenced on the pages of history—words that can teach us much about the joys and sorrows of being an Eastern Band Cherokee woman during the past two hundred years.

As Creek scholar Craig Womack points out, many Native students value knowledge in relation to the degree it makes a return to their own people possible. One question Native writers must ask, according to Womack, is, "[If we take] up the hypertheoretical jargon of postmodern theory, will we limit our audience to a handful of academics, effectively cutting ourselves off from Native people?" (205). Writing a scholarly work, adds Womack, becomes "a process of spiritual warfare wherein the writer must decide the purpose of that writing because she or he is writing for the survival of a community of people" (206). From the beginning, I have wanted this work to be one that is easily accessible to those outside academia—especially to many of the descendants of the Cherokee women whose letters and speeches have made this project possible. Numerous books and articles about Eastern Band Cherokees have been published, many of them well written and informative; historically, however, very few authors have used Cherokee informants or included Indian voices—especially those of women—in their studies. Not surprisingly, more and more American Indians are unwilling to read works written about them by authors who have never consulted tribal people for information. Many of the secondary works cited in this study, therefore, are by serious Native scholars who have maintained ties with their own people.

Also, I have aspired to reach a scholarly community of researchers, educators, and students who have a particular interest in American Indian Studies. In the words of Maori theorist Linda Tuhiwai Smith, "One of the many criticisms that gets levelled at indigenous intellectuals or activists is that our Western education precludes us from writing or speaking from a 'real' and authentic indigenous position. Of course, those who do speak from a more 'traditional' indigenous point of view are criticized because they do not make sense" (13–14). By including a variety of letters, diary excerpts, and speeches of Eastern Band Cherokee women—most of them products of Western educational systems, as well as participants in their own cultural traditions—I have sought to construct a more creative and well-rounded interpretation of their history and culture. At the same time, I have found the critical theories of numerous non-Native scholars useful in understanding the complex history of racial and cultural interactions in North America. One of my goals, therefore, has been to interweave Western and indigenous knowledge in ways that would foster an appreciation among readers for both styles of thinking and writing. Within the past decade, university professors in countries as diverse as Australia, Ghana, Hong Kong, and the United States have begun challenging Eurocentric education and are attempting to infuse Western curriculums with what they call "indigenous knowledge." According to Peruvian anthropologist Mahia Maurial, indigenous knowledge has three bases:

1. Indigenous knowledge is *local.*
2. Indigenous knowledge is *holistic.*
3. Indigenous knowledge is *agrapha.* (Semali and Kincheloe 63)

By *"local"* Maurial refers to knowledge that is derived from being immersed in one's culture—a knowledge that is re-created through generations of storytelling, working with the land, and keeping alive certain tribal traditions. Although the use of oral history (local knowledge) as source material is a sensitive issue in scholarly circles, I have chosen to include, for instance, Jack Hilderbrand's childhood recollection of the death of his great-grandmother, Nancy Ward. "Many historians and anthropologists," says Devon Mihesuah, "argue that Indians cannot accurately recount their past using oral traditions. They refuse to use informants, believing modern Indians' versions of their tribes' histories are 'fantasies.'" As Mihesuah hastens to point out, however, not all written records are reliable, either. "Are not the writings of some army officers, missionaries, explorers, and pioneers who encountered Indians exaggerated and biased?" she asks (2). Hilderbrand's memory may not produce an exact picture of Nanye'hi's death, but neither might the written report of a non-Native observer.

Not only is indigenous knowledge local, it is also *holistic*. Theory and practice are one. There is no division among "disciplines of knowledge." In this work, I have attempted to interweave ideas from the fields of anthropology and history and political science, music and literature and art, and psychology, social theory, and medicine—an approach that has at times proved daunting. Furthermore, I frequently invoke stories from the past to shed light on contemporary lives (and vice versa), for I agree with Okanagan elder John Kruger: "What [a] story does is speak in the *present* and bring the *past* forward, so we can have a *future*" (Awiakta 208). My greatest challenge, of course, has been in attempting to produce a work that will merit both tribal acceptance and academic accreditation.

A third basis of indigenous knowledge, according to Maurial, is that it is *agrapha,* not written down. In other words, indigenous knowledge is basically transmitted through oral tradition, not through the printed page. It suggests ways of knowing that cannot be documented in parenthetical citations or in bibliographic reference. Unlike Western knowledge, it cannot be found in archives, nor in laboratories. Because of my own childhood/adolescent experiences with missionary teachers and various letter-writing projects, for example, I understand something of the double bind the Cherokee girls at Brainerd Mission experienced: Their people had to be portrayed as helplessly pagan and uneducated if they were to receive educational assistance from their "friends at the North"; at the same time, the girls were compelled to emphasize the "civilized" status of the Cherokees in order to show that they were deserving of such support. Occasionally, therefore, my evaluation of a letter or a speech may seem more intuitive than scientific. This analytical strategy is based on prior knowledge, or what social scientists call "situated cognition," and is supported by numerous scholars as a key factor in interpreting data.[1]

In addition to indigenous knowledge, the role of storytelling in Indian culture cannot be overemphasized. Gerald Vizenor (Ojibwe) notes that "Native American Indian identities are created in stories, and . . . tribal consciousness would be a minimal existence without active choices, the choices that are heard in stories and mediated in names" (56). To be a storyteller, in other words, is to play a role in sustaining one's community, and according to Jace Weaver (Cherokee), "the single thing that most defines Indian literatures relates to this sense of community and commitment to it." It is what Weaver terms *communitism*—a combination of the words "community" and "activism" (*That the People* 43).

Because much of the women's discourse in this study falls under the rubric of storytelling, I often resort to metanarrative techniques in my discussion of these stories. Noting that writers engaged in ethnographic work are attempting to mediate between storytelling and information, Bonnie Sunstein declares:

> We need to become more like storytellers, artisans engaged in the preservation of informants' voices and narratives—spoken and written. And our academic emphasis on convention must be tempered by a greater attention to craftsmanship, to the rhetorical and aesthetic principles that protect the power and cohesion of people's stories. (179)

There is a growing trend among scholars—both Native and non-Native and representing a diversity of academic disciplines—to employ storytelling techniques in their books and dissertations, especially those dealing with boarding schools, American Indian literature, and epistolary practices. In fact, many of the secondary sources to which I have referred in this work have effectively combined academic discourse with personal narrative, anecdotal evidence, and humorous stories: David Wallace Adams, Genevieve Bell, Jon Brudvig, Brenda Child, Ann Ruggles Gere, K. Tsianina Lomawaima, Lucille Schultz, and Craig Womack, to name just a few.

The history of American Indians has been one characterized by struggle, and as Robert Warrior, Jace Weaver, Craig Womack, and other

Native scholars have pointed out, writing has become an essential means of resisting colonization and celebrating what Warrior calls "the fragile miracle of survival" (125). The critical writings of senior American Indian scholars Vine Deloria Jr., Elizabeth Cook-Lynn, and Carter Revard, as well as those of younger Indian scholars like Joanne DiNova, Daniel Justice, and Craig Womack, have greatly influenced my own thinking in this project.

Non-Native critics, too, have contributed much to my understanding of the discourse of Eastern Band Cherokee women. One of the most highly respected "pioneers" of American Indian Studies is A. LaVonne Brown Ruoff, who is, in the words of Gerald Vizenor, an " undeniable leader of serious research and education in tribal literatures" and one of the "most admired historical interpreters of contemporary novels and poetry" (91). Although Ruoff has not written specifically about Cherokee women, her helpful comments and suggestions have enabled me to focus my arguments more clearly and have greatly strengthened my work.

An eclectic group of scholars from outside the discipline of "literature" have written about Cherokees, and I have found that work indispensable as I have attempted to demonstrate cultural persistence in the discourse of Eastern Band females. To my knowledge, however, no previous study has been made of these letters and speeches; hence, I have attempted to utilize the theories and principles of numerous literary scholars (including several African American writers) in my descriptive analysis of the works included here. Sometimes I have disagreed with an author's stance; occasionally, I have found a writer's attitude toward Indians to be wholly offensive. In such cases, I have striven to support my own arguments and/or defense of American Indians with persuasive documentation, without showing disrespect for the viewpoints of others.

Research for this project has involved many months of studying old documents, trying to decipher barely legible letters on microfilm and pieces of age-brittled paper, contacting archivists and curators for obscure bits of history/biography, visiting places mentioned by Cherokee females in nineteenth-century letters, interviewing living Eastern Band Cherokee women, and reading literally hundreds of books and articles relevant to my study. Admittedly, I have only scratched the surface of Cherokee women's discourse, and certain segments of my work may seem to raise more questions than are answered. To quote Osage scholar Robert Warrior, however, "much of the point here is, in fact, to be convincingly suggestive rather than conclusive" (xv).

American Indians have been writing in English since the 1770s. Cherokee authors Elias Boudinot and John Rollins Ridge were publishing in the early 1800s, and Boudinot was editing a bilingual newspaper (the *Cherokee Phoenix*); John Milton Oskison, an early-twentieth-century Cherokee novelist, is just beginning to receive critical acclaim; Lynn Riggs's drama *Green Grow the Lilacs* (1931) was the play upon which Rodgers and Hammerstein's famous production *Oklahoma!* was based. Until only recently, however, the literary work of Cherokee women seems to have been limited to writing letters and personal journals. These latter documents, too, can enlighten us concerning prevalent attitudes, religious beliefs, and current events of the eighteenth and nineteenth centuries, and included in this project are some of the ancestral voices whose writings paved the way for what Native authors can do today. For centuries, Cherokee women have been writing protest letters and engaging in national speaking tours lobbying for Native rights and criticizing land theft. As Womack notes, "[Indians'] life stories, as well as their literary ideas, provide a useful study of the evolution of Native thought that has led up to contemporary notions of sovereignty and literature" (3).

Because the letters and speeches discussed in this work are often reflective of individual personalities, I have chosen to maintain the original spelling and grammatical structure of each work. While they may not evoke the same aesthetic satisfaction among some readers as Nathaniel Hawthorne's *The Scarlet Letter,* Walt Whitman's *Song of Myself,* Toni Morrison's *The Bluest Eye,* or even Sylvia Plath's *Letters Home: Correspondence, 1950–1963,* these letters and speeches and excerpts from diaries are nevertheless an important component of the American literary tradition.

Certainly, I do not pretend to have the last word on the discourse of Eastern Band Cherokee women. I do believe, however, that there are alternative ways of researching and writing about this discourse, and it is my hope that *Eastern Band Cherokee Women* can contribute significantly to ongoing discussions of American Indian literature.

Acknowledgments

Research and writing are daunting tasks, and I am deeply grateful for the guidance and support of others. Sarah Hill, Daniel Littlefield, Dana Nelson, and LaVonne Brown Ruoff have provided me with valuable advice, instructive comments, and the inspiration to keep writing.

Several individuals have been especially helpful to me in locating rare documents and other archival holdings. For their assistance and patient response to requests for information I express sincere appreciation to Sidney Farr, Gerald Roberts, and Shannon Wilson of Special Collections and Archives at Berea College Library; Barbara Landis of the Cumberland County Historical Society, Carlisle, Pennsylvania; Mike and Sue Abrams of the Cherokee Heritage Museum; Elizabeth Dunn of Special Collections, Duke University; Paulette Fairbanks Molin of the American Indian program at Hampton University; Debbie Green, Donzella Maupin, and Cynthia Poston of Hampton University's Archives; Barbara Duncan of the Museum of the Cherokee Indian Archives; and Helen Tanner of the Newberry Library. I am also indebted to the Newberry Library for a Francis C. Allen Fellowship.

Numerous members of the Eastern Band of Cherokee Indians have generously contributed their time and energies to this work. Foremost among these are former Principal Chief Joyce Conseen Dugan and former Director of Cultural Resources Lynne Harlan. Sometimes by telephone, other times in a busy office, or over a glass of raspberry tea at a local restaurant, they have shared their stories, provided me with crucial documents, and guided me through the intricacies of working with a people who have already been "studied to death."

Throughout the course of this study, I have been blessed with the unfaltering support of friends and family. My special thanks to Marilou Awiakta, Robert Blythe, Kathy Bullock, Joanne DiNova, Daniel Justice, and Cora Withrow. Also, I owe much gratitude to my children and grandchildren for their unconditional love during years of research, traveling, and preoccupied writing.

Finally, my sincere thanks to my editor at the University of Tennessee Press, Scot Danforth, for his rigorous—but always courteous—criticism of my work. Without his encouragement and assistance I could not have completed this manuscript.

To all of you, *gv-ya-li-e-li-tsi-si*—I appreciate you.

Abbreviations

ABCFM	American Board of Commissioners for Foreign Missions
AIRORF	American Indian Ritual Object Repatriation Foundation
ASP	*American State Papers*
BIA	Bureau of Indian Affairs
CIIS	Carlisle Indian Industrial School
COF	*Cherokee One Feather*
EBCI	Eastern Band of Cherokee Indians
HUA	Hampton University Archives
JCS	*Journal of Cherokee Studies*
JHP	John Howard Payne Papers
MCI	Museum of the Cherokee Indian
SF	Student file
SW	*Southern Workman*
T&T	*Talks and Thoughts*

Introduction

The storyteller keeps the stories
all the escape stories.
She says "With these stories of ours
we can escape almost anything
with these stories we will survive."

—Leslie Marmon Silko

As Elizabeth Cook-Lynn frequently observes in her essays and public speeches, the phrase "American Indian intellectual" sounds bizarre to many mainstream Americans. "While there are images of Jewish intellectuals, European intellectuals, British scholars, African novelists," Cook-Lynn points out, "there is no image of an American Indian intellectual. . . . It is as though the American Indian has no intellectual voice with which to enter America's important dialogues" (Mihesuah, *Natives* 111). Craig Womack (Muskogee Creek/Cherokee), however, makes the argument that although the term "Indian intellectual" is an oxymoron in dominant culture, American Indians "have produced written intellectual texts for centuries, not to mention indigenous-based intellectual knowledge so much a part of the oral tradition" (13). In fact, as early as the eighteenth century, several tribes dwelling east of the Mississippi began attempting to preserve histories of their interactions with Europeans and Euro-Americans. One method was to entrust designated individuals within a tribe with the task of memorizing important transactions, but written records were also maintained. For example, the Cherokee archives, located at Chota, the "mother town" of their nation, were established in 1750 and were placed in the care of Great War Chief Oconostota (Alden 240). Oconostota, well acquainted with the deceit of both the Americans and the British, placed great value upon keeping "talking papers," and when the Americans burned Chota to the ground during the Revolutionary War, they discovered a depository of letters, manuscripts, copies of treaties, and various commissions, buried beneath the former foundations of the Cherokee Council House (242).[1]

In addition to tribal histories, Indian authors have been writing sermons, protest literature, autobiographies, letters, speeches, and travel narratives since the eighteenth century. Indians have also engaged in rhetorical acts such as speaking out for Indian rights and protesting land theft, and these ancestral voices paved the way for what Native authors can write today (Womack 3). This written intellectual history is only beginning to be explored by American scholars. On the other hand, Anglo-Americans have always been fascinated with the oratorical skills of Indians and have, since the colonial era, continued to borrow Native American loanwords, making them an indispensable part of the English language.[2] Through the use of what Philip Deloria terms "theatricalized rhetoric," Americans have long "solidified their common understanding of themselves" by resorting to linguistic metaphors that have "suggested a way of thinking in which one could figuratively be what one was not." In his provocative work *Playing Indian,* Deloria demonstrates how white colonial rebels, for example, played Indian at the Boston Tea Party in order to claim an American Indian identity:

> By smearing their faces, speaking "ugh"-peppered pidgin English, and throwing tea from merchant ships, colonial rebels brought cultural understandings to life through dramatic performance . . . white, male Americans staked a unique and privileged claim to liberty and nationhood [by acting] through the channels cut by European traditions of carnival and misrule, traditions that they made uniquely their own through the use of Indian Others. (32, 33)

The men who performed these "wild Indian" antics personified what historian Robert Berkhofer Jr. refers to as the "white man's Indian." In his analysis, Berkhofer observes that whether Euro-Americans have viewed Indians as noble or savage, "the Indian as an image has always been alien to the White" (xv).

How did this "white man's Indian" develop in the Euro-American imagination? And what impact have such fabricated images had on the way many Americans perceive Indian eloquence? The "noble savage," along with his alter ego, the "diabolical savage," has been around since America was "discovered" in the fifteenth century, and images of "good" and "bad"

Indians abound in the literature of colonial America. In his *History of Plymouth Plantation* (1630–46), for example, William Bradford characterized Indians as "wild men" who inhabited "a hideous and desolate wilderness" (271). Puritan ministers Cotton Mather and Solomon Stoddard degraded Indians even further, equating them with wild beasts. Mather's tract, *Souldiers Counselled and Comforted* (1689), advised a group of colonists who had been offended by Indians: "Once you have but got the Track of those Ravenous howling Wolves, then pursue them vigourously; *Turn not back till they are consumed.* . . . Beat them small as the *Dust before the Wind*" (Stannard 241). In 1703, Stoddard formally petitioned the Massachusetts governor for financial assistance so that the colonists might acquire and train large packs of dogs "to hunt Indians as they do bears." His rationale was that Indians were not "as other people"; rather, Indians were wolves and were "to be dealt withal as wolves" (Stannard 241).

Other colonial writers were more charitable toward Indians. Thomas Harriot, in his *A Brief and True Report of the New Found Land of Virginia* (1588, 1590), acknowledged that within the limits of their own culture and technology, the "natural inhabitants" of the New World "seem very ingenious" (79). Roger Williams, best known perhaps for his work *A Key into the Language of America* (1643), believed that Native religion was one of "Satan's inventions"; yet he found the Indians of New England a harmonious people with a commitment to orderly government and justice (Bercovitch 78). At least one seventeenth-century English colonist claimed to *be* Indian. Robert Beverly (1673–1722) wrote in his *History and the Present State of Virginia* (1705), "I am an *Indian* and don't pretend to be exact in my language" (Bercovitch 98). Beverly is not, as Sacvan Bercovitch points out, identifying with real Indians. Rather, he is distinguishing himself as an American—a *natural* man whose dress, manners, and speech reflect the plain and unsophisticated lifestyle of an Indian (98).

By the nineteenth century, Indians had become a popular theme in the works of American novelists like Lydia Maria Child, James Fenimore Cooper, Catherine Sedgwick, and William Gilmore Simms. The prevailing theme in these novels, however, is the predicament of the poor Indian who becomes the helpless victim of "civilization"—a theme to which Cherokee writer Daniel Justice emphatically responds, "We're not a doomed race that sacrificed indigenousness for White civilization. . . . Rather, we are a diverse, ever-changing people with rich histories fully rooted in the Indigenous heart of this hemisphere" (5).

Early American writers seldom included Indian women in their works. When female characters were introduced, they joined other national symbols such as Pocahontas and Sacagawea—"good" Indian women who came to the aid of white Americans and recognized the inevitability of white conquest. Thus, notes anthropologist Elizabeth Bird, their stories, at a mythic level, explain to Euro-Americans their right to be here and help deal with "lingering guilt about the displacement of the Native inhabitants" (2). If we are to understand American history more completely, it is crucial that scholars perceive of Indian women of the nineteenth century (and yet today) as more than artifacts and that they recognize these women as real people capable of speaking for themselves.

One of the avenues of sociopolitical resistance open to American Indian women has been public and private discourse; in this study, I have chosen to focus on the letters, poems, diary entries, speeches, and memoirs of Eastern Band Cherokee women, dating from the late 1700s to the present. Although personal letters and diaries have long been used as primary sources of biography and history, only recently have such documents attracted serious attention among scholars. Therefore, like the frontier literature of Annette Kolodny, who admits that her work has contested the boundaries of literary history, my project may "make many literary historians nervous because it appears to beg the question of 'literariness'" ("Letting Go" 14).

In his critical work *Epistolary Practices* (1998), William M. Decker questions our right as scholars to assume the role of "voyeurs of lives" preserved in old correspondences. He concludes that "we may justify our more scholarly intrusions by arguing that our inquiry focuses not on *person* so much as on *systems* of representation" (5; emphasis added). However, the lines between public and private domain for many of the epistolary samples examined in this study were erased at the time they were written—especially those composed under the watchful eye of missionaries and school administrators during the nineteenth century. I am interested, therefore, in the individuals who wrote these letters, as well as in the discursive strategies they used. The letters and journals of ordinary Cherokee females have obviously not captivated the attention of scholars in the same way that the epistolary practices of Emily Dickinson or Gertrude Stein have, for instance. Nevertheless, the discourse of Eastern Band Cherokee (EBC) women is worthy of study as "literature," both because of the history it records and because of the cultural preservation it effects.

The Eastern Band Cherokees are a nation of 12,500 Indians who make their home on the 57,000-acre Qualla Boundary in the Great Smoky Mountains of western North Carolina. These are the descendants of a group of some 400 Cherokees who, in accordance with the federal treaty of 1819, lived on their own land in North Carolina and were exempt from the removal of 1838.[3] A group of fewer than 100 other Cherokees, along with their leader, Euchella, were allowed to join them, as a reward for helping federal troops round up Indians hiding in the mountains. Eventually, several hundred Cherokees who managed to evade the "roundup and removal" joined the band, bringing their tribal membership to about 1,400. Most of this small band of Cherokees who remained in their ancient homeland were full-bloods—Indians who had refused to intermarry with whites—and they spoke little or no English. They farmed small plots of land and supplemented their food supply by hunting and fishing. Unlike their western Cherokee relatives, they did not own slaves. They practiced traditional religion or Christianity—or sometimes a syncretic mix of the two. They opposed removal and many believed that Chief John Ross had betrayed them when he was unable to persuade the federal government to allow the Cherokees to remain in their homeland. They had no official relationship with the western Cherokees who had been removed, and they had little contact with the outside world (Ehle 386).[4]

As John Finger observes, the Eastern Cherokees may have had political differences among themselves, as well as with the main body of Cherokees from whom they were separated in 1819. On one matter, however, notes Finger, they were in one accord: their children needed education. After the removal, the Cherokees were without formal instruction, except for an occasional schoolteacher hired by their white friend William Holland Thomas for a few months at a time. In 1868, the U.S. government allotted one thousand dollars for books to distribute among the Eastern Cherokees, but without teachers and schools the books were meaningless (*Eastern Band* 130).

In 1875, Agent William McCarthy resolved to correct this problem. He recommended that the government hire Mary Manney, a schoolteacher in Robbinsville, North Carolina, for a five-month term at the Cheoah Boarding School in Qualla, and within a year McCarthy had four day schools in operation on the reservation. According to Finger, poverty was such an acute problem among the Cherokees that McCarthy urged the government to use the promise of clothing as an inducement for the children to attend school. The American government, however, was less than sympathetic and instead of complying with McCarthy's request, warned him against "giving handouts to destitute Cherokees" (131).

Of course, the Cherokees who are most visible in historical records are those who embraced Euro-American principles of "civilization" and who tried to re-create a Cherokee society conforming to those principles. Ironically, these Cherokees were also the ones who posed the greatest threat to white Americans who continued to encroach on their lands, and they were the first to be forcibly removed by the U.S. government.

Meanwhile, the assimilation programs of the U.S. government and the evangelistic efforts of Christian missionaries had little impact on the Eastern Band Cherokees, and they remained isolated from the dominant culture. Because they had no schools and, for the most part, were not writing in English, Eastern Cherokees were effectively silenced for a period of some thirty years following removal. All this changed, however, during the period of Reconstruction immediately following the Civil War. Under the new Reconstruction Constitution of North Carolina, Eastern Cherokees acquired the right to vote.[5] In 1868, they also wrote their own constitution and elected a chief and a council. That same year, the federal government recognized the Eastern Cherokees as an Indian tribe distinct from the Western Cherokees (Perdue, *The Cherokee* 90–91).

After the Civil War, the EBCI had little choice but to seek the help of the federal government in educating their children, including their girls. However, the teaching philosophies Jean-Jacques Rousseau gave the world on women's education had by this time become widely influential. Rousseau began by insisting on the fundamental differences commonly accepted between men and women and argued for a different education:

> The whole education of women ought to be relative to men. To please them, to be useful to them, to make themselves loved and honored by them, to educate them when young, to care for them when grown, to counsel them, to console them, and to make life agreeable and sweet to them—these are the duties of women at all times, and what should be taught them from infancy. (Woody 67)

By the late 1800s, white females were becoming more generally accepted in educational institutes, for as Thomas Woody observes in his *History of Women's Education in the United States* (1929), men came to regard women as "playthings rather than helpmeets, and believed they should be educated for show rather than trained in domestic duties" (244). Women of color, however, were expected not only to honor and obey their males but to be in subservience to whites, as well. Therefore, while white females of the late 1800s were studying physics and math and literature in American colleges and universities, females who were black or Indian attended industrial schools, where they learned to be domestics (Woloch 280).

It is little wonder, then, that the writing of Cherokee women has been stifled or that those letters and speeches that have been recorded arouse little apparent interest among academicians. With more Indians completing graduate school, however, the professions of history and anthropology and literature are witnessing more aggressive attempts at correcting inaccurate histories and at contesting what is commonly referred to as the "New Indian History."[6] For example, numerous tribal scholars are now recovering the written documents, as well as the oral histories, of ancestral Indians, and indigenous writers are becoming increasingly critical of white historians who fail to consult with tribal peoples concerning their histories.[7] Within the past decade, Native scholars Brenda Child (Ojibwe), Amanda Cobb (Chickasaw), and K. Tsianina Lomawaima (Creek) have published excellent studies on Indian boarding schools. These studies are based on hundreds of interviews with American Indians who attended government boarding schools or who are descendants of former boarding school students, as well as on letters and journals preserved by family members.

American Indians have often felt deprived of what Anishinaabe scholar Scott Lyons refers to as *rhetorical sovereignty*—the "inherent right and ability of peoples . . . to decide for themselves the goals, modes, styles, and exigencies of public discourse" (4). Consequently, the fabrication of frozen-in-history Indian images remains altogether too pervasive in American society, and the gifted orator, still highly valued in most Indian communities, continues to be supplanted in popular culture by the stereotypical grunting savage—an image that seems especially persistent in the fields of marketing and commerce.

In September 1996, for example, *Cherokee One Feather,* the official newspaper of the Eastern Band Cherokees, reprinted the following advertisement from the *Western North Carolina Real Estate Guide*:

> **Lookum for Special Tepee?** . . . We havum. You. Big Chief bringum tribe, seeum big cedar wigwam in village, on near-acre park. Happy

playground for whole tribe: Papoose pickum from 6 courts, swatum tennis balls (Russ showum how). Big chief swingum clubs on 18-hole golf course. Squaw poundum maize in kitchen, cookum over brick fireplace. Tribe cool off in big pool. Wigwam hasum many bedroom & bath. Big buy at **79,000** wampum. Sendum smoke signal for pow-wow—everybody danceum for joy, smokeum peace pipe forever.

This dumbing down of Indians denies the complex oratorical and literary traditions of the Eastern Band Cherokees—a people who for hundreds of years have defied the paternalistic attitude that Indians are "children," incapable of eloquent speech. In a public response to the Realtor's ad, therefore, Principal Chief Joyce Dugan reminded him that the perpetuation of the "Hollywood Indian" myth is one of the most detrimental factors to Native Americans' efforts to maintain their cultural identity in a constantly changing social environment. "Moreover," she added, "in today's era of politically correct advertising, I would be surprised if your prospective clients aren't equally offended."[8]

Apparently stunned by Chief Dugan's reaction, the dismayed Realtor replied in words that reverberate with the rhetoric of many nineteenth-century "friends of the Indian":

Please accept my apologies for any offense felt from this ad. Certainly there was no racial prejudice intended: on the contrary, the thoughts were out of fondness and empathy I have always held for the Native Indians.[9]

This North Carolina businessman's dismissal of racially offensive language as an unintentional blunder reflects a duplicity historian Jill Lepore characterizes as a "shiftiness in verbal behavior [that] can be traced to the earliest New World encounters and to questions about the humanity of the indigenous peoples of America" (xiv).[10] Even more disturbing, however, is the way such displays of "fondness and empathy" underscore the erasure of authentic Indians from the consciousness of a nation seemingly obsessed with "playing Indian."

In her autobiography, *Where Courage Is Like a Wild Horse*, Apache artist/writer Sharon Skolnick observes that although "the pressures and prejudices that helped to shape us decades ago still lurk just below the surface of the American psyche, fortunately, they are not the only influences that work powerfully on us" (xii). It is these "other influences"—the survival stories, the memories, the rhetorical strategies of a resilient people—that I want to explore. By examining the discourse of select Eastern Band Cherokee women, I hope to facilitate a richer understanding of the role female discourse has played in sustaining a dynamic Cherokee culture—their history, language, stories, dances, songs, crafts, and medicines.

Although the names of several nineteenth-century Cherokee men—names like Elias Boudinot, Major Ridge, John Ross, and Sequoyah—are occasionally mentioned in American history texts, scholars have, for the most part, ignored the lives and works of Cherokee women of the same era. Traditionally, the words of Indians—of any tribe—have not received much attention in white academic disciplines. As Lucy Maddox explains in her thought-provoking book *Removals*:

> The definition of American history that the academy has always found most usable has been able, so far, to accommodate only an admittedly ethnocentric version of Indian history. Similarly, our working definition of American literature has not yet been able to accommodate Indian texts, oral or written, very comfortably. And these prevailing definitions, of course, not only determine their own discourses but continue to privilege them over competing ones. (3)

By failing to consider the presence of Indians as a "significant factor in the debates about the definition of the American nation and about the production of a national literature," Maddox argues, literary criticism has continued to "remove" Indians from the primary sites of American cultural activity (flyleaf). This ongoing "removal" stems from a deeply ingrained belief that Indians are racially inferior—that their words have no place in "civilized" texts—and as early as the eighteenth century, American authors were employing satire as a means of attacking such biases. For example, Hugh Henry Brackenridge's novel *Modern Chivalry* (1792) describes a stranger, posing as an Indian treaty maker, who accosts Captain Farrago and asks to borrow the Captain's Irish servant, Teague O'Regan, to impersonate a Kickapoo "king." Since it is no "easy matter to catch a real chief, and bring him from the woods," the treaty maker explains, "it is much more profitable to hire substitutes and make chiefs of our own: And as some unknown gibberish is necessary, to pass for an Indian language, we generally make use of Welch, or Low Dutch, or Irish."

"How the devil," said the Captain, "do you get speeches made, and interpret them so as to pass for truth?"

"That is an easy matter," said the other; "Indian speeches are nearly all alike. You have only to talk of burying hatchets under large trees, kindling fires, brightening chains; with a demand, at the latter end, of blankets for the backside, and rum to get drunk with" (56–57).

As Brackenridge well knew, the speeches of American Indians were frequently dismissed by U.S. commissioners as quaint and politically naive, and he resorts to satire to ridicule the popular opinion that those who "know Indians" are just as qualified as a "real chief" to negotiate treaties and to address indigenous issues.

Being treated as children incapable of running their own affairs is hauntingly familiar to the Eastern Band Cherokees of North Carolina. In the anti-Indian climate of nineteenth-century America, political leaders like President Andrew Jackson and Gov. Wilson Lumpkin of Georgia felt it necessary to maintain rigid, impassable boundaries between "civilized" Anglo-Americans and "uncivilized" Cherokees in order to justify the removal of thousands of indigenous people from their ancient homelands. Like the North Carolina Realtor cited earlier, Jackson and Lumpkin claimed to have the best interests of Cherokees at heart, and many Indian people believed them. As the removal of Cherokees unfolded during the 1830s, therefore, it became an increasingly complex issue. Subsequently, Theda Perdue and Michael Green remind us, "not all Americans supported Cherokee removal; not all Cherokees opposed it; and the drama itself took place against a complicated backdrop of ideology, self-interest, party politics, altruism, and ambition" (vii).

Like many American Indians of today, nineteenth-century Cherokees often felt helpless against the power of the dominant society. Cherokee women, accustomed to being listened to with respect and to sitting on tribal councils, were gradually deprived of their right to speak publicly on issues affecting their people.[11] Furthermore, even women who dared to speak out in their own homes sometimes met with disastrous consequences. For example, in a journal entry dated February 13, 1817, Cyrus Kingsbury (founder of the Brainerd Mission School for Cherokees in southeast Tennessee) reports :

> Go out today on business—Meet with Charles Hicks, one of the principal Chiefs. He informs me an Indian on Highwasse [Hiwassee] river murdered his wife & children about a week since, supposed to be occasioned by a disagreement respecting removing over the Mississippi, he wishing to go, she not.

Perhaps the death of this woman motivated other Cherokee women to take public action, for in the same journal entry, Kingsbury notes:

> The women in these parts are about to draw up a memorial to the National Council against an exchange of country. This is done in cognizance of the hardships & suffering to which it is apprehended the women & children will be exposed by a removal. (Phillips 29)

On May 2, 1817, just a few weeks after the murder of their Cherokee sister and her children, a group of women, led by Beloved Woman Nancy Ward, met with tribal leaders in council, advising the men that they "thought it their duty as mothers to address their beloved chiefs and warriors." The women reminded the Cherokee men that each of them had been raised by a woman "on the land which we now have, which God gave us to inhabit and raise provisions," and that although the women had "never thought it our duty to interfere in the disposition of it till now," the time had come to "forewarn you all not to part with our lands."[12] The women further admonished the men to "cultivate and raise corn & cotton and your mothers and sisters will make clothing for you which our father the president [James Monroe] has recommended to us all." Moreover, the women advised the Cherokee men to "keep your hands off of paper talks"—an admonition suggesting the folly of forsaking a strong oral tradition, for inherent in their survival was the belief that language is sacred, that words have the power to bring about physical change in the universe (*Presidential Papers* 6453). In *The Man Made of Words*, Cherokee/Kiowa author Scott Momaday explains,

> By means of words can one quiet a raging [storm], bring forth the harvest, ward off evil, rid the body of sickness and pain, subdue an enemy, capture the heart of a lover, live in the proper way, and venture beyond death. Indeed there is nothing more powerful [than words]. (15–16)

As the Cherokees were rapidly learning, however, such a worldview is distinctly different from that of Western peoples. Consequently, observes Paula Gunn Allen in her groundbreaking work, *The Sacred Hoop* (1986), many scholars have been quick to dismiss as childish and superstitious the Indian belief that it is through "the sacred power of utterance" that the forces that surround and govern them can most effectively be shaped and molded to sustain their culture (56). In fact, critic Walter Ong declares,

"Without *writing*, human consciousness cannot achieve its fuller potential, cannot produce other beautiful and powerful creations" (14–15; emphasis added). Such a philosophy devalues and subordinates the power of orality among American Indians and perpetuates the popular notion that only a history that has been committed to writing is trustworthy.

Moreover, even among scholars who have in recent years begun to examine the recorded speeches, letters, poems, and stories of eighteenth- and nineteenth-century American Indians, only scant attention has been paid to women orators and writers. Likewise, many major textbook publishers, who have within the past decade introduced Native American authors to students of American literature, have included only a few token female writers, and I have searched in vain for selections by Eastern Band Cherokee women.[13]

Lucy Maddox suggests that because Indians leave most literary critics feeling "embarrassed, or bored, or quite uncritically pious," it is difficult to find a place for Indian writers in "civilized" texts, and that the alternative continues to be removal from these texts (178). If the analysis Maddox offers for the canonical exclusion of Native writers in general is accurate, it should come as no surprise that the words of Indian women evoke even greater skepticism and controversy among literary scholars than does writing attributed to Indian men. In fact, the two questions I have been asked most frequently since beginning my research on the oratory and literature of Cherokee women are (1) How can you be certain that these letters and speeches are authentic? and (2) What proof do you have that these words were not written by males using female pseudonyms?[14]

After examining hundreds of speeches, letters, poems, and memoirs written by nineteenth-century Eastern Cherokee women, however, I find no reason to doubt either the authenticity of their words or the major role these women played in resisting removal and assimilation efforts in that tumultuous era. Moreover, rhetorical strategies of women remain a potent force in sustaining Cherokee culture today. Hence, it is important that we look not only at how the cultural values of nineteenth-century women persist in the discourse of their twenty-first-century daughters, but also at the ways in which these voices have continued to disrupt the forces that have worked to "unravel Cherokee society."[15]

Researching the letters and speeches of ordinary Cherokee women has been at the same time fascinating and frustrating. A few—notably Nancy Ward and Arizona Swayney Blankenship—have become objects of scholarly study, but for the most part, the lives of Grandmothers—Cherokee ancestors—who paved the way for Cherokee women of today are of no more significance to the average American than the Third-World women described by George Orwell in his provocative essay, "Marrakech": "They rise out of the earth, they sweat and starve for a few years, and then they sink back into nameless mounds . . . and nobody notices that they are gone" (651).

That the writings and oratory of ordinary women—especially of Indian women—should fail to generate much interest among historians and literary critics is not surprising, since Western education, according to Susan Miller, has traditionally "deploy[ed] privilege to correct the power of the ordinary" (19). As early as the eighteenth century, however, common-place writing—civil records kept in "family books," for instance—had become "an infallible substitute for individual recollection" (28). Thus, the oral histories of American Indians have been often deemed inaccurate and invalid by Western scholars, and the written words of Indians have been relegated to a "contested space repeatedly demarcating class and educational boundaries" (29).

Furthermore, because *eloquence* is something of a vexed term in rhetorical studies, what has been considered as eloquence in Indian oratory over the years may need some elaboration. To rhetoricians like Cicero and Quintilian, for example, eloquence seemed to be "the study of stylistic ornamentation such as is found in the arts of poetry." Augustine believed wisdom to be more important than eloquence and suggested that one need not be a trained rhetorician in order to achieve eloquence; likewise, eighteenth-century rhetorician Hugh Blair, convinced that eloquence is a gift of Nature and "no invention of the schools," asserts the following:

> To be truly eloquent is to speak with purpose. For the best definition which . . . can be given of eloquence, is the art of speaking in such a manner as to attain the end for which we speak. Whenever a man speaks or writes, he is supposed . . . to have some end in view; either to inform, or to amuse, or to persuade, or, in some way or other, to act upon his fellow creatures. (Bizzell and Herzberg 818)

The eloquence of nineteenth-century Cherokee women, however, was based neither on style nor earnestness, but on a belief in their ability to transform the world in which they lived—a view clearly articulated by Okanagan writer Jeannette Armstrong in her essay "Land Speaking":

> To speak is to create more than words, more than sounds retelling the
> world; it is to realize the potential for transformation of the world . . .
> Speaking is a sacred act in that words contain spirit, a power waiting
> to become activated and become physical. Words do so upon being
> spoken and create cause and effect in human interaction. What we
> speak determines our interactions. Realization of the power in speak-
> ing is in the realization that words can change the future and in the
> realization that we each have that power. I am the word carrier, and I
> shape-change the world. (183)

The letters of nineteenth-century schoolgirls, therefore, painstakingly penned
in a second language, are a rich source of historical commentary, for as
Gloria Bird (Spokane) contends, writing remains, for Indians, "more than
a catharsis; at its liberating best it is a political act." Hence, what may
appear to the casual (or biased) reader of today as nothing more than
"simple" letters and speeches are indeed "political acts," designed to undo
damaging stereotypes about the Cherokee people, to rewrite their own history, and to mobilize their future ("Breaking the Silence" 30).

Letters and transcribed speeches—culled from Senate documents, religious periodicals, newspapers, historical archives, boarding school records,
and from Indian women themselves—are, therefore, central to this study
and are quoted extensively throughout each chapter. My emphasis on the
discourse of women is in no way intended to minimize the historical significance of similar works by Cherokee men; rather, it is a response to the general omission of Eastern Cherokee women in historical documents.[16]

As a child, growing up in the hills of East Tennessee, I was part of a
community in which a number of the residents were of Cherokee descent.
I felt very closely connected to the ancestors whose stories were told and
retold around the fireplace on cold winter nights. One of these stories, for
instance, was of my paternal great-grandparents, who were eleven years
old at the time of the forced removal of Cherokees in 1838 and who passed
on first-person accounts of soldiers rounding up Cherokees, of people
dying in overcrowded stockades, and of families being permanently separated by that catastrophic event.

Also, several well-known Cherokees once lived in my native homeland,
including the famed preacher and political leader Jesse Bushyhead, eloquent orator and military leader Major Ridge, world traveler Ostenaco,
and Beloved Woman Nancy Ward. In spite of the persistent cultural and
historical presence of Cherokees in my native county, however, American

Indians were ignored in the textbooks and classrooms of the schools I attended during the 1950s. Educators were far more concerned with the "Negro problem" in those days, and the few Cherokees still living in Polk County failed to excite much interest.[17] Once or twice each year, a group of Eastern Band Cherokees—dressed in the colorful regalia of Northern Plains warriors—traveled to Polk County from the Qualla Boundary in North Carolina to entertain local schoolchildren with their dazzling performance of Indian dance and song. Unfortunately, this superficial exposure to Cherokee culture was the only formal "Indian education" I would receive while living within a short drive of the largest federally recognized Indian tribe in the Southeast.[18]

In "My Grandmother Was a Cherokee Princess," Joel Martin remarks on the proliferation of representations of Indians in the antebellum white South—a surprising development, he argues, in a region that had expelled tens of thousands of Indians during the 1830s. "Having hated and 'removed' most literal Indians, southerners fell in love with figurative ones," Martin theorizes, and today, as then, "an astonishing number of southerners assert they have a grandmother or great-grandmother who was some kind of Cherokee, often a 'princess'" (136, 143).

This profusion of "Indian wannabes"—individuals with questionable American Indian heritage or who claim to have been Indian in a past life—has been a perpetual thorn in the side of Eastern Band Cherokees, and Executive Director of Cultural Resources Lynne Harlan undoubtedly expresses the sentiment of many when she advises the hordes of people now seeking tribal enrollment, "If your ancestors didn't hang with us when it wasn't cool, you shouldn't be trying to hang with us now" (personal interview, May 7, 1999). That the Tribal Council would approve *any* academic research among the Qualla Cherokees is, in fact, rather astounding in light of all the exploitation and misrepresentation foisted upon the people living there; thus, I am deeply grateful for the warmth and generosity extended to me during this study.

Cook-Lynn suggests that Indian scholars must ask one overriding question of themselves: "Is what I am teaching and writing and researching of value to the continuation of the Indian Nations of America?" ("The Radical Conscience" 13). Using Cook-Lynn's question as a beacon for this study has strengthened my resolve to give back to Eastern Cherokees a small portion of the wisdom and knowledge they have so freely shared with me.

The following chapters will evaluate some of the discursive strategies Eastern Band Cherokee females have utilized to fulfill what Alfonso Ortiz has defined as the primary roles traditionally assigned women in their culture: (1) mothers, (2) enablers, (3) transformers, and (4) healers (Awiakta, *Selu* 20).[19]

Chapter 1 opens with the story of a Cherokee woman from my own birthplace in Southeast Tennessee—the Beloved Woman Nancy Ward.[20] Women have traditionally been revered among the Cherokees as the life-givers of the Nation, and although I pay special attention to the oratory of Ward, I also discuss two captivity narratives that emphasize the rights and privileges of mothers in determining the fate of those taken captive by the Cherokees as American settlers began to encroach more excessively upon Indian lands. Also, I examine a letter written to Benjamin Franklin by a Cherokee woman in 1787—during a time when the voices of Indian women were being steadily muted by a European-style government—and draw parallels between changing constructions of gender and the gradual loss of rhetorical power among Cherokee females.[21]

Just as eighteenth-century skeptics refused to believe that the young African American poet Phillis Wheatley was capable of writing her *Poems on Various Subjects, Religious and Moral* (1773), modern-day critics often scoff at the idea of studying the words of "uneducated" Cherokee orators who were Wheatley's contemporaries.[22] Because "writing, especially after the printing press became so widespread, was taken to be the *visible* sign of reason," explains Henry Louis Gates Jr., people of color were "reasonable," and hence "human," only if they demonstrated an ability to write. Thus, "while the Enlightenment is characterized by its foundation on man's ability to reason, it simultaneously used the absence and presence of reason to delimit and circumscribe the very humanity of the cultures and people of color which Europeans had been 'discovering' since the Renais-sance" (8).

It is not surprising, therefore, that as nineteenth-century Cherokee females came increasingly under the influence of Western education, they learned to value the written word. In chapter 2, I invoke the Cherokee creation story of Selu and Kana'ti to illustrate woman's role as an enabler of her people, and to explore ways in which Cherokee schoolgirls used writing as a means of sustaining their culture.[23] I argue that even young girls in early nineteenth-century mission schools were deeply concerned about the survival of their people, and that Brainerd Mission students such as Catharine Brown and Nancy Reece became adept at finding ways to fight for the rights of the Cherokees through the letters the missionaries assigned them to write to the benefactors of these schools.

As numerous historians have noted, the Cherokees, more than any other tribe, showed a willingness to adopt Anglo-American political institutions and cultural values; hence, by the late 1800s, Cherokee women, educated in predominantly church-affiliated schools, often seemed to echo the patronizing attitudes of their white mentors. Chapter 3 investigates boarding school letters and records for evidence of cultural assimilation, but as in the case of students at Brainerd (chapter 2), I argue that in spite of the schools' concerted efforts to assimilate Indians, these young Cherokee women relied upon the strength of their cultural traditions to improve and transform their own schools and communities. In the words of Frances Rains, such women "found ways to resist practices meant to destroy them and their cultures. . . . They stood before their oppressors with the dignity of truth and insights that their positioning as 'Other' gave them, and in so doing attempted to bridge the chasm of ignorance, the crevasse of complacency, over 100 years ago" (319).

For instance, Lottie Smith Pattee, a young Cherokee graduate of the Hampton Institute in Virginia, worries in an 1894 letter to Cora Folsom (her former dorm mother) that she (Pattee) and her Sioux husband will not be able to live comfortably on the thirty dollars a month he is earning. "Of course," the young woman writes, "if we were to live like Indians perhaps we could get along. But we don't wish to live that way" (HUA). Once she has children of her own, however, Lottie relies heavily upon the strength of her Cherokee traditions to filter the advice of her boarding school mentors and to speak out for the rights of Indians.

Unlike Lottie, who was systematically assimilated into "the cult of true womanhood" and taught to look down upon her own culture, contemporary Cherokee women are frequently found actively battling for the right to preserve their culture. Furthermore, unlike nineteenth-century Cherokees, who gradually paid less and less attention to the voices of their tribal women, the Eastern Band of Cherokees voted overwhelmingly in 1995 to elect a woman—Joyce Conseen Dugan—as their Principal Chief. During her inaugural speech, Chief Dugan stressed the importance of community and insisted that her inauguration be "not a celebration for the chief or the vice chief, but a celebration for . . . the principal people . . . the first step in giving the government back to [the people] and the start of the healing process."[24]

Chapter 4, therefore, explores ways in which Chief Dugan has relied upon the power of "quiet actions" rather than "loud words" to help restore balance and emotional healing among her people and to protect their cultural heritage, and I argue that the fires of oratory burn as brightly today as they have for thousands of years.

While, according to James Berlin, all rhetoric involves self-discovery, and a writer's style is a reflection of his or her personality (169), it is essential in the study of the letters and speeches of Cherokee women to remember that the purpose of American Indian oratory/writing is never merely self-expression. Rather, as Paula Gunn Allen argues, Indian writers seek "to embody, articulate, and share reality, to bring the isolated private self into harmony and balance with this reality . . . and to actualize in language, those truths that give to humanity its greatest significance and dignity" (55). In this study, I have been more concerned with the words of the colonized than with the words of the colonizer. Some readers may feel alienated at times by what they deem "unscholarly" writing—a narrative style that seeks to interweave "survival stories" with frequent quotes from the letters and speeches of "ordinary" Cherokee women. Still others may feel impatient with what is perceived as "academic jargon" in some sections of the narrative.

My primary purpose, of course, is to demonstrate how selected letters, journals, and speeches—spoken and written by women whose names, for the most part, remain as obscure as their words—reflect the tenacity of Cherokee females. The women represented in this study have chosen to define themselves by speaking their minds rather than allowing others to define them in manipulative and detrimental ways.[25] Even words in the wind, they would argue, are a powerful force, and the discourse of Eastern Cherokee women continues to play a vital role in preserving and sustaining their culture, for as Marilou Awiakta so eloquently declares:

Our courage
is our memory.

Out of ashes
peace will rise,
if the people are resolute.
If we are not resolute,
we will vanish,
And out of ashes
peace will rise.

In the four directions . . .
Out of ashes peace will rise.
Out of ashes peace will rise.
Out of ashes peace will rise.
Out of ashes peace will rise.

Our courage
is our memory. (*Selu* 7)

Chapter 1 *Mothers of Men*

"Nothing will ever be the same," she said, and those
were the last words she spoke.

—from Robert Conley's
War Woman

In 1955, I entered Polk County High School in Benton, Tennessee, a small
town some eight miles north of the mountain community in which I lived,
and every school day for four years I rode a yellow county bus along the
same predictable route: Highway 411. Frequently, as our bus approached
the Ocoee River bridge just south of Benton, some self-appointed guide
would point to Hancock Hill and remind the rest of us that "an old Indian
woman is buried up there." Although I was determined to learn the story
of this mysterious Indian woman and to visit her resting place there high
above the river someday, I finished high school without ever setting foot on
the site or even learning her name.

Today, the formerly unmarked grave of Nanye'hi (circa 1738–1822),
the famous Beloved Woman of the Cherokees, is covered with a stone pyramid, and a bronze tablet declares her the

Princess and Prophetess
of the Cherokee Nation
The Pocahontas of Tennessee
The Constant Friend
of the American Pioneer[1]

Among many Cherokees, Nanye'hi continues to be honored as a coura-
geous mother and grandmother, a War Woman, a woman "so special that
the Great Spirit often chose to send messages through her" (Mankiller 207).
Euro-Americans, on the other hand, refer to her as Nancy Ward and tend

to think of her primarily as a Cherokee "Pocahontas" who was instrumental in saving the lives of thousands of white settlers on the Tennessee frontier. Today, numerous biographies, children's stories, and scholarly articles attest to her greatness, and people travel from all over the world to visit the grave of the *Ghighau,* or "Most Honored Woman."

My intent goes beyond investigating Nanye'hi's contributions as a cultural broker; rather, this chapter lays the groundwork for a discussion of themes in the letters and speeches of nineteenth-century Cherokee women and for exploring the relentless sociopolitical challenges faced by Eastern Band women during the past two centuries. I focus on the words of Nanye'hi and Katteuha, two Beloved Women generally characterized as "traditional" Cherokees.

The very term *traditionalism,* of course, is complicated, for it is often associated with spirituality, not politics—a philosophy that, according to First Nations writer/activist Lee Maracle (Salish), arises from European attempts to interpret indigenous society as opposed to their society. Without politics, Maracle explains, a nation is lawless; therefore, to say that Indians were lawless is to say that they were indeed savages. While Europeans have traditionally enforced laws with police, military troops, and other means, the indigenous people of the New World understood that laws were obeyed not because of armed force but because the people agreed with the laws. Therefore, says Maracle,

> I can understand democracy. The will of the people was sacred to our leaders. This is one of our strongest traditions. No Native person accepts his or her leader's direction as a command. Conversely, only fools accept that a society that requires force to ensure proper social conduct is a democratic one. Without the voice of the trammelled and the dispossessed, democracy is but an echo in the canyons of the minds of lunatics. (40–41)

As their letters and speeches demonstrate, spirituality and politics (or the sacred and the secular) were not separate spheres for Nanye'hi or Katteuha, and their discourse establishes a model for the letters and speeches examined in subsequent chapters. I am arguing against what scholars often view as diminished power and cultural decline among Cherokee women and for what Nancy Shoemaker describes as resistance to "the Euro-American gender ideal" (20).

In an article published by the *Polk County News* in 1938, John Shamblin wrote, "Like the eagle, the Cherokees have all gone. Some of them went to the wild and wooly [*sic*] west when the pale face took possession of this country and some of them had gone to the happy hunting grounds before this time." Shamblin further notes that the ashes of one of these long-departed Indians—the friend of the "palefaces," Nanye'hi—"reposes today beside that of her son Five Killer and brother Long Fellow" (1).[2] Shamblin, like most white writers of his day, believed that Indians were becoming extinct, and almost certainly he would have been shocked at the idea of Cherokees reading his words a half century later.[3] In addition to ignoring the fact that several thousand Indians were living in Qualla, North Carolina—less than eighty miles east of Polk County—Shamblin romanticizes the "copper-colored Cherokees" by attributing such terms as "paleface" and "happy hunting grounds" to a people who had been literate in both Cherokee and English for at least one hundred years. In fact, some scholars argue that the stereotypical Indianisms *paleface* and *happy hunting ground* were coined by white literary authors, not by the Cherokees.[4] Shamblin's use of such terms, therefore, suggests not only his adherence to the "vanishing red man" theory but also his belief in the "children of the forest" myth brought over by the Puritans.

If whites knew so little about the Eastern Cherokees in 1938, how impenetrable must have seemed the cultural barriers that Nanye'hi encountered in her contact with white Americans during the late 1700s/early 1800s. In Nanye'hi's lifetime, for example, the Women's Council was powerful, both politically and spiritually. Among other powers, they had the right to speak in the men's council and the right to participate in decision making. Every public speech attributed to nineteenth-century Cherokee women emphasizes the belief that women are the life-bearers, and are therefore to be revered. Yet, when Nanye'hi, the War Woman of Chota ("Mother Town" of the Cherokees), addressed a treaty conference, she violated "the Anglo-American convention that barred women from speaking publicly on political matters" (Perdue, "Nancy Ward" 85).[5] When Cherokee men insisted that their women be allowed to join them in negotiating with British and American leaders, they were derisively accused of having a "petticoat government."[6] In fact, throughout the early colonization of the Cherokees, the British worked hard at lessening the power of women in Cherokee affairs, and within five years after Nancy Ward's death, the

Cherokees themselves had deprived women of sitting on the Tribal Council or voting (see 1827 Constitution of the Cherokee Nation, Sections 4 and 7).

Because the Cherokees had no centralized political system in the eighteenth century, the patriarchal and coercive power of Euro-American government was strangely unfamiliar to them.[7] In fact, not until the English began to dominate their trade and alliances did the Cherokees even have tribal chiefs or tribal councils, for custom and public opinion sufficed to maintain order (McLoughlin, *Cherokee* 10–11). Each Cherokee town was self-governing, and anyone—male or female—could speak in the town council meetings. Cherokee women were held in such high regard that the penalty for killing a woman was double that for killing a man. The role of the Beloved Women was to sanctify food, drink, and places in the landscape by singing, dancing, and praying, while the War Women were chosen to control the activities of their warriors. These women were particularly respected among their contemporaries, owing to their age and healing abilities (Parker 118–19). Thus, the systematic efforts of the Americans to "civilize" the Cherokees rested on the overthrow or subversion of what Paula Gunn Allen refers to as "the gynocratic nature" of their traditional system. Adair's ridicule of the Cherokees' "petticoat government," Allen argues, was a direct jab at the power of the Beloved Woman, Nanye'hi, for the honor accorded her in tribal councils was an affront to the white man's belief in universal male dominance (32).

Cultural insults, however, did little to deter the Ani-yun-wiya—the Real People, as the Cherokees called themselves. In fact, as Rennard Strickland (Cherokee/Osage) argues, traditional Cherokee thought on legal matters survived long after their adoption of written laws, for "to a people who felt that every rock and every living thing involved an earthly manifestation of a spirit world, conceiving of law as 'social engineering' was impossible" (183). For example, Cherokee women had traditionally enjoyed complete control of their property, and this property could not be managed by their husbands without consent; in spite of written laws that later supplanted this tradition, the equality of women remained a basic social goal (100). Hence, in November 1785, at the Treaty of Hopewell (South Carolina), prominent Cherokee males refused to continue negotiations with the U.S. commissioners gathered there until Cherokee tradition was honored and the voice of their Beloved Woman was heard.

To understand the full significance of Ward's brief speech, however, we must first examine the oratorical approach taken by Onitositaii (Old

Tassel), the primary spokesman for the Cherokees at Hopewell. As history records, Onitositaii was experienced in debating legal issues—an argumentative style known as *forensic* rhetoric and one very familiar to the commissioners. For days, Onitositaii, one of the chiefs of the Upper Town Cherokees (those who lived in the towns in North Georgia and East Tennessee that wished to abide by the treaty), had been asking for payment for lands taken illegally from his people and had repeatedly expressed the unwillingness of the Cherokees to cede more land.[8] Each day, when Onitositaii tired of talking, he simply announced, "I have no more to say," or "We have said all we intend today . . . if the commissioners have anything to say, we will hear it." Often, the patience of Onitositaii wore thin, and he was notorious for calling the Americans "rogues and liars."[9]

Finally, exasperated with the fact that his words seemed to be falling on deaf ears, Onitositaii spurned political decorum and announced, "I have no more to say, but one of our beloved women has, who has born and raised up warriors." Based on the premise that truth and justice are universal values, Onitositaii argued with the Americans that the Cherokees had been deceived and defrauded and that any "deed" the U.S. government possessed was a forged document. The commissioners quickly asserted their legal authority in their reply to the proud Cherokee Chief:

> Your memory may fail you; this [deed] is on record, and will remain forever. The parties being dead, and so much time elapsed since the date of the deed . . . puts it out of our power to do anything respecting it; you must therefore be content with it, as if you had actually sold it. (*ASP* 1:42)

Onitositaii was powerless against the Americans and their written documents, for following well-established European traditions, the commissioners used the "law" to "legally" dispossess the indigenous peoples of much of their territory and to diminish their sovereignty (Wilkins 3). Realizing that nothing he said would influence the commissioners to rescind their government's actions, Onitositaii turned to the War Woman, Nanye'hi, whose reputation commanded respect—even among the Americans—and who was as skillful with words as she once had been with military weapons.[10]

The War Woman of Chota (Nanye'hi) then addressed the U.S. commissioners:

> I am fond of hearing that there is a peace, and I hope you have now taken us by the hand in real friendship. I have a pipe and a little

tobacco to give the commissioners to smoke in friendship. I look on
you and the red people as my children . . . I am old, but I hope yet to
bear children, who will grow up and people our nation, as we are now
to be under the protection of Congress, and shall have no more dis-
turbance. The talk I have given is from the young warriors I have raised
in my town, as well as myself. They rejoice that we have peace, and
we hope the chain of friendship will never more be broke. (*Gazette* 1)

The War Woman gave the commissioners a string of beads, a pipe, and
some tobacco, and the Hopewell Treaty negotiations concluded.[11] The
Cherokees ceded large tracts of their land, while the U.S. government
pledged to protect the Cherokee Nation.

The famous eighteenth-century Mohegan missionary Samson Occom
once reminded white Methodist leaders of "the reciprocity that structure[d]
his relationship with the Christian colonial mission." Similarly, Nanye'hi
emphasized that the U.S. government's promise to protect the Cherokees
was not without cost to her people.[12] Occom refused to ingratiate himself
before Christian "superiors" who seemed to believe that they were doing
him a favor by awarding him a mere pittance in exchange for his working
as a full-time missionary among his own people. Instead, he reasoned, "I
am not under obligations to them, I owe them nothing at all; what can be
the Reason that they used me after this manner?" ("Narrative" 946). With
similar dignity, Nanye'hi remonstrated that government protection was a
trifling benefit in the face of the near-total loss of Cherokee lands.

After observing the commissioners' supremacist stance with Onitositaii,
Nanye'hi adroitly shifted to a device commonly used by Cherokees and
known in ancient Greece as *epideictic* rhetoric. This style of argumentation, according to Cynthia Sheard, "testifies to the importance of establishing a common ground as a basis for persuading a [listener] to think or to do
whatever a [speaker] deems necessary, urgent, productive, or otherwise significant." As Sheard further notes, this style of speaking is based on an
assumption, popularized by rhetorician Chaim Perelman, that "good reasoning is not enough to persuade others to our visions; we must also address
our common humanity" (766).

Consequently, when the War Woman of Chota asserted "I look on you
and the red people as my children," she issued a poignant reminder that
every individual was brought into this world by a woman and that "red
people" share a common humanity with white people. Furthermore, she

gestured toward subverting the patriarchal power assumed by the "Great White Fathers" in their dealings with Onitositaii, as well as in establishing for herself a position of authority in that gathering.

Wambdi Wicasa, director of the American Indian Culture Research Center in Marvin, South Dakota, contends that basic philosophical differences between the two cultures—Euro-American and Indian—led to very disparate understandings of the legally binding contracts they made. According to Wicasa, the trouble began when American leaders looked on the treaties and called them *contracts*—agreements made in suspicion and requiring the parties to set "limits" to their own responsibility. Indian leaders, on the other hand, referred to these treaties as *covenants*—agreements made in trust and sealed with tobacco or a string of beads ("Covenant versus Contract"). When the Beloved Woman concluded her speech with "We hope the chain of friendship will never more be broke," she was using the language of a covenant, suggesting the Cherokees' willingness to live in peace with the Americans.

By assuring the commissioners that her words were spoken in behalf of "the young warriors I have raised in my town," she indirectly reminded them that she, a woman, had been selected to represent even the men of her town. Thus, she alluded to a question posed by the Cherokees in a previous meeting with the Americans: Where are your women?[13] Richard Lanham's argument that epideictic rhetoric is "fundamentally playful" does not seem applicable in Nanye'hi's case, for hers are not the words of a "playful" orator (164). Rather, they are the forthright and unsentimental assertions of a Cherokee woman acutely aware of the Americans' determination to undermine female leadership among her people.

Only two years after Nanye'hi's widely publicized speech at Hopewell, the words of yet another Cherokee woman made national news. In September 1787—the same month the Federal Constitutional Convention sent its new constitution to Congress—Benjamin Franklin, then governor of Pennsylvania, received a letter signed "From KATTEUHA, The Beloved woman of Chota."[14] Katteuha, like Nanye'hi before her, introduces herself in the letter as "the mother of men," and in the tradition of her people, she encloses some tobacco, inviting Franklin and his "Beloved men" to "smoake it in Friendship."

Subsequent letters between Katteuha and Franklin, and recorded in the *Pennsylvania Archives,* provide no immediate context for the following comments from the Beloved Woman:

Brother,

I am in hopes my Brothers & the Beloved men near the water side will heare from me. This day I filled the pipes that they smoaked in piece, and I am in hopes the smoake has Reached up to the skies above. I here send you a piece of the same Tobacco, and am in hope you & your Beloved men will smoake it in Friendship—and I am glad in my heart that I am the mother of men that will smoake it in piece.

Brother,

I am in hopes if you Rightly consider it that woman is the mother of All—and that woman Does not pull Children out of Trees or Stumps nor out of old Logs, but out of their Bodies, so that they ought to mind what a woman says and look upon her as a mother—and I have Taken the privelage to Speak to you as my own Children, & the same as if you had sucked my Breast—and I am in hopes you have a beloved woman amongst you who will help to put her Children Right if they do wrong, as I shall do the same—the great men have all promised to Keep the path clear & straight, as my Children shall Keep the path clear & white so that the Messengers shall go & come in safety Between us—the old people is never done Talking to their Children—which makes me say so much as I do. The Talk you sent to me was to talk to my Children, which I have done this day, and they all liked my Talk well, which I am in hopes you will heare from me every now & then that I keep my Children in piece—tho' I am a woman giving you this Talk, I am in hopes that you and all the Beloved men in Congress will pay particular Attention to it, as I am Delivering it to you from the bottom of my heart, that they will Lay this on the white stool in Congress, wishing them all well & success in all their undertakings—I hold fast the good Talk I Received from you my Brother, & thank you kindly for your good Talks, & your presents, & the kind usage you gave to my son. (181–82)

As a Beloved Woman, or Ghighau, Katteuha held the highest authority in the Cherokee Nation and was considered holy. Furthermore, in her capacity as a diplomat, she, like other Beloveds, frequently traveled north to Philadelphia, Detroit, and the towns of the Iroquois Confederacy (Parker 123–24). It is possible, therefore, that Katteuha and Ben Franklin had met; almost certainly she would have been aware of Franklin's outspoken support of Canasatego, the Onondaga sachem who had spoken for the Six Nations at the Treaty of Lancaster, Pennsylvania, in the summer of 1744.[15]

Perhaps Ben Franklin seemed to be the Cherokees' last hope in sustaining such equality for the "mothers of men" in the New Republic. At any rate, it is significant that Katteuha felt confident enough to address the eighty-one-year-old Franklin, who was said to be nearly as eminent as George Washington at the time (Bernhard et al. 167).

As in the speeches of Nanye'hi, the motif of woman as the "mother of men" is prevalent in Katteuha's letter, and she reiterates the responsibility of women to "put [their] Children Right if they do wrong." Written during an era scholars have described as one of the most transformational periods in Cherokee history, Katteuha's letter to Franklin employs language that may appear to modern readers to be laced with quaint Indianisms; to a Cherokee orator or writer, however, it is a letter rife with cultural symbolism. For example, Katteuha writes in the same letter, "the great men have all promised to Keep the path clear & straight, as my Children shall Keep the path clear & *white* so that the messengers shall go & come in safety Between us." In the conclusion of her letter, Katteuha urges the men to pay particular attention to her words, delivered "from the Bottom of my heart," and to "Lay [them] on the *white* stool in Congress" (emphasis added). The word "white" in Katteuha's pledge to "keep the path clear & white" between her people and "the Beloved men in Congress," as well as her reference to a "white stool," is symbolic, denoting peace and happiness. As Alan Kilpatrick notes, "to the Cherokee psyche the color of white celebrates a condition of tranquility and felicity." Also, in Cherokee tradition, the color white is frequently used in sacred formulas to render harmless "the evil intentions that emanate from the souls of humans." Thus, the word "white" may well be used to indicate, metaphorically, that "the reciter is now enshrined in an impervious state of psychological calm," and that, whether the men of Pennsylvania hear her words or not, Katteuha is fulfilling her spiritual role in keeping the traditions of her people alive (75).[16]

Katteuha must have been aware, also, of Franklin's duplicitous behavior toward Indians. For example, on June 25, 1764—twenty years *after* his outspoken support of Canasatego—Franklin wrote the following in a letter to his London friend Richard Jackson:

> I am afraid our Indian War will become perpetual (as they begin to find they can, by Plunder, make a Living of it), without we can effectually Scourge them, & speedily. We have at length concluded to send for 50 Couple of true Bloodhounds to assist in hunting [Indians]. If any

Gentleman of your Acquaintance has such, I wish you would persuade them to spare 'em to us. Mr. Neate a Merchant of London, I think, is apply'd to, to collect them. (Van Doren 170)

In light of this letter, and others in which Franklin lamented the number of whites who were choosing to live among Indians, Katteuha's repetitious use of the word "white" may have had yet another stimulus.[17] The groundbreaking work of Henry Louis Gates Jr., *The Signifying Monkey: A Theory of African-American Literary Criticism* (1988), suggests one possible purpose: signifying. Signifying is, in black discourse, a general term for several modes of boasting, lying, or indirect insult—or, as Kimberly Benston puts it, "When one Signifies, one tropes-a-dope" (Gates 52). Among American Indians, as with African Americans, signifying is also a way of encoding messages or meanings. Therefore, when Katteuha remarks that "the old people is never done Talking to their Children—which makes me say so much as I do," her comment is directed at no one in particular—a strategy Claudia Mitchell-Kernan refers to as "obscuring the addressee" (Gates 82). Because of Franklin's age, however, and because of his "whiteness," Katteuha's letter could be construed as an act of resistance to being treated as a child, always forced to listen to the words of the white "fathers" in Congress. If Franklin and his colleagues happen to "get" her meaning and are offended, she is free to maintain that she is speaking symbolically, or alternatively, as Gates points out, she can say, "if the shoe fits, wear it" (83).

Long before activists like Susan B. Anthony, Carrie Chapman Catt, and Elizabeth Cady Stanton, Cherokee women were publicly fighting for the rights of their people. For example, during the Revolutionary War, a Cherokee War Woman named Gatun'lati captured a party of Tories, while Cuhtahlatah (Wild Hemp) led Cherokee warriors to victory after her husband was mortally wounded. In July 1783, fourteen Creek and Cherokee women joined forces and spoke at a Detroit council meeting to request aid against the Americans who were stealing their land. According to the minutes of that meeting, their request was granted by Maj. Arant Schuyler de Peyster (Parker 126).

As is explained in the *Study Guide for the Native American/Hawaiian Women of Hope*,

Besides being life givers and life sustainers, [women] served on councils, held leadership roles, owned land and other property, created and maintained the home, exercised the right to vote, tilled the soil, nurtured children and other family members, bestowed names, healed the sick, comforted the suffering, composed and sang songs, told stories, engaged in diplomacy and trade, fought against enemies, made peace, selected, counseled, or removed leaders, cooked, gathered, fished, herded, stored, trapped, traveled, guided, sewed, quilled, mended, quilted, and taught. In short, the traditional female role in tribal nations was (and is) powerful, the balancing half of male power. ("Women of Hope")

Katteuha's letter to Benjamin Franklin, though cloaked in politeness, is a vigorous defense of the humanity of Indian women and a timely reminder that females of all races are indispensable to the welfare of a nation. Unfortunately, no further record of Katteuha seems to exist. Less than two years after the publication of her letter to the governor of Pennsylvania, however, a contingent of Cherokee chiefs from the village of Hiwassee (East Tennessee) complained to Franklin that times "have altered greatly . . . and now we are Reduced to the lowest degree of want and Missery By a Set of Bad People, who wants to Drive us into the sea." Furthermore, the chiefs reminded Franklin, "when the Northward Indians & French was at ware with you, then you co[u]ld send for us to help you, which we allways did without hesitating; now the Shawneys Lives at home, in Peace, and . . . we have hardly land sufficiant to stand upon" (*Pennsylvania Archives* 584).

In light of these ongoing encroachments on Cherokee land, it might be argued that the words of the Beloved Women were merely a transient novelty for their non-Indian audiences, and that the protests of the Hiwassee chiefs confirm the ineffectiveness of letters and speeches by women like Nanye'hi and Katteuha. Clara Sue Kidwell (Choctaw/Ojibwe) reminds us, however, that, as in all the changes forced upon American Indian people through "the historical patterns of intervention by government and religious organizations in [their] affairs," one very significant element of indigenous culture has persisted to the present: the woman's role as mother and keeper of the home. That persistence of values, from ancient Indian societies to contemporary times, contends Kidwell, "provides a source of power for American Indian women within their own societies, despite the relative powerlessness of Indian people in American society today, [for] the necessity of those roles, and the respect accorded them, continues today" ("Power" 114).

According to the eighteenth-century trader Alexander Longe, when a baby girl was born to the Cherokees, "all the female relations look[ed] on the child to be their proper daughter." Women were so highly respected in Cherokee culture, in fact, that Longe concluded "the women Rules the Roost and weres the brichess" (32). Matrilineal ownership of land, control over their resources, and female-centered households gave the Cherokee women an autonomy that allowed them to support themselves and their children independently (Hill 33). Consequently, to equate this particular form of female power with the Euro-American principles of domesticity is to misinterpret traditional Cherokee views of women altogether. In fact, notes Rebecca Tsosie, even contemporary Indian women "find an identity . . . which emphasizes their own special bond to the female life-forces of the universe, [and] . . . have always perceived their regenerative qualities in close concert with the earth's cycles" (32).[18] Hence, it was from this perspective that both Nanye'hi and Katteuha sought to impress upon their Euro-American listeners/readers the regenerative power of a woman's *words,* as well as of her body—a concept which contrasted sharply with the views of the "cult of true womanhood" that emerged in the mid-nineteenth century.[19]

According to Karen Anderson, most nineteenth-century whites believed that "civilized womanhood" would have a special appeal for Indian women, freeing them of the "drudgery and degradation whites associated with Native American gender systems." One of the "paradoxes of coerced change" embodied in the acculturative policies of white leaders, therefore, was that, in order to "emancipate" Indian women, they often had to curtail women's traditional powers (37–38).

Lt. Henry Timberlake observed in his *Memoirs* (1765) that the power of the Beloved Women was so great that "they can, by the wave of a swan's wing, deliver a wretch condemned by the council, and already tied to the stake" (94). Failure to understand the status of women within Cherokee communities, or to acknowledge the power of their words, therefore, often led to dire consequences for white men who found themselves at the mercy of these women. In fact, the underestimation of Cherokee women's oratorical power is perhaps best reflected in two distinctively different captivity narratives from eighteenth-century Georgia—the state that would eventually prove most aggressive in removing the Cherokees.[20]

According to one of these narratives (1761), surgeon David Menzies, who was captured by the Cherokees while en route to treat "a gang of negroes" on a Georgia plantation, was presented to the mother of one of their head warriors who had recently died in a "skirmish." Menzies, claiming to understand the Cherokees, "having some knowledge of their tongue," states that he was "overjoyed, as knowing that I had thereby a chance not only of being secured from death and torture, but even of good usage and caresses." When he was introduced to his prospective "mother," however, his fantasies of a Cherokee "Pocahontas" were joltingly displaced by a woman he describes as sitting

> squat on the ground, with a bear's cub in her lap, as nauseous a figure as the accumulated infirmities of decrepitude, undisguised by art, could make her, and (instead of courteously inviting her captive to replace, by adoption, her slain child) fixed her blood-shot haggard eyes upon me; then, rivetting them to the ground, gargled through her throat my rejection and destruction. (22)

All hope evaporated for Menzies as his vision of a beautiful redemptress was overshadowed by "barbarians [who] brought me stark-naked, before a large fire, kindled in the midst of the diabolical heroine's hut." Abruptly, the solicitous manner of the surgeon who "understood Cherokees" faded. Substituting yet another product of the European fantasy, the "savage beast," for his original image of the "noble savage," Menzies erupted with a string of epithets—words the bereaved Cherokee mother had undoubtedly read in his demeanor, long before he uttered them: "the old ferocious savage," "my canibal mistress," "old hag," "old woman in a drunken stupor," "inhuman she-tyrant" (23).

According to Cherokee tradition, Menzies would have been presented to a *skaigusta*, or female war captain, to which all prisoners must be delivered alive. These captives were turned over to the *skaigusta* as slaves, whom the women could adopt, punish, or expel, as they saw fit (Parker 119). Unfortunately, Dr. Menzies underrated the power this Cherokee mother possessed to decide his fate, and except for the interference of another band of Indians, he would have been "roasted" to death.[21]

A second captivity narrative—published in 1785 by black evangelist John Marrant—reflects quite a different picture. Marrant's narrative, in spite of its "Pocahontas" motif, suggests not only a decline in the power of female rhetoric among southeastern Cherokees, but the subtly changing role of the women in dealing with captives, as well.

Marrant, who had "just turned fourteen, and without sling or stone," wandered into Cherokee territory in Georgia while trying to escape the persecution of family members who opposed his recent conversion in one of evangelist George Whitefield's revival meetings. At the time of his capture, Marrant, like David Menzies, professed to know something of Cherokee culture and language, having "acquired a fuller knowledge of the Indian tongue" from the man with whom Marrant had spent weeks hunting deer (21).[22] Unlike Menzies, however, young Marrant fully expected to be killed by his captors; thus, his brief hours of confinement were spent "blessing [God] and singing his praises all night without ceasing" (23).

As his story unfolds, Marrant preaches to the Cherokees. After declaring him a witch, the chief promptly orders that the boy "be thrust into the prison, and executed the next morning" (27). Meanwhile, the chief's nineteen-year-old daughter, who has pleaded in vain with her father to spare Marrant's life, becomes critically ill, and the young prisoner is summoned once again to what he mistakenly refers to as the "king's house." After Marrant's fervent prayers, the daughter is healed, the chief embraces Christianity, and John Marrant is adopted into the Cherokee Nation.

Because Marrant's writing style conforms to the standard design for the captivity narrative, he elaborates very little on Cherokee culture.[23] As suggested earlier, Marrant's narrative alludes to a number of ways in which the traditional role of Cherokee women had begun to diminish by the late 1700s, particularly in the matter of dealing with captives. However, his cultural ideas of gender—particularly since he was so heavily influenced by the beliefs of Euro-American Christians—may have led him to ignore or misinterpret the actions of the Cherokees into whose hands he fell.

For instance, since it was traditionally the women of each clan who decided which captives would be adopted, and since it was the War Woman's role to determine who would burn at the stake, the absence of females in Marrant's lengthy narrative is noteworthy. Also, details describing Marrant's arrival at the Cherokee village indicate that the men may have purposely prevented any women from coming near the boy, for he notes that some fifty men surrounded him at once and carried him to one of their chiefs.[24] Furthermore, Marrant recalls, "my companion of the woods attempted to speak for me, but was not permitted; he was taken away, and I saw him no more" (21).

A second factor to consider when pondering the dearth of female discourse in Marrant's narrative is the impact of slave trade upon the Cherokees during this particular time. As several scholars have recognized, "slavery" had existed primarily for social reasons among the Cherokees.[25] In fact, throughout much of the eighteenth century, Cherokee women had adopted captives to repopulate clans depleted by war, famine, and disease. Once slave trade became popular in the United States, though, the nature of Cherokee warfare changed dramatically and, in the words of Theda Perdue, "reward joined revenge as a major motivation" (*Cherokee Women* 68).

Consequently, John Marrant—healthy, young, and black—represented a valuable commodity in the hands of his captors; however, as Perdue notes, the struggle over the control of prisoners often became so intense during that era that "some warriors preferred a dead captive to one who fell into the hands of the women" (70). This would explain the Cherokee men's eagerness to keep Marrant's presence secret, for tradition would almost certainly have prescribed that the women, who had for hundreds of years invoked motherhood as their primary source of power, had a voice in deciding the fate of young John Marrant. At any rate, when the chief's daughter—the only Cherokee female mentioned in Marrant's narrative—failed to sway her father from his fierce determination to kill the young captive, the executioner himself interceded and, according to Marrant, "assured [the chief] that, if he put me to death, his daughter would never be well" (27). The Cherokee executioner's warning simultaneously embodies a call for the chief to return to tradition and to honor the words of his daughter, lest the Nation lose a vital source of cultural strength and suffer the ominous consequences of scorning that spiritual power.[26]

By the late 1700s, even Nanye'hi, the Beloved Woman of Chota (Tennessee) was finding her ability to maintain harmony and order among the Cherokees increasingly insecure, since shortages of food, clothing, game, and ammunition compelled them to engage in trade with the Americans (Parker 141). Nanye'hi, whom biographer Pat Alderman describes as "all Indian and, by Cherokee standards, neither saint nor sinner," frequently endured opposition from within the Cherokee Nation, as well as from without (45). In fact, many of the younger Cherokee warriors, angered by the Beloved Woman's claim that "the white men are our brothers," and by her attempts to accommodate a rapidly growing number of white settlers in Cherokee country, refused to listen to her cry, "all for peace," and organized their own war parties for dealing with the encroaching whites.[27]

Still, Nanye'hi persisted in using her oratorical powers to persuade men—both Indian and white—of the critical role women play in the survival of a nation. On July 26, 1781, at the Long Island Treaty Meet in East Tennessee, she addressed a group of U.S. commissioners who, only a few months before, had destroyed Chota, along with the Cherokees' winter food supply. Perhaps, because she had been married to (and eventually abandoned by) a white man, Nanye'hi was already familiar with the subservient status Euro-American culture assigned women. Concerned about the portentous impact of those views on her own people, the Beloved Woman rose from her seat and spoke:

> You know that women are always looked upon as nothing; but we are your mothers; you are our sons. Our cry is all for peace; let it continue. This peace must last forever. Let your women's sons be ours; our sons be yours. Let your *women* hear our words. (Alderman 65; emphasis added)

Deeply moved by the dignified Cherokee woman's speech, Col. William Christian was chosen to respond. "Mothers," he said, "we have listened well to your talk. . . . Our women shall hear your words. . . . We will not quarrel with you, because you are our mothers" (65).

"Despite Col. Christian's tolerant response," concludes Sara Parker, "[Nanye'hi's] words fell into an abyss" (147). Nevertheless, history records that the Beloved Woman's speech at Long Island that day did accomplish one purpose: the occasion was "one of the very few Cherokee-White peace treaties (if not the only one) when no demands were made for Indian territory" (Alderman 65).[28]

Treaty after treaty, however, was broken by the U.S. government and, by the final decade of the eighteenth century, violence and destruction were so rampant in Cherokee territory that President George Washington issued a proclamation in the *Connecticut Courant* offering a reward of $500 for each person apprehended and brought to justice for "invading, burning, and destroying a town of the Cherokee nation" (1). However, Washington's proclamation had little effect, it seems, for Cherokees, including women and children, continued to be randomly murdered, and the perpetrators rarely brought to justice; "squatters" were moving into Cherokee territory by the hundreds; and chronic food shortages made it imperative that the men stay home to hunt, fish, and assist with crops.[29]

As Cherokees became increasingly susceptible to threats and bribes, a few individuals began selling their homeland to land speculators and traders. Consequently, a political system emerged, which, as Theda Perdue points out, had little room for Beloved Women like Nanye'hi. Instead, "male warriors, who could enforce national decisions, and the descendants of traders, who could deal more effectively with whites," began to centralize power in the Cherokee Nation. The title of Beloved Woman became an anachronism ("Nancy Ward" 96).

The world, as the Cherokees had known it before the coming of the European "boat people," was undergoing vertiginous changes—changes that were forcing Cherokee women to transform and be transformed, "weaving new worlds from old"—and the morale of the Cherokees was at an all-time low (Hill 34). In a letter dated July 29, 1818, Secretary of War John C. Calhoun assured Gov. Joseph McMinn, an agent for Cherokee removal in Tennessee, "It is in vain for the Cherokees to hold the high tone which they do, as to their independence as a nation, for daily proof is exhibited that, were it not for the protecting arm of the United States, they would become the victims of fraud and violence" (National Archives microfilm, roll 14); just five months later, Calhoun reported a dramatic decline in the fighting spirit of the Cherokees. Writing once again to Governor McMinn, he concluded, "That high spirit of independence which they assumed some months since has subsided into an acknowledgment of their dependence on the Government of the United States; and whatever may have been their former opposition to the fair execution of the treaty, they appear now disposed to act correctly" (*ASP* 2:4).

Nanye'hi's political power, however, rested not in her ability to "act correctly" in the eyes of the American government, but in her position as a mother in a society where, according to Perdue, "references to motherhood evoked power rather than sentimentality" (*Cherokee Women* 101). Thus, Nanye'hi refused to allow the political transformations brought about by acculturation to stop her from speaking out on behalf of her people.[30] On May 2, 1817, in response to an American proposal that would result in the removal of the Cherokees to lands west of the Mississippi River, the great War Woman of Chota made her last recorded speech—this time, to her own people. Quite aged now and too ill to attend the Amovey Council meeting in person, Nanye'hi sent her son, Five Killer, carrying her distinctive walking cane to represent her, along with a written plea to Cherokee leaders to "not part with any more of our lands" (McClary 10).[31] In spite of her physical exhaustion, the War Woman's oratorical powers remained strong, and once again she reminded the head men and warriors of their relation and responsibility to their Cherokee mothers:

The Cherokee ladys now being present at the meeting of the Chiefs and warriors in council have thought it their duty as mothers to address their beloved chiefs and warriors now assembled.

Our beloved children and head men of the Cherokee nation we address you warriors in council we have raised all of you on the land which we now have, which God gave us to inhabit and raise provisions we know that our country has once been extensive but by repeated sales has become circumscribed to a small tract, and never have thought it our duty to interfere in the disposition of it till now, if a father or mother was to sell all their lands which they had to depend on which their children had to raise their living on which would be indeed bad and to be removed to another country we do not wish to go to an unknown country which we have understood some of our children wish to go over the Mississippi but this act of our children would be like destroying your mothers. Your mothers and sisters ask and beg of you not to part with any more of our lands, we say ours you are descendants and take pity on our request, but keep it for our growing children for it was the good will of our creator to place us here and you know our father the great president will not allow his white children to take our country away, only keep your hands off of paper talks for it is our own country for if it was not they would not ask you to put your hands to paper for it would be impossible to remove us all, for as soon as one child is raised we have others in our arms for such is our situation and will consider our circumstance.

Therefore children don't part with any more of our lands but continue on it and enlarge your farms and cultivate and raise corn and cotton and we your mothers and sisters will make clothing for you which our father the president has recommended to us all we don't charge anybody for selling any lands, but we have heard such intentions of our children but your talks become true at last and it was our desire to forewarn you all not to part with our lands.

[Nanye'hi] to her children Warriors to take pity and listen to the talks of your sisters, although I am very old yet cannot but pity the situation in which you will hear of their minds, I have great many grandchildren which I wish them to do well on our land. *(Presidential Papers, 6452–53)*

Nanye'hi's speech articulates what she sees as the most crucial aspect of her people's survival, as well as the areas in which she believes her people can afford to compromise their cultural heritage: Cherokee men can adhere to the President's "civilization" recommendations by farming, and their

women can sew and spin in the fashion of white women, without sacrificing the essence of who they are. However, unless they "keep [their] hands
off of paper talks" and refuse to part with more land, the Cherokees will
be permanently uprooted from the place of their ancestors—an event that
causes Nanye'hi to fear for the very survival of the Cherokee Nation.

In their introduction to *Great Documents in American Indian History*
(1973), editors Wayne Moquin and Charles Van Doren write, "In pre-
twentieth-century material, we have to rely almost entirely upon the tran-
scriptions by white redactors of what Indians said. What has come to us,
therefore, is almost as much the product of who wrote it down as it is of the
actual author" (xvii). Such an analysis, however, suggests that the words of
Indian orators like Nanye'hi cannot be trusted as "authentic." Rhetorician
Lucille Shultz reminds us of the danger of making such assessments—a
danger that critics like Hayden White, Michel Foucault, and James Berlin
have cautioned against repeatedly: "pretending—even for a moment—that
there is but one story, one way of reading the past; and of the danger in
pretending—even for a moment—that the storyteller can stand in a neu-
tral space or in a space outside the story" (4).

Responding to such scholarly pretensions, Wilma Mankiller, former
Principal Chief of the Cherokee Nation (Western), observes the following:

> An entire body of knowledge can be dismissed because it was not writ-
> ten, while material written by obviously biased men is readily accepted
> as reality. The voices of our grandmothers are silenced by most of the
> written history of our people. How I long to hear their voices! (20)

Nanye'hi's message, accompanied by the signatures of twelve other
women—including her daughter, Caty Harlan, and her granddaughter,
Jenny McIntosh—implies a consensus among the female constituents of
Amovey that the sale of Cherokee lands must cease. It also suggests a pre-
scient awareness of the future need among Cherokee women to hear the
voices of the grandmothers, the traditional source of authority among the
people, hence Nanye'hi's insistence that the speech be delivered and transmitted. In the speech—her final message to the Cherokee people—she
emphasizes a number of traditions that continue to play a vital role in cultural persistence and that help to explain the resistance of many contemporary Cherokees to assimilationist policies.

First, Nanye'hi reminds the Nation that, according to Cherokee belief, women and the land are inseparable; thus, to sell or to abandon one's birthplace is analogous to destroying one's mother—a state of affairs modern Cherokee poet Awiakta likens to a dying tree:

> Women die like trees, limb by limb
> as strain of bearing shade and fruit
> drains sap from branch and stem
> and weight of ice with wrench of wind
> split the heart, loosen grip of roots
> until the tree falls with a sigh,
> unheard except by those nearby. . . .
> (*Abiding* 28)

Secondly, Nanye'hi's message conveys a potent warning against the adoption of Euro-American concepts of ownership. Asking her people to remember that, according to their own oral history, they are on land given them by the Creator, not property acquired through "paper talks," Nanye'hi indirectly invokes the Cherokee creation story:

> The first woman, as well as the first man, was red. The red
> people, therefore, are the real people, as their name *yv-wi-yu*
> indicates. (JHP 1:5)

Finally, by informing the Council that she has "great many grandchildren which I wish . . . to do well on our land," the Beloved Woman sends a poignant reminder to the Cherokees that they are a matrilineal society, and that it is the women who should be deciding how their descendants will live.[32]

When Nanye'hi died in 1822, those gathered around her deathbed testified that "a light rose from her body, fluttered like a bird around the room, and finally flew out the open door." Watched by Nanye'hi's startled family and friends until it disappeared, the light was last seen moving in the direction of Chota—mother town of the Cherokees—marking, in the words of biographer Ben McClary, Nanye'hi's passing "from life unto legend" (1).[33]

Described in Carolyn Foreman's *Indian Women Chiefs* as "daring, fascinating, influential and beloved by all," Nanye'hi was unquestionably an extraordinary woman and a valiant leader (83). Even so, she was a controversial figure in her day—and remains so today among the Cherokees. For example, Nanye'hi's act of sending her British son-in-law, Ellis Harlan, to warn the white people of the Watauga region of an impending attack by the militant Chickamauga Cherokees in 1781, as well as her informing British commanders about the activities of the Chickamaugas on other occasions, marks her as a traitor to some Cherokees. Such an accusation, however, belies an ignorance of Cherokee culture. It was, in fact, a legal requirement among the Cherokees, as among many other Indian nations, that warning be given of an impending attack. As Clara Sue Kidwell (Choctaw/Ojibwe) argues, the Beloved Woman was actually playing her role as it was defined in her own culture—advocate for peace—and "to that end she protected American settlers and informed British military agents of the hostile intentions of Cherokee men" (103). Furthermore, Sara Parker points out that Nanye'hi was a member of the White Council of Chota, a group charged with "keeping the town and themselves pure and in compliance with Cherokee laws." This meant, therefore, that they could neither shed blood themselves, nor could they sanction any bloodshed within the town limits of Chota (134).

Thus, like Whirlwind, the brave and headstrong protagonist of Robert Conley's fascinating novel, *War Woman*, Nanye'hi was as frequently misunderstood and hated by some as she was revered and immortalized by others.[34] Because of the strong character of Nancy Ward, however, eighteenth- and early-nineteenth-century Cherokee women were accorded increased respect, and they played a significant role in Cherokee affairs. Each clan chose women's councils, which often had the power to override the authority of the chiefs (Hoig 15).[35]

Hoig argues that this trend did not continue long past the time of Nancy Ward, and he views the recent rise of Cherokee women to positions of leadership as "more a reflection of [their] own personal ability and the belated acknowledgment of women's value by modern Western society in general than of Cherokee tradition" (15). Wilma Mankiller's own philosophy, articulated in her short story "Keeping Pace with the Rest of the World," suggests otherwise. In the story, Pearl, a Cherokee woman whose grandmother, Ahniwake, has just died of a heart attack, leaves the hospital and goes home to grieve. Entering her darkened living room, Pearl sits gazing into the fireplace as she and her grandmother were accustomed to doing:

She leaned forward and looked more closely. There, in the back of the flames, she saw Ahniwake with old man Charlie Christie on one side and Levi Buckskin on the other. Ahniwake looked very happy but Pearl began to weep. They could not speak to each other across the worlds that separated them but Pearl knew the message Ahniwake was sending. Once again she heard Ahniwake saying, "As long as the Cherokee people honor our ancestors and our Creator, the roots, herbs, and medicine songs will be available to us. These things will be shown to our people again. They are never really lost as long as we are not lost." (Harjo and Bird 406)

Although the lifestyle of Cherokees has changed drastically since the days of Nanye'hi, their women have remained notoriously independent, nourished by the spirits of ancient mothers and grandmothers. Despite all outward appearances, contemporary Cherokee women have persisted in reclaiming and revitalizing their cultural traditions, believing that, in the words of Linda Hogan (Chickasaw):

> This land is the house
> we have always lived in.
> The women,
> their bones are holding up the earth
> (Green 158)

American history continues to portray Indian women like Nanye'hi as "saviors and guides of white men and agents of European colonial expansion" (Kidwell, "Indian Women" 98). The letters and speeches of Nanye'hi and Katteuha, however, preserve a cultural legacy that persists today, for

one does not lose culture. It is not an object. Culture changes, sometimes for the better, sometimes for the worse, but it is constantly changing and will do so as long as people busy themselves with living . . . Sound waves do not leave the earth's atmosphere. The living voices of the dead remain trapped in the air we breathe and travel on the wings of their own waves. (Maracle 110, 114)

The letters, diaries, and speeches discussed in the following chapters reflect the same courage, forthrightness, and determination that Nanye'hi and Katteuha demonstrated at the turn of the nineteenth century. Sometimes perceived of by white scholars as fully acculturated, almost never characterized as "traditional," these orators and writers represent an array of Cherokee mothers, schoolgirls, nurses, teachers, basket weavers, and political leaders who have continually had their status as "mothers of men" challenged. Like Nanye'hi and Katteuha, however, they have continued to use their power as Cherokee women to protest the injustices of colonization, and the cry of each new generation resounds in a line by poet Joy Harjo (Muskogee Creek): "We have just begun to touch the dazzling whirlwind of our anger" (*Mad Love* 8).

Chapter 2 *Time Flowing Back on Itself*

When the missionaries came . . . they had the Bible and we
had the land. They said, "Let us close our eyes and pray."
When we opened our eyes, we had the Bible and they had
the land.

—Bishop Desmond Tutu

. . . You ride my plasma
Like a platelet,
Eldest kinswoman,
You cry to me through smoke
Of tribal fires.
I echo the primal voice,
The drumming blood.

—from Mary Tall Mountain's
"The Figure in Clay"

Hundreds of years before Albert Einstein's theory of relativity caught the
imagination of the Western world in 1905, the idea that we move in a con-
tinuum of past, present, and future was prominent in Cherokee thinking.[1]
Central to an understanding of this worldview, and of the role women play
in sustaining it, is the creation story of Selu and Kana'ti—mother and
father of humankind and inhabitants of a place beyond time and space.[2]

According to one version of the story, Kana'ti (The Lucky Hunter) and
his wife Selu (Corn) lived with their only son at a place called Pilot Knob.
Every day, the young son of Kana'ti and Selu went down to the river and
played with a boy the old people called I'nage-utasun'hi (He Who Grew Up
Wild), a boy with magical powers who had sprung up from the blood of wild

game, which Selu washed off at the river's edge. Eventually, Kana'ti and Selu took Wild Boy home with them and tamed him. Just as the Edenic serpent enticed Adam and Eve to eat the forbidden fruit of the Tree of the Knowledge of Good and Evil, however, Wild Boy persuaded his new brother to help him discover the source of game and corn that sustained them each day by spying on the first Cherokee man and woman.

When the two boys followed Kana'ti into the mountains, they discovered that he kept all the animals shut up in a hole underneath a large rock. When he needed fresh venison for his family, Kana'ti simply lifted the rock, then used his bow and arrow to kill an escaping deer. One day, the two young adventurers decided to try their own luck with bows and arrows. They became so excited about shooting game, however, that they forgot about covering the hole where the animals lived, and all the creatures escaped into the mountains. Kana'ti, though furious with the boys for their mischief, punished them lightly, then informed them that, for the rest of their lives, they would have to work hard, tracking animals all over the woods in order to have fresh meat.

When the boys arrived home, they were tired and hungry, but since there was no meat, Selu had to prepare a meal of corn and beans. Soon Wild Boy became just as curious about the source of this food as he had been about the game Kana'ti had always provided. "Let's hide and watch our mother when she goes to the storehouse for corn," Wild Boy challenged his brother. What they saw, however, disturbed the boys greatly. Selu was standing in the middle of the room with a basket in front of her. When she rubbed her stomach and armpits, corn and beans fell into the basket, filling it to the top. The boys decided that their mother was a witch and that she was trying to poison them, so they immediately began plotting to kill her.

Selu knew their thoughts, though, and with typical Cherokee forthrightness, she confronted them. "So you are going to kill me?" she asked. The boys may have squirmed uncomfortably in the face of such a direct question; nevertheless, feeling entirely justified in their intentions, they answered, "Yes. You are a witch!"

Unlike her husband, who undoubtedly felt that having to work for the rest of their lives at hunting was punishment enough for the boys' curiosity, Selu began giving the youngsters explicit instructions for surviving after her death. "After you've killed me, you must clear a large piece of land and drag my body around the circle seven times," she explained. "Then drag me seven times across the ground inside the circle, and stay up all night and watch. In the morning you will have plenty of corn." The boys did as they were told, and everywhere Selu's blood fell on the ground, corn sprang up (Mooney 242–45).

Arguing that it promotes violence and killing, many Euro-American audiences find the story of Selu the Corn Mother rather disturbing. Conversely, the story has been used for centuries among Cherokee people to teach children the consequences of disrespect, and how they can help to restore harmony among the people. "Used as it was originally designed," Cherokee/Appalachian writer Marilou Awiakta reminds us, "the story is a timeless and reliable compass to right relationships with Mother Earth, with the human family and with oneself" (*Selu* 16).

Certainly, the story of Ginitsi Selu, enabler and sustainer of her people, would have been familiar to most Cherokee girls who attended early-nineteenth-century mission schools. Taught by Christian missionaries, however, that such stories were "pagan myths," the girls were faced with a troubling question that continues to plague Indian communities today: If I become a Christian, must I reject my Native culture? Or, is it possible to be both Cherokee and Christian? Also, chipping away at the very foundation of their identity as the rising generation of Cherokee women was the Christian concept of womanhood, a view that prescribed learning the domestic skills typically performed by Anglo-American women of the nineteenth century. Thus, as historians Joyce and Gary Phillips observe, schools like the Brainerd Mission School in East Tennessee encouraged young female students "to abandon traditional ways and to take on the white manners and customs" by awarding them certificates of merit for "laudable accomplishments in the 'civilized' labors of white women" (12).

By the late 1820s, the Brainerd Mission had gained international recognition as a center for educating Indians; from a tiny one-room school in 1817, it had expanded to eight schools, with a faculty and staff of thirty-five missionaries and teachers, overseeing some two hundred Cherokee boys and girls. A typical school day began at 5:30 a.m. and ended at 9:00 p.m. and included lessons in arithmetic, English, geography, history, and the Bible. Additionally, the students were required to perform gender-specific labor tasks—"domestic" chores such as dressmaking and cooking for the girls and "masculine" work such as farming for the boys (Coleman, "Cherokee Girls" 125).

It is important to keep in mind that, although the students whose letters appear here identified (and were identified by their teachers) as Cherokee, many of them also had white ancestry. As such, they must have faced some of the same identity issues that confront many bicultural children today. Moreover, these young girls were constantly compelled to weigh the merits of their own Cherokee culture against the Western traditions they were being taught—a task not impossible to imagine today, for the cultural tensions of the early 1800s continue to impact American Indians, particularly those living on reservations. In fact, in my current position as a tribal college professor, I interact with students every day who—almost two hundred years later—are still contending with the frustration of trying to succeed in mainstream schools and jobs without sacrificing their cultural traditions and sense of identity.

Primary documents from the Brainerd Mission School are replete with stories of the successful acculturation of Cherokee students, and the letters of young girls, in particular, seem to affirm their eagerness to become thoroughly "civilized." As many Cherokees argued, on the other hand, learning the ways of the white man did not have to be an altogether negative experience; education in their schools could indeed become a means of empowerment.[3] In fact, a closer examination of these "schoolgirl letters" reveals anecdotes and subtexts that suggest that what many scholars have dismissed as the tragic acculturation of young Cherokee scholars may indeed have been a form of religious adaptability that enabled them to survive both personally and communally.

Brainerd Mission, located seven miles east of present-day Chattanooga, and two miles from the Georgia state line, was founded on January 13, 1817, by Reverend Cyrus Kingsbury, a native of New Hampshire. Under the auspices of the American Board of Commissioners for Foreign Missions (ABCFM)—a nondenominational organization composed primarily of Presbyterians and Congregationalists—the mission quickly attracted other missionaries. On January 3, 1818, Rev. Ard Hoyt, a native of Connecticut, and Rev. Daniel Butrick, from Massachusetts, arrived with their families at Brainerd, and later that month, seventeen-year-old Catharine Brown, who had enrolled in the Brainerd Mission School on July 9, 1817, became their first Cherokee convert (Starr 81–82).[4]

Catharine, according to Reverend Kingsbury, had a "blooming complexion" and comely features, complemented by "easy manners" and a modest demeanor when she arrived at Brainerd to attend school. "With all her gentleness and apparent modesty, however, [Catharine] had a high opinion of herself, and was fond of displaying the clothing and ornaments in which she was arrayed." Furthermore, Reverend Kingsbury worried that the young Cherokee's "feelings would not easily yield to the discipline of our schools, especially to that part of it which requires manual labor of the scholars" (R. Anderson 14–15).

Catharine, however, surprised her teachers by being "attentive to her learning, industrious in her habits and remarkably correct in her deportment." Moreover, she was able to progress within sixty days from "reading words of one syllable . . . to read[ing] the Bible intelligibly, and, in ninety days, could read as well as most persons of common education" (R. Anderson 15).

A visitor to the Brainerd Mission School, Gen. Calvin Jones of Raleigh, North Carolina, was likewise impressed with Catharine's demeanor. On November 13, 1818, in an article published in the *Raleigh Register*, Jones wrote the following:

> [One of the Brainerd students] was a young woman of much merit; she read well, conversed sensibly, was grave, dignified, and graceful in her manners, handsome in her person, and would be an ornament to almost any society. I was told that at their female society meetings, when asked to pray, she always unhesitatingly did so, and in a manner peculiarly fervent and eloquent; her name is Catharine Brown. (119)

Only a few months after entering the Brainerd Mission School, Catharine's life was disrupted by the threat of her family's forced removal from their Alabama homeland to the state of Arkansas. According to the *Brainerd Journal*, the parents of Catharine called on the missionaries on November 4, 1818, at which time Mr. Brown expressed tearful concern that the white people would not allow him to remain on his farm. Already, marauders had stolen most of his cattle, horses, and hogs, and he felt that his only recourse was "to go over the Mississippi." To the consternation of the missionaries, the elderly father announced that he would return in about ten days to get Catharine to go home and prepare to accompany her family to Arkansas (Phillips 91).

It was during this time of emotional upheaval that young Catharine began writing letters to various missionaries and supporters of Brainerd Mission—letters which the mission preserved as evidence of the piety of their first Cherokee convert, but which often reflect as much about the letter writer's strong ties to Cherokee traditions as they do about her religious beliefs. For example, in a missive dated November 1, 1818, and addressed to Mrs. Williams at Elliot, Catharine writes:

> I expect my father here every day. I do not know whether I shall go to the Arkansas, or not. I feel grieved when I think of leaving my Christian friends, and of going far from all religious people, into a wild howling wilderness, where no star shines to guide my wandering feet to the Babe of Bethlehem; where no warning voice is heard to keep me in the straight path that leads to heaven. When I look to that dark region, I start back; but when I think of my two brothers there, and my dear parents, who are soon to go, I feel reluctant to stay behind, and leave them to perish alone. (R. Anderson 31)

Catharine Brown's letter demonstrates remarkable competence in grammar, vocabulary, and orthography for a student, who only a year earlier, could read and write only a few words in English. Furthermore, the young Cherokee's mastery of the Christian vernacular reflects the "civilized" language of a stellar student whom the missionaries at Brainerd so proudly "regarded . . . as the first fruit of their missionary labours, and loved her, as well on that account, as on account of her pious and amiable conduct" (R. Anderson 19). Still, she clings tenaciously to the Cherokee tradition of placing the needs of family and community above her own desires and is insistent in her unwillingness to "stay behind, and leave [her family] to perish alone."

Catharine's letter to Williams is also a compelling example of acculturation; her portrayal of "a wild howling wilderness," where the light of Christianity has not yet penetrated, is a model of Puritan imagery. Yet, here was a Cherokee girl who had spent her entire life in the mountains of southern Appalachia and who had fled to those mountains when her life was in danger, employing the metaphor of a "howling wilderness" to describe territory inhabited primarily by Indian people.[5]

Furthermore, her reluctance to remain behind in the relative safety of the Brainerd Mission while the rest of her family was forced to settle in the "dark region" to which the U.S. government was removing them, hints at the inner conflict she experienced in being caught between two disparate cultures. In spite of her strong attachment to the missionaries, Catharine confronted her parents a few days after writing to Williams and begged them to let her stay at Brainerd. Cherokee women, however, sensing that their matrilineal powers were rapidly being eroded, proved more resistant to cultural change than did their men, and Catharine's mother was especially unhappy about the missionaries' influence on her daughter. Several months later, Catharine told Mr. and Mrs. Williams, "My mother said if I remained here, she did not expect to see me again in this world. Indeed, she wished she had never sent me to this school, and that I had never received religious instruction" (R. Anderson 45).

In a change of heart that Catharine considered "an evident answer to fervent believing prayer," her parents finally relented. Catharine reported to the missionaries that as she entered the room where her mother and father were sitting one evening, Mr. Brown announced: "Kate, we know you feel very bad about leaving the missionaries & going with us to the Arkansas—we have been talking about it—we pitty you, & have concluded that you may go back [to Brainerd]" (Phillips 111).

Another possible key to Catharine's ambivalence in the matter of leaving her homeland may lie in the journal of young Daniel Butrick, an unmarried missionary, who confessed that his "carnal" attraction to the beautiful Cherokee girl left him feeling extremely guilty.[6] On one occasion, he confided to his diary, "My wicked passions rage, the storm beats on my foundering bank, and gaping waves and towering surges threaten my immediate ruin" (Johnston 7).

Although Butrick spent a great deal of time with the Brown family when he was at Creek Path, Catharine rarely mentions him in her letters to the other missionaries. In a letter dated July 18, 1820, however, she notes that Butrick and John Arch (a Cherokee student) have just left Creek Path to carry out a three-month preaching assignment elsewhere in the Cherokee Nation. "I cannot sufficiently express my gratitude to God, for sending out missionaries to this distant land," Catharine writes, "and willingly would I offer myself for their assistance, were I qualified for a religious teacher" (R. Anderson 65–66).

As it turned out, the Brown family did not remove to Arkansas until some four years later, an interval during which Catharine is credited with having been instrumental in the "formation of schools, and to the stated preaching of the Gospel, at Creek-Path, the place of her father's residence, and to the hopeful conversion of nearly all her family" (34). Her growing concern for the evangelization of the Cherokees is especially evident in letters she penned after returning to Brainerd in May 1819. On May 30, she wrote to a Mr. and Mrs. Hall, of Knoxville, Tennessee, "My heart bleeds for my people, who are on the brink of [spiritual] destruction. O pray for me, my dear brother and sister" (37). In July of that same year, Catharine confided in a letter to Mr. and Mrs. Williams her desire to "be made the means of turning many souls from darkness unto marvellous light." "I hope you will pray for [my parents], and also for me," she wrote, "that I may be useful to my dear people. My heart bleeds for their immortal souls" (45).

By October, she seems to share the missionaries' view of her people as "heathen." Writing to Mr. Moody Hall at the Taloney Mission in northern Georgia, Catharine declares,

> O how I feel for my poor Cherokee brethren and sisters, who do not know the blessed Jesus, that died for us, and do not enjoy the blessings that I do. How thankful I ought to be to God that I have ever been brought to the light of the Gospel, and was not left to wander in darkness. O I hope the time is at hand, when all the heathen shall know God. (46)

A cursory reading of Catharine Brown's letters and diary may leave the impression that assimilation has claimed every vestige of her Native culture and values. In fact, her physician, Dr. Alexander A. Campbell, once observed that Catharine was so "graceful and polite, and humility and benevolence beamed from her countenance" in such a way that some of his acquaintances "were unwilling to believe she was an Indian" (69).

Certainly, the words of Catharine Brown convey a piety and devotion that set her apart, even among Christians; yet, she allows neither her devotion to Christ nor her love for the missionaries to alienate her from her own people. Rather, she uses every opportunity to share her newfound faith with family and friends, consistently reminding missionaries and supporters of the ABCFM of her deep concern for the spiritual welfare of the Cherokees. Consequently, Catharine's entire family, as well as several of their neighbors, eventually converted to Christianity.

It is worth noting here that the Cherokees were a monotheistic people long before the arrival of white missionaries, and religion permeated every aspect of their lives. Alexander Longe, after living among the Cherokees fifteen years, wrote in 1725: "They owne one Supreme Power that is above the firmament, and that power they say was he that made the heavens and the earth and all things that is therein and governs all according to his will and pleasure" (Longe 3). Later, during the Green Corn Feast, Longe witnessed Cherokee hunters sacrificing a portion of their kill to the fire. Upon asking the priest why he "burned that piece of meat in the fire, he told me that it was to the great king above and that it was burnt in honor and obedience to him being supreme lord and emperor of all visable and invisable" (11).[7]

The principles of Christianity, therefore, were not as foreign to the Cherokee religion as the missionaries may have expected. Conversely, as William McLoughlin points out, many Cherokee converts were able to "find in Christianity the same sense of community loyalty, family loyalty, and national loyalty that had sustained them in the past," and they bridged the gap between ancient traditions and new religious beliefs, not by altering their identity as Indians, but by enhancing it ("Evan Jones" 120). Furthermore, because Cherokees did not divide religion and culture into separate spheres, Catharine Brown's concern for the welfare of her people could as easily be attributed to her Cherokee values as to her newfound faith in Christ.

When tuberculosis so weakened Catharine's body that it became necessary for her to abandon her studies at Brainerd and return home to her family in 1820, she refused to give up and die. Rather, she started a school for girls in her home village of Kusa-Nunnahi (Creek Path), a settlement established around 1785 by Chickamauga Cherokees who wanted to put more distance between themselves and the rapidly expanding white frontiers.[8] On the day before her departure from Brainerd, she wrote the following in her private diary:

> Tomorrow morning I shall leave this school, perhaps never to return. It is truly painful to part with my dear Christian friends . . . This is the place where I first became acquainted with the dear Saviour. He now calls me to work in his vineyard, and shall I, for the sake of my Christian friends and of my own pleasures, refuse to go, while many of my poor red brothers and sisters are perishing for lack of knowledge? O no, I will not refuse to go. (R. Anderson 53)

Initial enrollment in the Cherokee mission school at Creek Path was twenty pupils, but attendance grew rapidly, and soon many of the mothers of Catharine's students were also coming to her for instruction. Describing Catharine's work, missionary William Potter wrote, "The spiritual interests of the family lay nearest her heart, and she sometimes spent whole evenings in conversation with them on religious subjects. . . . She endeared herself to our hearts and she was most tenderly loved by all the children" (Walker 182).

Laura Potter, who—along with her husband, William—resided with the Brown family for two months while waiting for their own housing in Creek Path, was impressed with yet another facet of Catharine's personality. After describing the young girl's deep devotion to her parents, Mrs. Potter writes, "Nor did she forget the poor *slaves* [emphasis added]. Having, at her own expense, put a spelling-book into the hands of each of the younger ones, she began with zeal to teach them to read" (R. Anderson 57). Although the Brainerd missionaries undoubtedly influenced Catharine's attitude toward slavery, they seem to have left the teaching of slave children to the discretion of individual teachers. Another factor to consider, however, is that Creek Path, part of the Cherokee Nation, was located within the boundaries of Alabama—a state that only a few years later (1832) officially enacted a law against teaching literacy to black slaves. As reflected in their Constitution of 1827, Cherokee leaders, too, were beginning to discriminate against blacks.[9] Thus, teaching slave children required at least some degree of courage on the part of Catharine and is yet another instance of female resistance to a loss of Cherokee cultural values.

Tuberculosis eventually took its toll on Catharine Brown, but even as she lay dying, she seemed more preoccupied with the welfare of the Cherokee people than with her own impending death. In a letter to her brother David on June 13, 1823, she wrote:

> It was my intention to instruct the people more than I have done, when I returned from Brainerd; but when I got home, I was not able to do it. It was a great trial to me not to be able to visit our neighbours, and instruct them. But I feel that it is all right. It is my prayer that you may be useful to our poor people. (R. Anderson 100)

On July 18, 1823, only a few weeks after dictating her final letter to David, Catharine died. Surrounded by friends and family, she is said to have looked steadily at her weeping mother for a moment, "filial love beaming from her eyes," and then to have "expired without a groan, or a struggle" (R. Anderson 102).

Predictably, the missionaries took credit for "her expansion of mind, her enlargement of views, her elevated affections, her untiring benevolence" (R. Anderson 118). As Robert Walker reminds us, however, the missionaries had been astounded to learn that even before she came to Brainerd, "at a time when she had no religious conceptions," Catharine Brown had "regarded the preservation of her character far above that of injury or loss of her body" (177).[10] She was, in fact, the epitome of the moral integrity and strength the Brainerd missionaries sought to foster in their students. Yet, in spite of what appear to be "textbook examples of internalized oppression," in her letters and diary Catharine Brown never fully adopted what theologian James Treat (Muscogee Creek) refers to as the "theological blindnesses of [her] missionary trainers," nor for one moment did she abandon her Cherokee identity. As Treat reminds us, "Native people have a long history of adopting and adapting the literary tools and techniques of the dominant culture" (10). To cite the letters of Catharine Brown, therefore, as a classic example of Cherokee acculturation is to deny the author of those letters the right to embrace Christianity as her own religion, or to use the language of her teachers to instruct her own people.

Curiously, the *Brainerd Journal,* which so carefully chronicles the life of "the first fruit of our missionary labours," and which records the deaths of numerous other Cherokees, is completely silent concerning the demise of Catharine Brown. In fact, the journal entry for July 3, 1823, is devoted entirely to pondering the feasibility of travelling "40 miles up the river" to buy corn (*selu*) versus buying for the same price at a local warehouse (365). Catharine Brown would surely have found it ironic that her former instructors, who denounced the Cherokee creation story as a pagan myth, should be preoccupied with discussions of the monetary value of *selu* while the body of their first Cherokee convert was being prepared for burial.

Gradually, the name of Catharine Brown seems to have been reduced to a mere memory as the missionaries found other Cherokee girls to serve as examples of missionary achievement at Brainerd. One of these young women seemed particularly destined to follow in the footsteps of Catharine Brown and to establish herself early in life as a devout Christian and an outstanding student. Lydia Lowery, age fifteen, enrolled at Brainerd in April 1818—about ten months after Catharine Brown's arrival at the school—and is mentioned frequently in the *Brainerd Journal* in conjunction with Catharine. According to the *Journal* entry for January 26, 1819, Lydia had been "under particular instruction as a candidate for baptism," and was, at that time, being "considered as a candidate for full communion, in all the ordinances & privileges of the church of God." The writer of this particular journal entry further states that "[Lydia's] whole deportment since the apparent [conversion] has been such as to give increasing evidence that it is real & saving" (Phillips 105). Although the journals do not devote nearly as much space to the life of Lydia Lowery as they do to that of Catharine Brown, it is evident, nevertheless, that she was also an ideal candidate for Brainerd Mission's select group of Cherokee students. Lydia, the daughter of a prominent couple, Maj. George Lowery and Lucy Benge (a half-sister of Sequoyah), was intelligent, open to the teachings of Christian missionaries, and amenable to the ideas of Euro-American domesticity.[11]

Unlike her friend Catharine, Lydia seems to have left behind no letters and no diary; instead, she was kept busy during her spare time serving as an interpreter for the missionaries and for new students who spoke only Cherokee. One important sample of her writing, however, still exists: Lydia Lowery lays claim to the honor of being the author of the first Cherokee hymn. Though no specific date is cited for the composition of this hymn, George Foster, nineteenth-century writer/bibliographer, documents some of the circumstances that apparently inspired the song of the "little Cherokee scholar, Lydia Lowery." In a highly romanticized account, Foster describes "that nature-loving Cherokee girl, who at that time was numbered among the very brightest of that then uncivilized tribe," going for a walk one Sabbath morning after lessons, throwing herself beside a "brook which was rippling in the deep forest," and repeating the following line from Psalm 23: "He leadeth me beside the still waters." In the words of Foster, Lydia then "fell to wondering about the Great Spirit of the Pale Face," promptly fell asleep, and dreamed. In her dream "a vast concourse of Cherokee people" were seated in a semicircle, and "in their midst stood a wonderful being, giving praise to the Great Spirit, the whole congregation repeating again and again the words after him, in joyful Cherokee song." When Lydia awoke, she remembered the exact words the congregation of her dream had chanted. Immediately, she went to share them with missionary William Chamberlain, who translated her words from Cherokee into English:

> God and I are friends,
> I will not be afraid of Him.
> Though all the world be against me,
> I will still be confident. (20–21)

Within both the context of Lydia's dream and her own life as a student at Brainerd Mission School, the lyrics of this simple hymn speak volumes, especially in light of the impending removal of her Cherokee people.

Furthermore, Lydia speaks of God as a personal "friend" with whom she feels both comfortable and confident. She breaks from the conventional language of her classmates, whose letters are rife with statements characterizing God as a fearsome master and a wrathful judge. One wonders, for example, what perceptions of God must have influenced the following confession of ten-year-old Lucy McPherson, written to a Mrs. Conner in a letter dated June 11, 1828: "I think you wish to know my feelings. I feel as though I am a great sinner and very wicked sinner . . . When I sing I always felt very bad it seems that I was mocking God" (JHP 8:41).

As African American music professor/scholar Kathy Bullock reflects, music is one avenue by which oppressed people "can gain power over their condition." Especially among tribal peoples, explains Bullock, music has always permeated every aspect of life:

> There are songs for grinding corn, for hunting, fishing, for planting, harvesting. A baby shows his first tooth, a child reaches puberty, a visitor to the home or community is greeted, for each occasion there is music. Music, then, is functional, designed for a particular purpose outside its own edification. In fact, some tribal languages do not have a word for music, when defined as an abstract art form that one listens to for its own sake. (3)

It is understandable, then, that the Brainerd school girls should be puzzled by the refusal of one of their teachers to join them in singing hymns during evening vespers. Nancy Reece reports in a letter:

> Many times Miss Ames has the girls all take their seats before evening worship after they have laid aside their work for the purpose of singing, then we often ask her why she does not learn to sing. How glad we should be to have our teacher sing with us. One of the scholars promised her if she would learn to sing she would give her a Cherokee cotton frock. (JHP 8:20–21)

What may appear at first glance to be merely a playful bribe on the part of the girl, who offers Miss Ames a cotton frock in exchange for her singing with the scholars, takes on more serious overtones when one considers the special role music has always played in Indian culture.[12] As Debra CallingThunder so eloquently puts it, "The words of the grandparents have bound us together, those of us who are like a victory song, like an eagle feather, like the thunder when it laughs" (46). While Lydia Lowery's "little hymn" certainly demonstrates her ability to use Christian music as a means of binding her people together "like a victory song," she manages, at the same time, to embody the spirit of Selu and the song of the Grandmothers conceptualized by Cherokee/Appalachian poet Awiakta:

> I love and work and sing.
> I listen to the Spirit.
> In all things I speak my mind.
> I walk without fear.
> I am Cherokee. (*Selu* 93)

By the time Lydia Lowery was seventeen years old, she was married and actively engaged in missionary work herself. Other Cherokee students began assuming the role of Brainerd notables. Since the missionaries were required to carry on voluminous correspondence with benefactors and patrons of the Brainerd Mission, they often called on their students to assist them. Since letter writing was considered a "feminine" task, most of the letters preserved from Brainerd school days were written by Cherokee girls. One of the most prolific of these writers was Nancy Reece, daughter of former warrior and Cherokee leader Charles Reece. Characterized by the missionaries in 1823 as a nine-year-old "half-breed : . . apt to learn & apt to work," Nancy quickly established herself as a favorite among the missionary teachers (Phillips 423). Little is known of Nancy's mother, but according to the *Brainerd Journal* entry for January 25, 1817,

> Charles Reece . . . has had three sisters for his wives at the same time, one of whom is dead; & he has left the other two on account of the insolence of their mother—has left a good plantation, & a valuable stock of cattle, for them & his children, & taken another woman with whom he has begun anew in the world. (28)

Nancy would have been only three years old at the time of this journal entry and may have been one of the children for whom Charles Reece had provided when he left his wives. It is more likely, however, that she was the daughter of the woman with whom her father had "begun anew in the world," for in a letter addressed to Rev. John Johnston (January 1, 1829), Nancy writes:

> Miss Ames says I may relate something of my father's family he is an elder of this church he is an interpreter, he has eight children at this

school besides myself, my brother Samuel has gone through his course of his studies he united with the church before he left he now resides with his mother who married a Cherokee man; but he is not contented and thinks of leaving soon, his mother is an opposer to religion and wishes him to work on the sabbath. (JHP 8:24)

Although Nancy's letters seem void of any mention of her mother, she does refer frequently to her father, and in a letter dated December 25, 1828, she proudly states, "when my father comes on sabbath days he talks in Cherokee [for] those children who do not talk english" (JHP 8:22).

Whether she was abandoned by her biological mother or simply did not feel close to her, Nancy bonded quickly with the missionaries and seems to have thought of more than one of her female teachers as a surrogate mother. In a letter written May 16, 1828, for example, the young student (now fifteen years old) describes the emotional pain she suffered when Mr. and Mrs. Dean, a missionary couple at Brainerd, left the mission due to the illness of Mrs. Dean, without informing Nancy that they were leaving. Distressed even further by news of the death of Mrs. Dean, received later from New Jersey, Nancy writes to Mrs. Coleman, a relative of the deceased:

> It is a year since I wrote to you; But I understand that you have not recieved [sic] the letter. In my other letter, I mentioned the love I had towards Mrs. Dean, and how much good she has done me. I mentioned that they left their son here. I took care of it while it was here and at my fathers. They had it there five or six months. I loved both of their children very much as well as I do my brothers and sisters. When Mr. and Mrs. Dean went away I was not here. I was at my fathers taking care of their son. I wished to see them before they went away. They were father and mother to me, and it almost makes me shed tears to think about them and how many pleasant hours I spent in working with her and playing with Chester. (JHP 8:1)[13]

Nowhere in her letter does Nancy specifically mention the recent death of Mrs. Dean; in fact, she devotes most of her two-page message to describing routine activities at school. That she thinks of the Deans in familial terms, however, is quite evident, and her disappointment over not having seen them before they left Brainerd—though couched in polite terms—is palpable. Furthermore, Nancy's letter indicates that the Deans left their three-year-old son, Chester, with the Reece family when they returned North. How long the Deans may have been separated from their child is unclear, but the very act of placing their child in the care of a Cherokee family seems antithetical to the Mission's declaration that "the children should be removed as much as possible from the society of the natives, and . . . be boarded by the missionaries and teachers, be entirely under their direction and have their pious, orderly and industrious example constantly before them" (Walker 22–23).[14] Surely the young letter writer was aware of the mission's practice, if not their philosophy, of removing Cherokee children from the homes of their families and immersing them in the culture and family values of the Anglo-American missionaries. By reminding Mrs. Coleman, therefore, of the Deans's willingness to entrust the life of their own son to the care of a Cherokee family, Nancy demonstrates her subtle understanding of one of the incongruities of Western culture: a willingness to utilize "the society of natives" when advantageous while invalidating the civilization of that same society.

Further evidence of Nancy's insight and maturity is demonstrated in a letter written on July 27, 1828, to Mrs. Elizabeth Preston in Boston. Informed of the death of Mrs. Preston's little daughter, Rebecca, and, more recently, of a young son, Nancy confesses, "I never lost any near relative but my grandmother; she died this year. I thought I felt bad as though she had been my near relative but I expect it is harder for mothers to part with their children." Later, in the same letter, she describes some children who attend the Brainerd Mission School and explains how the Cherokees take care of their own:

> I think you would be pleased to sit in our school room and see us attend to our studies, you would see some tawny girls, though some are white as any children. Some have lost father or mother and some both. But orphans among the cherokees have generally some kind friends, who do not think right if they do not take them and give them victuals and clothes and often they do as well by them as they do by their own children. (JHP 8:12)

Without pious phrases or insincere rhetoric, Nancy uses her letter of condolence as a means of impressing upon Mrs. Preston the fact that Indians, too, grieve over the loss of a loved one, and that even orphans can expect to be well cared for among the "pagan" Cherokees.

In yet another letter, Nancy notes the relative success with which the missionaries convert small children to Christianity. "I have thought much on the subject of religion," she declares, "have felt it was important to seek

God while young. I often think of little children who seek God for new hearts when they are not [even] five or six years old then I think of some young ladies who are not christians and ask myself why it is so and then I answer it is because [the younger children] sought God right" (JHP 8:13). Although there seems to have been a paucity of female guidance in Nancy Reece's own family, she manifests a decidedly maternal interest in the spiritual welfare of younger Cherokee students at Brainerd and is quick to observe that the sooner children "seek God for new hearts," the stronger their faith as they mature.

Traditional American Indian systems, as Paula Gunn Allen points out, did not rely upon external social institutions such as schools and churches to teach their children essential values. Rather, Indian children were traditionally "oriented toward internal governing mechanisms"; thus, it often became the responsibility of tribal females to guide their young in developing a spiritual belief system (206). Nancy's compassion for children may have developed as a result of the lack of closeness she apparently experienced with her own mother. Or she may simply have possessed unusually strong maternal instincts. Whatever the reasons, Nancy's extraordinary concern was undoubtedly intensified by the Calvinistic teaching she received at Brainerd—an indoctrination that left Nancy with serious concerns for the destiny of her own soul, as well. In a letter addressed to a benefactor in the North and signed "From your unworthy young friend," she writes, "Sometimes I feel as though my sins were forgiven, and other times I am doubtful" (JHP 8:8). In a letter to a Mrs. Coleman, Nancy elaborates:

> There has been more attention to religion at this Station and in this neighbourhood than usual. Among others the girls of this school have thought more about the Saviour and that they were sinners. Some of them think that their sins are forgiven. I have thought more than I did and sometimes I think that my heart is changed and at other times I am doubtful. . . . I pray that there may be a survival of religion here. (JHP 8:1)

Nancy seems also to have shared these religious doubts with her friends, for on May 1, 1828, Mary Ann Vail, daughter of one of the Brainerd missionaries, casually mentions to a correspondent, "Nancy Reece hopes her sins are pardoned" (JHP 8:4).

Numerous letters from Nancy's younger classmates attest to the fact that she was not alone in succumbing to the fear and anxiety instilled in

Cherokee children by their Christian teachers.[15] As Apache writer and former mission school resident Sharon Skolnick quips, "Fear of hellfire [can do] wonders to alter [the] depraved character of little children" (20). Unlike Skolnick, however, who had the benefit of a kindhearted housemother to counter some of the fiery sermons to which she was subjected, Nancy was forced to address her concerns to missionaries who seemed to offer little reassurance of God's love, or on the matter of her eternal destiny.[16]

While both Catharine Brown and Nancy Reece express a common interest in the salvation of their Cherokee people, a subtle shift in the girls' affinity with their parents seems evident by the time Nancy begins writing letters some five years after the death of Catharine: Whereas Catharine's letters and diary reflect a fundamental interest in maintaining ties with her Cherokee parents, as well as with her siblings, the letters of Nancy Reece place far less emphasis upon parental ties and focus almost entirely upon the children of the Cherokee Nation. Furthermore, Nancy never even mentions her mother—traditionally the parent whose family controlled the lives of Cherokee children—and she devotes considerable space in her letters to describing her interactions with various surrogate mothers assigned her by the mission.

Undeniably, vertiginous changes were taking place in family and kinship structures among the Cherokees; however, family relationships and the changing role of Cherokee children were not the only cultural concerns addressed by the children at Brainerd Mission. For example, in a letter dated May 20, 1828, fifteen-year-old Elizabeth Taylor expresses an interest in the work of Miss D. Gould, an artist living in the North:

> I inquired of Miss Ames about your education. She told me you understood all the useful branches of learning, and you could paint. The cherokees are not acquainted with the art of painting. If you please, I should be very glad to have you send me a small peice [sic] of your painting, and write my name on it. (JHP 8:9)

Elizabeth's eagerness to receive an inscribed painting from Miss Gould may have stemmed merely from a teenage fascination with collecting. On the other hand, she seems to be as interested in learning about Anglo-American culture as many white Americans were in studying Indian societies.

A few weeks later, Elizabeth describes various aspects of Cherokee culture in a letter to Abigail Parker, a friend of her teacher at Brainerd. She prefaces her remarks with the following explanation: "[Our teacher] wishes me to give you an idea of the customs of the Cherokees; as she has not time. I am willing to do it because I think when christians know how much we need the means of knowledge; They will feel the importance of sending missionaries." Then the young scholar proceeds with:

> The unenlighted parts of this nation assemble for dances around a fire. The one that goes before sings; a woman follows after having herself adorned with shells which make a rattling noise when she dances the others follow after dancing around a fire in a ring, and keep up their amusements all night. (JHP 8:13)

Although Elizabeth Taylor issues a predictable disclaimer, attributing these activities to "the unenlighted parts of this nation," she restricts her comments to a mere description of the dance and refrains from making any remarks that might be interpreted as judgmental of Cherokee culture. Furthermore, while Elizabeth does make a distinction between "civilized" and traditional Cherokees, she is careful not to express any condemnation of those who still cling to ancient customs: "Many about this station are more civilized. Some come to meeting and appear as well as white people," she writes. "Others dress in the Indian manner with maucassins for shoes, and handkerchiefs round their heads for turbans."

Finally, in a rather startling maneuver, the young Cherokee concludes with the following observation: "But I have learned that the white people were once as degraded as this people; and that encourages me to think that this nation will soon become enlightned" (JHP 8:14). Elizabeth's primary purpose in writing, therefore, seems to have been threefold: (1) to demonstrate her ability as a "civilized" Cherokee girl to write in the English language, (2) to exchange cultural knowledge with non-Natives, and (3) to persuade other missionaries to come South and impart their "means of knowledge" to the Cherokees.

That the girls at Brainerd were able to maintain a polite tolerance for the stereotypes and prejudices of their white teachers is evident in several letters. Eleven-year-old Lucy McPherson, for example, wrote to one of the school's patrons, "One of the missionaries said when she first came into this Cherokee Nation she felt afraid the Cherokees might come with their tomahawks to kill them" (JHP 8:59). Of course, the fears of that missionary— like those of many a newcomer to a region or culture—were undoubtedly based on the stories she had heard and the stereotypical notions she harbored. Still, it must have seemed puzzling to these young Indian girls that people of the North still entertained such fears, even after such leaders as Sequoyah (inventor of the Cherokee syllabary), Elias Boudinot (editor of the bilingual *Cherokee Phoenix*), Rev. Jesse Bushyhead (Baptist minister), and John Ross (Principal Chief of the Cherokee Nation) had proven the Cherokees to be a highly "civilized" people. Culture shock was also common among the missionaries, and in another letter Nancy Reece reports to Mrs. Thankful Holton: "Miss. Ames has read a part of her letter where she is describing the Cherokees. It appears to me that you cannot avoid laughing where she is telling [Miss Parker] the manner of their living" (JHP 8:29).

Despite overwhelming evidence of advances in European culture among the Cherokees, the Brainerd missionaries, like many other nineteenth-century Americans, believed that the only way to save the Cherokees from certain removal was to "civilize" their children. Lamenting the lack of available overseers for their female students, for instance, a Brainerd administrator writes: "Considering the dark shades from whence these dear girls have so lately been brot., they do much better, than we could have expected; but they, as well as the boys, need some one with them every hour" (Phillips 99).

Within the confines of their rooms at night, these "dear girls" may have wondered aloud about some of the words and actions of their teachers; however, cultural constraints dictated a veneer of courtesy and compliance in their public behavior, as well as in their handwritten letters, which rarely betrayed negative thoughts or feelings. Like Selu, who chose to forgive the indiscretions of her son and Wild Boy in order to provide them with strategies for survival, the Brainerd girls seemed able to circumvent the cultural misconceptions and superior attitudes among their teachers by refusing to think of themselves as helpless victims. Unwittingly, perhaps, these Cherokee girls recorded not only their views on Cherokee history and culture, but also various insights into the lives of the missionaries—an Indian perspective, very rarely found in nineteenth-century literature.

Occasionally, the girls found the missionaries' standard of womanhood somewhat amusing. "We went to the boys school," Polly Wilson wrote to a friend, "and they came in ours, and Mr. Elsworth told me that I better alter my voice he said I spoke like a man" (JHP 8:39). More often, however, the girls seemed to view domesticity as a necessary part of their Christian training, and Lucy Campbell must have encouraged the hearts of her teachers when she wrote:

The Missionaries schools do a great deal of good they teach us how to
behave as Christian people do and how to study as white children do,
and how to take care of families that when we go home we can take
care of our mothers house, and to teach poor children who can not
come to Missionaries school. (JHP 8:49)

Eager to impress upon white patrons the extent to which her parents
have become "civilized," Sally Reece, a younger sister of Nancy, notes in a
letter to Rev. Daniel Campbell, "My Father works in the field Mother spins
and weaves" (JHP 8:45).

As Phillips and Phillips point out, "Had these girls remained at home
with their mothers, they would have learned the age-old Cherokee stories
of Selu, the first woman, teaching the tribe to plant crops, as the women
labored in the field planting corn" (13). Instead, the female students learned
to embrace Christian principles which the missionaries believed would
"transform an idle, dissolute, ignorant wanderer of the forest into a labori-
ous, prudent and exemplary citizen" (1823 *Annual Report* of the ABCFM).
The girls were required not only to make their own clothing but also to sew
and mend for the male students. The girls must learn these domestic skills,
explains Nancy Reece, "so they can do such work when they go home, to
assist their parents. They can then take care of their houses and their brothers and sisters and perhaps can learn their parents something that they do
not understand" (JHP 8:22). The girls were not always enthusiastic about
mastering these skills, however, and in another letter, Nancy Reece com-
plains, "Sometimes I think we have got all the sewing done then [Miss
Ames] will find some thing else which she says is necessary to be done"
(JHP 8:18).

On several occasions the girls inform their correspondents of a policy
requiring that they now work Saturdays, during hours that were formerly
set aside for play. In keeping with the work ethic they have been taught,
however, the Cherokee girls are quick to credit the missionaries with teaching them the joy of serving others. Once again, it is Nancy Reece who is
most articulate concerning the lessons they are learning. In a letter to Rev.
David Green, she writes:

Miss Ames asked some questions like these, who are you sewing and
kniting for? we answered for ourselves, then she asks who pays you?
we answered the Board, then she said do you think that you are doing
the Board a great service to work for your selves and they pay you for

it. . . . I felt little mortified but I did not say any thing for several days and then I asked her if I could not do something to get money for the Society myself. (JHP 8:25–26)

Nancy goes on to explain to Rev. Green that Miss Ames "thinks that it may be that such things can be sent to some place where people do not know that Indian children can learn like white children and that christian people will be so well pleased that they will purchase them, then we shall have more money to send you" (JHP 8:26).

Not only were the girls required to work long hours, they also were expected to show gratitude for the privilege of learning the domestic skills of their white sisters. Apparently the Cherokee scholars were a bit slow in expressing their thanks, for in a letter addressed to Jeremiah Evarts, the fifteen-year-old daughter of missionaries, Mary Ann Vail remarks on the gradual improvements her parents and other missionaries observe among the students. Reflecting an attitude of superiority and self-righteousness that the Cherokee girls must have found exasperating at times, Mary Ann writes, "[The children] appear to have more gratitude for the privileges they enjoy; but we ought not feel satisfied with this while they are walking the downward road to destruction" (JHP 8:16). A few months later, in a letter addressed to a group of young scholars in Georgia, Nancy Reece is a paragon of gratitude as she declares, "I am glad that we have a society, for I think if we did not have one we shall be spending our time foolishly. We all ought to exert ourselves and try to do all we can to pay what has been done for us" (JHP 8:27–28). Hence, regardless of how she may have felt about toiling from daylight till dark, Nancy Reece learned to ingratiate herself with those who appeared to hold the fate of the Cherokee people in their hands, and it is likely that she taught the younger girls to do likewise. One of these younger girls was twelve-year-old Polly Wilson, who confesses in a letter to Mr. Evarts:

I will tell you what I used to think last year and I am willing to own my bad thoughts to you. When I was reproved I thought that I would run away from school and when they asked me to work I used to think it was very hard and that I was obliged to work for the good of the missionaries. But I do not think so now and feel sorry that I did not have better feelings. I think that I feel more grateful. I feel as though we ought to be very thankful indeed to God for his kindness that he sent the good missionaries, we should have been ignorent and known nothing. (JHP 8:51)

While many missionaries maintained a steadfast confidence in the Cherokees' potential for rising above "heathen darkness" and becoming fully civilized, most persisted in their absolute intolerance of Cherokee cultural practices. One Presbyterian missionary outlined the task of nineteenth-century missionaries to the Indians quite succinctly when he wrote, "We must teach them to *think, feel, act,* and *work.* We must form their whole character—all their religious, moral, intellectual, social, and industrial habits. This is the work to be done" (*American Indian Correspondence* 5). Thus, as Michael Coleman so aptly concludes, the missionaries had "a many-sided effect on their pupils. They generated within them a sense of spiritual and cultural self-loathing; yet they also worked to convince the girls that they could be as good as whites" (128).

Since the traditional role of females as political activists and public speakers in the Cherokee Nation was being subsumed by the principles of "true womanhood" taught by Christian missionaries, the Brainerd girls adapted by "speaking" through the letters they were assigned to write. Their rhetoric, even as it became more apparently pious and self-deprecating, simultaneously became more politically infused. Almost without exception, the girls sought to convince their readers of the "progress" of the Cherokees, usually conflating "civilization" and Christianity as naturally as did their instructors. "I think the Cherokees are more civilized than they were a few years ago," writes eleven-year-old Lucy McPherson (JHP 8:47), but in a letter to Jeremiah Evarts, she worries about her own "awful and wicked" condition and expresses considerable anxiety concerning the spiritual and political future of the Cherokee Nation:

> If the Cherokees should be removed from their native land and be driven into a far country and seperated from each other we cannot expect God will be our friend in this time of affliction if we have not given up our hearts to him. (JHP 8:53)

That removal was uppermost in the minds of early-nineteenth-century Cherokee children is abundantly clear in the letters of the Brainerd school girls. Despite the fact that the girls' letters often imply a distancing of themselves from their "unenlightened" brethren, moreover, they consistently identify with the Cherokee Nation and view themselves as separate from "the country of the Christians." For example, two years before the Indian Removal Act of 1830 was passed, Elizabeth Taylor wrote to her cousin Flora McDonald, "I do not know when I shall see you. I suppose you have heard talk of the Cherokee going to the Arkansaw, it is uncertain whether they will go or not." Imagining the removal of her people from their own land, however, must have been difficult for a fifteen-year-old girl who had spent her entire life in the Appalachian homeland of the Cherokees. In fact, Elizabeth informs her cousin, "We scarcely ever see any white people excepting the missionaries and a few travellers. Our neighbors are all Cherokees . . . I often think of my dear friends . . . and wish to see them very much. But I am perfectly willing to stay in this nation" (JHP 8:3).

Because they could read, the young girls at Brainerd were acutely aware of the determination of men like President Andrew Jackson and Gov. Wilson Lumpkin of Georgia to remove the "irreligious savages" from the Southeast.[17] "I see much in the papers of the Cherokee removal," reported Nancy Reece in a letter to a northern minister. "I think the missionaries and most of the children think that such a separation would be the most trying season that they ever met with" (JHP 8:26).

On another occasion, Nancy addresses a group of young [white] Georgia scholars, whose instructor is a friend of Brainerd missionary, Delight Sargent. More intrepid, perhaps, in addressing adolescents like herself than in writing to adult benefactors and religious leaders, the young Cherokee writer politely reproves these students. She has heard that "a great many people in Georgia had become Christian." In fact, she "did not know that there were so many that were christians," and she cannot believe that "these christian people wish us to remove." It was her understanding, she writes, that the Christians "wish us to be civilized and be like other Christian people." Obviously, Nancy cannot reconcile the rumored spread of Christianity in Georgia with what is being reported by the press concerning the Cherokees, for she announces, "I have read much in the papers about the Georgians wishing the Cherokees to remove from their native Country" (JHP 8:27).

Like Nancy Reece and Elizabeth Taylor, most of the Brainerd schoolgirls found it incomprehensible that those "from a christian land" would wish to remove civilized Indians from their midst. In fact, one visitor to the school (Gen. Calvin Jones, mentioned earlier in this chapter) observed that the Indians with whom he conversed "seemed to feel the sentiment of patriotism strong in their bosoms, to deplore the fall of their once wide extended and powerful nation, and to be anxious that the little of it which remained, should be saved from annihilation" (121). Spurred on by teachers who were, in general, opposed to removal, the girls wrote compellingly of the accomplishments of Cherokees, and they clung tenaciously to the idea of Native sovereignty. In respectful but unequivocal terms, eleven-year-old Lucy Reece advises a northern Ladies Society, "I think that this nation will [soon] be civilized so that this people can teach themselves as the white people do in their own country" (JHP 8:33).

At times, the Cherokee girls—especially the younger ones—seem completely bewildered by the strange confluence of civilization, Christianity, and Indian removal in their lives. For example, in a letter to a little girl her own age, ten-year-old Lucy McPherson asks, "But where is the spirit is he gone from us? Do you think about the Spirit Mary Coe? Does your Father think about the Cherokees? Do pray for me, my Friend" (JHP 8:42). Also, the younger girls often seem to link death and removal, and their letters serve as a poignant reminder of the missionaries' emphasis on "behaving with propriety" in the face of grief.[18] Nine-year-old Susan Taylor, for instance, is apologetic for the grief she is experiencing after the death of several friends, a brother that she loved dearly, a grandmother, two uncles, and a cousin. In a letter to Jeremiah Evarts, Susan confesses that following these losses, "I felt very bad but I could not help it," but, she hastens to add, "I must not murmer because [God] took them away for it is right. perhaps it was that we might think more about dying." Moving immediately to the topic of removal, Susan reflects, "Death may come when we will not think it will. if we should remove I don't know what would become of us we would be scatered about it may be that we never see the missionaries any more who have been so kind to us and have done so much for us" (JHP 8:5).

To understand the reasoning behind the coalescence of physical death and removal from the land in Susan's letter, one must understand some-thing of the Native American worldview. As Cherokee/Chickasaw writer Geary Hobson points out, in many American Indian languages, the words "land" and "people" are indistinguishable and inseparable (11). Thus, to be uprooted from the *land* of their ancestors meant being uprooted from the *souls* of their ancestors, and one of the primary incentives for the large-scale acculturation of the Cherokees was to avoid removal to the West. Hence, if the missionaries expected the Cherokees to view death as a "wake-up call" from God, even the young girls must adapt their thinking to that of the Christians.

When a little Cherokee boy died of burns in November 1829, for example, nine-year-old Christiana McPherson reported to Jeremiah Evarts:

> I have lately heard that I had a little cousin burned to death he was but a child. I then thought death was near us.—how time passes it is now a year since my Grandmother died. she was an old woman. She belonged to this church her soul has gone to God and her body is now mouldering in the grave . . . I wish to be a good girl while I live in this world and when I die to go and be where God is (JHP 8:54)

Like Christiana, twelve-year-old Polly Wilson is profoundly affected by the death of this little boy, and in a letter to her brother John, a student at the Creek Path Mission in Alabama, she writes:

> I cannot say much but I will speak a few words to you. Love your God pray to him and you must not play on the sabbath; think about God, and you must mind your teachers and love your schoolmates. You must not quarrel with them . . . I will try to visit Creek Path next Summer if I live. . . . Aunt Peggy McCoy's little boy is bunt to death by catching fire to his clothes. This is another call for us to repent of our sins. I hope you will think of this. (JHP 8:43)

In the same letter, Polly reminds her brother, "I think it is about five years since I saw you last." The fact that she admonishes her brother to live a good life, then relates the details of their young cousin's death by fire, suggests that Polly may be worried about her brother's mortality, as well as her own. Yet, she "cannot say much" about her grief over the death of their cousin, nor about her fears concerning death—only that she hopes John will think seriously about his spiritual life and will behave as a Christian. Furthermore, one of their own Cherokee preachers, Stephen Foreman, had told them that "God sometimes takes children away from those that don't think anything about God [in order] to make them think about Him" (JHP 8:51). Thus, the Brainerd girls had little recourse but to maintain the same attitude toward death that Nancy Reece expressed concerning removal: "I hope we shall not murmur if it is God's will that such a thing should take place" (JHP 8:26).

Although the girls often resorted to self-abasement and professions of their wavering faith, they had no qualms about using their positions as "showcase scholars" to persuade men in high places of the virtues of the Cherokee people. Sometimes they resorted to flattery, as is evident in twelve-year-old Ann Bush's note of January 22, 1828, to Jeremiah Evarts, corresponding secretary of the ABCFM. "Respected Friend," she writes, "I felt as though I wished to write to you, because I knew you was a friend to us." Then, with the charisma of a seasoned politician, Ann informs Reverend Evarts that she remembers not only his visit to Brainerd but also the words that he spoke while he was there. Finally, after expressing her gratitude for all that the missionaries have done for the Cherokees and acknowledging the need of her people for "new hearts," she closes with, "We heard you was at Washington and I think you are pleading for the Cherokees that they may stay in their own country" (JHP 8:50). Evarts, who initially supported voluntary Indian removal, later changed his mind and publicly opposed removal, under any circumstances.[19] Who knows what effect the letter of a young Cherokee girl may have had on him?

Perhaps even greater cajolery was at work in the letter of Christiana McPherson, who took it upon herself to write to a man characterized by many as the most notorious Indian hater in the East: President Andrew Jackson.[20] While her classmates dutifully penned religious poems and passages of scripture designed to sway the president of the United States to look favorably upon the Cherokees, Christiana wrote:

> Sir.
> We heard that the Cherokees were going to send you a mink skin and a pipe. We thought that it would make you laugh; and the Scholars asked our teacher if they might make you a present and she told us that she did not know as there was any thing suitable in the whole establishment. Then she looked among the articles of the girls society and told me that I might make you a pocket book. Will you please to accept it from a little Cherokee girl aged nine years. (JHP 8:31)

Significantly, Christiana does not even allude to removal in her letter to the president. Instead, she simply follows the example of her elders and allows her gift to "speak" in behalf of the Cherokees. As voice and speech coach Patsy Rodenburg asserts, "Rhetoric, when linked with an individual's inner truth and need becomes a potent force" (14), and little Christiana McPherson had apparently learned already that there is "a time to keep silence, and a time to speak" (Ecclesiastes 3:7).

James Ronda and James Axtell argue that nineteenth-century missionaries were skilled propagandists who served as "potent agents for social change" among American Indians. Furthermore, "because the missionaries were usually dedicated and self-sacrificing, historians have revered them more than they have understood them" (1, 2). Many Native scholars, on the other hand, insist that Christianity is the one element of Western culture that has caused the most irreparable damage among Indians. As Geary Hobson puts it, "Europeans, like farmers in a hurry to get a late crop in, plowed under tribal religions with zeal as they sought to make the Indian into their own image" (3). Consequently, the missionaries' effectiveness as cultural revolutionaries often leads scholars to focus upon the widespread acculturation of Cherokees, and to ignore the resilience of traditional beliefs and customs that has enabled them to continue as a sovereign Nation. As Suzanne Fournier and Ernie Crey observe, few Indian children escaped boarding school education with their cultural identity intact:

> Children [often] returned home strangers who could trust no one; far from being "improved," they were demoralized, victimized and often unable to bond with their families or elders, so that their sad stories stayed locked up within them. (62)

Dismissing the conditions under which Indian students were educated may lead one to underrate the vibrancy and strength of young Cherokee girls like those at Brainerd, who found ways to capitalize on their role as "missionary scribes" and to speak for their people through the medium of letters.

According to one version of the Selu story, the Corn-Mother told her sons that they had plotted to kill her because their minds were bewildered by their incapacity to understand her powers. "In killing your mother under the pretense of her being evil," she told the boys, "you yourselves will fill yourselves with evil. But your mother will remain a mother to you, even though you kill her; take heed, therefore, and treasure up her words." Selu then informed them that though they would incur the guilt of her murder, they would not be able to destroy either her or her love for them, that she would still be alive, both on earth and in the skies. "Make invocations to me," she admonished the young men, "and when I hear you, I will take fast hold upon your mind and bring it back to what it ought to be" (JHP 1:26–28).

Although the voice of Selu was silenced by the missionaries, the Cherokee girls at Brainerd School did not forget the essence of her story, and even in the face of impending removal, they remained steadfast in their belief that the Real People would continue in the future as they had in the past. Could these girls have addressed men and women of generations to come—especially those who would be critical of the girls' Christian orthodoxy—they might have invoked the words of British writer Olive Schreiner, who wrote at the beginning of the twentieth century:

> You will look back at us with astonishment! You will wonder at passionate struggles that accomplished so little: at the, to you, obvious paths to attain our ends which we did not take; at the intolerable evils before which it will seem to you we sat down passive; at the great truths staring us in the face, which we failed to see; at the truths we grasped at, but could never get our fingers quite around. You will marvel at the labour that ended in so little;—but what you will never know is how it was thinking of you and for you, that we struggled as we did and accomplished the little which we have done. (*Woman and Labor* 23)

They were only children, but the Brainerd scholars served as unwitting agents of continuity and change during an era of unprecedented upheaval in the Cherokee Nation. Intelligent, spiritual, and proudly Indian, this handful of little schoolgirls left a legacy in letters that are a tribute to the indomitable spirits of Cherokee women of all ages—past, present, and future.

Chapter 3 *Boarding School Blues*

For a time we forgot
The sounds of ghost
            dancers
On the plains, drums
Ancestral, resolute
Converging in the distance

For a time we forgot
            the Voices
For a time we believed
The tinny pulpit voices
            instead
Could see only their pink
Fisted bibles
Raised as if poised
            to strike
And for a time we were afraid
But now I believe the sounds grow large
And now I see the Northern Lights gone wild
And between the shivering folds of pink paranoia
I hear the Voices, softly now:
            Tear down their fences
            They can't think without lines

—Joanne DiNova, "Seventh Fire"

In June 1744, the College of William and Mary in Virginia invited the Indians of the Six Nations to send twelve young men to their college to be "properly" educated (Carroll 240). Like many Native Americans, however, leaders of the Six Nations had already become disillusioned with the educational devices of the Americans. Shortly after receiving the invitation from William and Mary, therefore, they responded with the following letter:

> Sirs,
> We know that you highly esteem the kind of learning taught in Colleges, and that the Maintenance of our young Men, while with you, would be very expensive to you. We are convinc'd, therefore, that you mean to do us Good by your Proposal; and we thank you heartily. But you, who are wise, must know that different Nations have different Conceptions of things; and you will therefore not take it amiss, if our Ideas of this kind of Education happen not to be the same with yours. We have had some Experience of it. Several of our Young People were formerly brought up at the Colleges of the Northern Provinces; they were instructed in all your Scienes; but, when they came back to us, they were bad Runners, ignorant of every means of living in the Woods, unable to bear either Cold or Hunger; knew neither how to build a Cabin, take a Deer, or kill an Enemy, spoke our Language imperfectly, were therefore neither fit for Hunters, Warriors, nor Counsellors; they were totally good for nothing. We are, however, not the less oblig'd by your kind Offer, tho' we decline accepting it; and, to show our grateful Sense of it, if the Gentlemen of Virginia will send us a Dozen of their Sons, we will take care of their Education; instruct them in all we know, and make Men of them. (Carroll 240)

Many nineteenth-century Cherokees remained equally suspicious of the missionaries' motives for establishing schools for Indians. Repeatedly, Cherokee leaders informed missionary preachers that their interest was in education, not Christianity. When the Moravians, the first missionary group to enter the Nation, had asked the chiefs in 1799 for land on which to build a mission station, the chiefs agreed, but only on condition that the Moravians would, within a three-year trial period, start a free boarding school for any Cherokee children who wished to attend. When at the end of three years no school had been opened, the chiefs ordered the Moravians to pack up and leave (McLoughlin, *Cherokees and Christianity* 20).

About the same time, Presbyterian minister Gideon Blackburn approached the chiefs with an offer to start schools for Cherokee children in Tennessee. Promising not to engage in preaching to the students, Blackburn received the council's approval, and in 1804 he founded the Highwassee Mission in Blount County, Tennessee. Reverend Blackburn devoted much of his time to keeping financial supporters abreast of the progress of his schools, lamenting in one report that "so many [Cherokee children], who are capable of shining in the circle of a Bacon or Newton should lie neglected in the smoaky huts of the wilderness" (*Panoplist* 140).

Blackburn, like most assimilationists, believed that if the Cherokees' worldview, or what came to be known as their "system of values," could be changed, they would adopt the ways of the white man and become civilized. Two requirements for civilization on which there was widespread agreement were conversion to Christianity and the adoption of the English language; thus, Christianity and education frequently merged into a single requirement (Maddox 23). After visiting Blackburn's "little charge of Cherokees" in 1807, U.S. Indian agent Return J. Meigs wrote to Reverend Blackburn:

> I heard them read, —saw their writing and books of arithmetic, and heard them sing sundry hymns . . . little Cherokees with books in hand, intelligence sparkling in their eyes, with real character depicted in their faces . . . We look back! We look forward! We look back to the time when all was darkness. We look forward when all shall be light. The diffusion of knowledge among the children of your schools will multiply in arithmetical progression; and then the wilderness will indeed blossom like the rose. (*Panoplist* 140)[1]

However, Meigs had mixed feelings concerning the intelligence of the "little Cherokees," as the conclusion of his letter reflects in the following tribute to Mr. Dinnon, a teacher in Blackburn's school:

> It is my opinion, that out of one hundred teachers, you cannot find two, who would be willing, or perhaps able, to give the uncommon attention he has done to the hard and trying business of instructing the ignorant savages; in leading their minds from barbarism to the mild and gentle principles of christianity. (140)

By all accounts, Gideon Blackburn was a successful schoolmaster, and although there was considerably more religion than education in his school, he seems to have gained a general acceptance among the Cherokees (DeJong 64). His undoing, however, was in attempting to deceive the Cherokee leaders into giving up more land to the government. Taking it upon himself to meddle in Cherokee politics, and to campaign in the Cherokee Nation for laws that would Christianize the Indians, he boasted in some of his fund-raising letters that he was "single-handedly turning the Cherokees into a Christian tribe" (McLoughlin, *Cherokees and Christianity* 21). In fact, Blackburn claimed to have taught more than three hundred Cherokees to read and write English; yet, only five years after opening, the Presbyterian mission schools suffered a sudden and mysterious demise— a circumstance historian William McLoughlin attributes to the embarrassment of Reverend Blackburn's alleged involvement in illegal whiskey trade among Creeks and Cherokees.[2]

Whiskey trade, it turns out, was only a front for a more subversive activity—one the Cherokees saw as yet another affront to the sovereignty of their nation. In 1809, Blackburn agreed to undertake a secret mission for the federal government, a venture that entailed exploring the navigable waterways between Tennessee and the Gulf of Mexico, mapping out possible routes for white bargemen to travel back and forth through the Cherokee and Creek Nations. Concealing the real purpose of his mission, Blackburn rented a boat, loaded it with 2,200 gallons of whiskey (which he made in his own distillery in Maryville, Tennessee), and announced that he was undertaking a business venture to sell whiskey in Mobile, Alabama. In exchange for his part in the subterfuge, Blackburn hoped to "persuade the government to give him a large tract of Cherokee land for his own use." The Indians were not fooled by the minister's deception, however, and when he entered the Creek Nation, Chief Big Warrior stopped the boat and confiscated Blackburn's cargo. When the whole story came out, Blackburn's reputation was ruined, and he was forced to close down his schools (McLoughlin, *Cherokees and Christianity* 21–22).

Anti-mission sentiment among the Cherokees continued to mount, and by 1824, some of the chiefs were urging that missionaries from the American Board of Commissioners for Foreign Missions also be driven out of the Cherokee Nation. Although Charles Hicks, one of the chiefs who supported the work of ABCFM, specifically requested that the mission board ask permission of the Cherokee Council before bringing more missionaries to Brainerd, the Christian leaders apparently did not consider it necessary to do so. The board of ABCFM went so far as to publish a report in *The Missionary Herald* containing "an estimate of mission property at Brainerd, including improvements of land, to a considerable amount." When the Cherokees read this report, they complained to Charles Hicks, "This is what we always told you, that these missionaries would claim the land for themselves." Additionally, they accused Hicks and other pro-

Christian chiefs of "being in league with the missionaries in order to enrich themselves" (McLoughlin, *Cherokees and Missionaries* 193).

As numerous scholars have argued, the missionaries were highly instrumental in teaching the Cherokees vocational and academic skills that would enable them to deal more effectively with white men.[3] On the other hand, attitudes of white supremacy and ethnocentrism often interfered with the missionaries' ability to find acceptance among the people they claimed to cherish. Deciding whether the missionaries were, in the long run, friends or enemies of the Cherokees is not the objective of this study, for as McLoughlin concludes, that has to be "left up to the individual judgment of those who sift the conflicting evidence" (12). As removal became more and more inevitable, however, distrust between the Cherokees and the missionaries escalated.[4] Families of the young girls who attended Brainerd School (see chapter 2) eventually learned that "civilization" was not the key issue, after all, in the U.S. government's proposed removal of the Cherokees. Indeed, no matter how enthusiastically they adopted the laws and manners of the Anglo-Americans, the Cherokee people could not thwart the greed and determination of land-hungry settlers.

The scope of Cherokee removal has been addressed in hundreds of books and articles.[5] In spite of such rapid acculturation that they became, in the words of historian Mary Young, the "mirror of the American Republic," the Cherokees were still widely considered by whites an inferior race with an innately "savage" nature, and few Anglo-Americans seemed to mourn their fate (501). For those Americans who did protest removal, the popular press seemed always ready with an answer. For example, on August 28, 1838, in response to critics who charged that the Cherokees were subjected to "harsh treatment by the forces ordered to superintend their emigration," the *Daily National Intelligencer* (Washington) printed the following disclaimer:

> As we have seen several statements implying that [the Cherokees] are subject . . . to harsh treatment . . . we take pleasure in imparting, on unquestionable authority, the following facts: The whole of the Cherokees were, on the 31st ultimo, collected in four camps . . . they are perfectly content to emigrate as soon as the cool season shall return. [They are] well-fed, clothed, furnished with tents, physicians, medicines. The Indians are cheerful and confide unreservedly in the General. (3)

According to the eyewitness reports of missionaries and Indian people themselves, however, the Cherokees were, in general, neither "cheerful," confident, nor well cared for during this chaotic and tragic chapter of American history.[6] Moreover, the "whole of the Cherokees" had by no means been "collected"; in fact, primarily through the efforts of a white man, William Holland Thomas (1805–93), several hundred Eastern Cherokees gained legal rights to land in North Carolina and were able to remain in their ancestral homeland.[7] For awhile, it seemed as if the Cherokees who stayed behind might be allowed to live in peace, but as William Anderson asserts, "Corruption and greed soon subverted whatever philanthropy might have originally motivated policy makers, and as with removal, many Cherokees [continued to suffer]" (xiii).

Still, many people of European descent lived peaceably among their Indian neighbors, and one of the difficulties pertaining to the forced removal of southeastern Cherokees was that they must sever ties with local whites who had been their friends and neighbors. The threat of such a separation seemed especially painful for Cherokee children like Jane Bushyhead, who had attended school with white children. In the spring of 1838, while her father, Rev. Jesse Bushyhead, was in Washington still pleading the Cherokee case against removal, fourteen-year-old Jane penned the following letter to Martha Thompson, a former classmate at the Kingston Academy in Maryville, Tennessee:

> Beloved Martha,
> I have delayed writing to you so long I expect you have relinquished all thought of receiving any thing from me. But my Dear Martha I have not forgotten my promise. I have often wished to enjoy your company once more but it is very uncertain whether I shall ever again have that pleasure. If we Cherokees are to be driven to the west by the cruel hand of oppression to seek a home in the west it will be impossible. My father is now in Washington City. He was one of the delegates who went to Florida last Oct. We do not know when he will return. Not long since Mr. Stephen Foreman received a letter from father. He was absent when the letter came and before he arrived the [American] troops had been there and taken it to the Agency giving it to General Smith and he handed it round for all to read. It is thus all our rights are invaded. About two months ago my youngest brother died. He was sick almost two months. I was not at home when he died but they sent for me to attend his funeral. He was burnt very badly last fall and

it is very likely his death was occasioned by it however we do not exactly know. It will not be long before our next vacation. Then we expect to go home. Perhaps it may be the last time we shall have the privilege of attending school in this nation, but we are not certain. If we should remove to the Arkansas I should still hope to continue our correspondence.

Your Sincere friend,
Jane Bushyhead (*JCS* 3.3:7)

Like several of the young girls at Brainerd, Jane seems to link removal with death. In fact, the impending threat of Cherokee removal and Jane's concern for the safety of her father blend almost imperceptibly with news of the death of her little brother.[8] Adding to the pathos of the letter is the young Cherokee's longing to see her friend, and her subsequent despair in recognizing that if the Cherokees are removed to the West, "it will be impossible" to "enjoy your company once more." Only a few months after she wrote this letter, the worst fears of the Cherokee schoolgirl were realized: she and her family were forced to walk the thousand-mile route that was to become known as the Trail of Tears, and Jane was permanently separated from her friend Martha, as well as from her beloved homeland in East Tennessee (MSS 87–81, MCI Archives).

Introduction of Boarding Schools

Whites continued to interfere in the affairs of the Cherokees, and in order to hasten the assimilation of Indian children into American culture, the federal government initiated a boarding school program in the late 1870s. In an address delivered October 5, 1912, at a convention of military leaders in Columbus, Ohio, Capt. Richard Henry Pratt provided his audience with extensive details pertaining to the founding of these boarding schools— a history that sheds considerable light on Pratt's own views pertaining to "the Indian problem." According to Pratt, his ideas for educating Indians materialized in 1875, when Gen. Phil Sheridan devised a plan that would remove in chains to Florida "the ringleaders and most criminal" Indians in the West—a group of prisoners of war from the 1874 Red River War on the Southern Plains. Seventy-two prisoners were selected and transported to St. Augustine, Florida, where they were placed in confinement in the old Spanish fort San Marco (also known as Fort Marion) and were isolated indefinitely from their families and other tribal members.

Pratt, who was at that time a first lieutenant in the Tenth U.S. Cavalry, was placed in charge of these prisoners, and after watching a number of the Indians suffer "the greatest depression" and die, he proposed to General Sheridan that "while under this banishment they should be industrially trained, educated and civilized so far as possible." Two years later, "charitable people from the North" agreed to pay the expenses of the most promising of these young men if Pratt could find schools in the East willing to educate them (6). In the words of Pratt, however, "Correspondence with a number of agricultural and industrial schools failed to secure entrance for any of them anywhere, until Hampton Institute in Virginia was suggested" (7).[9]

Though wary at first, Gen. Samuel Chapman Armstrong, founder of Hampton Normal and Agricultural Institute, agreed to accept seventeen of Pratt's prisoners, and in 1878, the first American Indians enrolled in an institution that would educate more than 1,300 members of sixty-five tribes during the next forty-five years.[10]

Hampton's educational philosophy "combined cultural uplift with moral and manual training, or as Armstrong was fond of saying, an education that encompassed 'the head, the heart, and the hand'" (Adams, *Education* 45). Indian children who attended Hampton were isolated from family and friends by hundreds, and in some cases thousands, of miles. Stripped of traditional language, dress, and family values, Indian children were forced to learn new social and cultural values in an assimilation program that dominated the Indian educational scene for nearly fifty years (DeJong 264).[11]

This idea of removing Indian children from their parents, argue Suzanne Fournier and Ernie Crey (Stó:lo), originated with European clerics who—"accurately perceiving that they were encountering a powerfully intact civilization in the New World (though they considered it pagan and inferior)—focussed from the beginning on undermining the bond between Indian children and their families."[12] Predictably, this deliberate policy of separating and forcibly assimilating Indian children into the mainstream, has "pervaded every era of aboriginal history . . . and profoundly injured [Indian] people both historically and today" (17).

History shows that nineteenth-century clergymen worked hand in hand with military leaders and other government employees to enforce assimilation policies among the Indians, and that this coalition of "Friends of the Indian" often found themselves at odds with one another.[13] For example, when Pratt finally managed to enlist some Cheyenne girls to attend Hampton, they were dissuaded at the last minute by missionaries who feared the intermarriage of Indian girls with black men at the predominantly black institution. Thus, Captain Pratt's first effort to recruit Indian *girls* to Hampton was disappointing, largely due to cultural taboos against miscegenation (Lindsey 35).

Still other Hampton supporters were opposed to Indian coeducation on the supposition that funding the education of Indian girls would be a waste of money. In 1878, Commissioner of Indian Affairs Ezra Hayt publicly rejected the idea of coeducation at Hampton, primarily because he "questioned the morality of allowing Indian women to mix with black men" (Trennert 274). Samuel Armstrong countered Hayt's argument by invoking a comment of First Lady Lucy Hayes (wife of President Rutherford B. Hayes), who during a commencement address at Hampton had declared that "the condition of women is the true gauge of civilization" (Lindsey 35).

In spite of the ongoing controversy surrounding coeducation, the government approved a stipend of $167 per student for fifty Indian youths "of both sexes and in equal numbers, between the ages of 14 and 20," and after recruiting Indian students at six agencies in Dakota Territory, Pratt arrived at Hampton with forty boys and nine girls on November 5, 1878 (Hultgren and Molin 18). Most of the Indian students at Hampton, in fact, were from the West, but by the time the Hampton Indian program ended in 1923, sixty Eastern Band Cherokees had attended school there.

In addition to other problems, persistent stereotypical notions of "bloodthirsty savages" resulted in widespread fear of American Indians, and as Adams points out, Armstrong's public assurances that the Indians were harmless were not always persuasive. Several teachers and trustees were openly skeptical about accepting Indians at Hampton, and the black students refused to volunteer as mentors for the seventeen Indian students initially brought to the institute. When Armstrong pressed for an explanation, one student rose and spoke for the group: "We want to but we're scared—we're afraid they might scalp us." Eventually, Armstrong, was able to get the volunteers he wanted, but he remained privately worried. In a letter to

Pratt, he wondered how he should go about disciplining "an objectional Indian." Within two months after the admission of Indians to Hampton, however, Armstrong joked in a letter to one of the institute's trustees that although the Indians were once "terrible cutthroats," they were now "said to be tamed" (45).

In her study of "before" and "after" photographs of Indian girls who enrolled at Hampton, Laura Wexler concludes that these young scholars were to be "reconstituted not just as imitation white girls but as white girls of a particular kind." They were to be "imprinted with the class and gender construction of the [ideal Victorian female]" (170). As tribal sovereignty, therefore, was attacked on the political front, Indian individuality was attacked in the dormitory and classroom (Lomawaima 99).

Postbellum Conditions in the Qualla Boundary

Sociologist Abraham Makofsky observes that, as in the rest of North Carolina, the Cherokee economy was shattered after the Civil War. Agricultural prices were so severely depressed that most Cherokees were forced to abandon farming. Some of the Indians hired on as laborers for local white farmers, but the pay was meager and poverty was widespread (37).

Also destroyed by the Civil War was the comprehensive school system the Cherokees had managed to build after the removal. In fact *no* Indian schools were left in the Qualla Boundary by the time the war ended. In 1875, however, the Tribal Council appointed Rev. William McCarthy as school superintendent, and within a year three day schools and a boarding school were in operation on Cherokee lands. According to Makofsky, "internal divisions prevailed, and the educator was ousted" in 1876; dissension within the tribe and continuing quarrels with government educators finally led a federally appointed school superintendent to pursue a policy of sending students to out-of-state boarding schools and colleges. It was during this period that Eastern Band youth began attending Carlisle in Pennsylvania, Chilocco in Oklahoma, Hampton in Virginia, and Haskell in Kansas (38).

Cherokee Women at Hampton Institute

Many nineteenth-century reformers saw Indian "prejudice" against whites as a major reason for educating Indians in black schools. For instance, Rev.

Hollis Frissell, principal of black education at Hampton, taught his white audiences that Indian children were bred to hate whites. While blacks had been subdued by slavery, Frissell said, Indians believed themselves to be "natural aristocrats," superior beings, "like men who came to England with [William] the Conqueror, whose names were written in the Domesday Book entitling them to land and to lives of luxury while others labored" (Lindsey 92). The *Southern Workman* (September 1879) would later state that "[Hampton's] colored students, selected as they are from a wide range, furnished the best practicable conditions for building up wild Indians in ideas, decency and manhood" (90).

Although it was the Indian Office's policy after 1891 to educate Indians in local white public schools, only 359 Indian students were attending these schools by the end of the century (Lindsey 93). Moreover, it is a well-known fact that Indians attending most reservation or boarding schools were forbidden to speak their Native languages.[14] The struggle to maintain their cultural integrity in an environment where they were considered inferior to both blacks and whites, therefore, was profound for the Cherokee students who attended Hampton. Divested of their Cherokee language, isolated from their families, and forbidden to indulge in cultural practices such as dancing or wearing Native jewelry, many of them never completed their studies at Hampton.[15]

In this chapter I focus on three Cherokee females who attended Hampton Institute during the "Indian Program" era (1878–1923): Lottie Smith, Arizona Swayney, and Louisiana (Lula) Owl. Well aware that failure on their part would be attributed to their Indian heritage, while any success they enjoyed would be credited to their white ancestry, these Cherokee women maintained an Indian identity that focused on sovereignty and cultural survival for their people, not on making names for themselves. On the other hand, they often conformed to white cultural expectations, they intermarried with Euro-American men, and they enjoyed privileges some of their poorer relations in Qualla never dreamed of possessing.

As early as 1783, according to Moravian missionary Martin Schneider, every white trader he met had a Cherokee wife, and as Wilma Mankiller points out, this "mingling and intermarriage with whites" had a critical effect on tribal development (25).[16] While many scholars tend to focus solely on the declension of Cherokee women who have intermarried with white men, others argue that this mixing of the races was, for indigenous women, a survival strategy.[17] For example, Beth Brant (Mohawk) contends that women like Nancy Ward and Pocahontas had their own destinies to fulfill, and that the white men they married would have become part of a Native household or family group—a "kind of assimilation that is never discussed or written about" (91). Whether their primary motive was survival or not, history confirms that even prior to contact with Euro-Americans, Cherokee women were making alliances, trading, intermarrying, and exchanging cultural traditions with people outside their own Nation.

The feelings and emotions of Indian women have, for the most part, gone unaddressed in historical works, so tracing the outlines of what Aurora Morales labels "a woman-shaped hole in the record" can be a "powerful way of correcting imperialist history" (7). Furthermore, Mihesuah is right, I think, in suggesting that "without the inclusion of feelings and an understanding of motivations, the histories of Indian women are boring, impersonal, and more important, merely speculation and not really Indian history" (*Natives* 47).

There is no such thing as a monolithic Cherokee woman, of course, and cultural ambiguity is prevalent, sometimes even within the same family. Lottie Smith, Zona Swayney, and Lula Owl, however, experienced events and crossed cultural borders that continue to impact the ways their descendants think and act and feel, and their letters and speeches provide meaningful keys to understanding the lives of Eastern Band Cherokee women today.

Of these three Hampton students, only Lottie did not return to the Qualla Boundary to live. Consequently, her letters focus more on family crises, or on the difficulties of teaching on alien Indian reservations, than on issues pertaining to her own Cherokee people. Because Lottie's letters and news reports provide a much-neglected Cherokee female perspective on history and culture, however, I have devoted considerable space to her words in this chapter.

Lottie Smith (1870–1966)

In August 1889, Chief Nimrod Jarret Smith of the Eastern Band Cherokees agreed to send his nineteen-year-old daughter, Lottie, to Hampton.[18] The *Southern Workman,* official journal of Hampton Institute, noted the arrival of this "Cherokee girl from the sunny southland" with the following commentary: "Lottie is quite a musician, and she helps to make the evenings at Winona [Lodge] very pleasant with her sweet songs" (October 1889). In addition to being an accomplished musician—skilled at playing the piano, organ, and guitar, as well as possessing "a sweet voice"—Lottie was said to be "well grounded in the three Rs," and she wasted no time in putting her writing skills to work as a staff member of the Indian newspaper at Hampton, *Talks and Thoughts*.[19] Shortly after arriving at Hampton, Lottie published a short account of life in Cherokee, North Carolina. "The most interesting thing at Cherokee," she declared, "is the school." Describing the Cherokee Training School for her classmates and teachers in Virginia, she wrote:

> Anyone going there for the first time will be surprised if they have not heard about the place before . . . There are 40 boys and 40 girls in the Home besides outside scholars . . . The boys work on the farm, and in the house the girls do the cooking, washing, ironing, and sewing. Cherokee is one of the happiest places you can find anywhere. (*T&T*, Dec. 1889)

Lottie Smith, age nineteen, 1899.
Courtesy Hampton University Archives.

Extracurricular writing, such as letters and school newspapers, contends Lucille Schultz, allowed students to write in ways that classroom-based assignments did not. These texts, Schultz notes, "address subjects and issues that were rarely included in classroom-based writing, the texts are informal and for the most part, self-sponsored, and the texts had a specific audience (other than a teacher)—most often an intimate audience of family, friends or the writer's self" (130–31). In the tradition of the Cherokee girls whose letters from Brainerd, some fifty years earlier, had kept outsiders informed of the accomplishments of their people, Lottie alludes to the adoption of European gender roles among her people. Conspicuously absent from her narrative, however, is any mention of religion. Furthermore, since *Talks and Thoughts* is read by a predominantly Indian audience, she is not burdened with the same cultural constraints her Brainerd predecessors had faced a half-century earlier—especially with the need to disparage her own people or to affirm white supremacy. Instead, she boasts:

> The [Cherokee] boys have a Brass Band; they learn very fast and take a great deal of delight in practicing. Soon after the Indian boys got their Band, the white young men at Bryson City, which is about 10 miles from Cherokee, thought they would have a band too. So they sent for it and a teacher also. Our boys did not have a teacher, but while the Bryson City band learned three pieces in three months, our band learned seven in three weeks. (*T&T*, December 1889)

Though praise for their own culture and people also characterized the earlier letters of the Cherokee schoolgirls at Brainerd, their comments were often exploited by the missionaries as a means of showcasing the civilization efforts of the Mission. Lottie, on the other hand, gives credit where credit is due: to the Cherokee boys who, even without a teacher, were able to make incredible progress in their musical accomplishments.

In December 1890, the *Southern Workman* announced that Lottie Smith would be one of the editors of *Talks and Thoughts* for the coming year, but in March 1891 the *Workman* printed the following notice:

> One of Winona's favorite "Elder sisters," Lottie Smith, returned to her home in Cherokee, N.C., on the 12th. The evening before she left a "high tea" was given her by a few of the girls in one of the small Indian cottages, and the night before that her three room-mates in Long Room gave her a parting "spread" there. We all miss her bright face,

sweet voice and gentle ways, but we know she is making sunshine where it is perhaps needed more, and rejoice with her that she is able to do so well what her hand has found to do. (SF, HUA)

No reason is given in the above account for her leaving Hampton, but just a month earlier—while still at Hampton—Lottie had written a letter to the *Workman* in which she seemed concerned for the future of the Cherokee Training School in her home state of North Carolina:

The school is very good, but we need better books and blackboards. We have a good Superintendent and we want to keep him always, because now he understands how to work with the Indians. The Indians are trying to be like the white man all the time, and I think if the schools are kept up and all the children have a chance, after a few more years we will be civilized. We feel that you have already done a great deal for us and we thank you for it. (February 1891, 154)

The difference in the tone of this letter, written primarily for a white reading audience, is profound. It is significant, too, that her ingratiating comment about Indians "trying to be like the white man" is couched in a not altogether subtle appeal for help, implying that Lottie is keenly aware of the role the term "civilized" plays in tugging at the heart (and purse) strings of potential donors.[20] Lest her letter be misconstrued as a mere plea for charity, however, Lottie closes with, "We are glad to have a chance to work and earn our own living."

Her withdrawal from Hampton Institute, in the middle of a school term, seems even more baffling when one considers that Lottie Smith was a popular student, an accomplished scholar, and the recipient of a full scholarship. Was she so concerned about the education of Eastern Cherokee children that she decided to forgo her own education and return home to teach? A letter to the *Workman* some two weeks after Lottie left Hampton seems to suggest that this was indeed the case. She writes:

I have been away from Hampton two weeks lacking one day. It seems like so many years. I think of you so much, sometimes I can't keep the tears back. But all the [Cherokee] children and teachers treat me with perfect kindness. Yet I do want to see all the people at Hampton again.

Today I began my school. I have sixteen in my room. They are all small but they are bright. I felt a little embarrassed at first, but I soon felt at home with them. I think they will be very obedient and nice. (SF, HUA)[21]

Obviously, Lottie is engaged in teaching the children of her own tribe. Less than two months later, however, the following announcement appeared in North Carolina newspapers, shedding a different light on her seemingly abrupt departure from Hampton in March:

Wednesday was a gala day at the Training school on the Indian Reservation in Swain County. Any one approaching the picturesque headquarters would, from a distance, have observed flags flying at full mast, and heard notes from a brass band echoing through the mountain valleys. A nearer approach would have disclosed the children of the well-ordered school in holiday attire and many signs of some unusual event, which was nothing less than the marriage of Miss Lottie, the third daughter of Chief N.J. Smith, to Capt. John P. Pattee, recently graduated from the well known school at Hampton, Va. . . . The bride is not only famed for her beauty and accomplishments, but also for the more enduring attractions of "worth and truth." The groom, who is a Sioux, has distinguished himself in many ways throughout his course at Hampton . . . but, it is safe to say, in no way more than by the winning of this coveted Cherokee prize. The couple . . . will in a few days start for South Dakota where Capt. Pattee's property and interests are. (*SW*, May 1891: 25)

In keeping with traditional principles of descent, Cherokees traced their lineage through their mothers, and when a Cherokee couple married, they moved to the home of the bride (French and Hornbuckle 7). Thus, Lottie Smith's move to South Dakota, "where [her husband's] property and interests are," marked not only a departure from Cherokee custom, but also the beginning of a lifelong separation from her own people in western North Carolina.

Shortly after her marriage to John, Lottie Smith Pattee wrote to their friends at Hampton from her new home in Crow Creek, South Dakota:

We don't write much, because we are busy most all the time. John is president of the "Hampton Boys' Society." They meet every month to know how they might help their people. They have asked to have the dancing stopped. . . . [22] I wish you could visit our little home. It is too little in the kitchen and dining room to be comfortable. But we make out very nicely. We want to have our sitting room and dining room fit-ted up so that Hampton boys and girls can come in and read or play games. [23]

> Take a great deal of love from your Hampton children.
>
> John and Lottie (SF, HUA)

Expressing hopes and dreams somewhat typical for a new bride, Lottie's letter also makes it clear that she and John still feel strongly connected to Hampton, a sentiment she expresses in almost every letter she writes. In a note to her former teacher Josephine Richards, dated February 26, 1893, Lottie writes glowingly of their work in Crow Creek, comments on the growth of their baby daughter, Cora, and boasts of the Sioux people's love for her young husband. "John is lending a hand to the returned students and all his people," she writes. "I know this, because, if some of them get in trouble, they come to John to get his advice as to what is best to do. If they did not have confidence in him they would not come to him." Their memories of Hampton seem to sustain the young couple in their work, as the following lines demonstrate:

> . . . We talk and think about our dear Hampton friends a great deal. We read every line in "Talks and Thoughts" and SOUTHERN WORKMAN for Hampton news. We are always interested in everything that goes on there. (61)

The person to whom Lottie was obviously most attached at her beloved alma mater was Cora Mae Folsom—dedicated nurse, teacher, journalist, student adviser, drama director, and museum curator—whose tenure spanned all but three of the forty-five years Indian students were enrolled at Hampton (Hultgren and Molin 45). Although it may be that some of Lottie's letters home simply have not survived, existing records suggest that correspondence with her own family in North Carolina seems to have gradually tapered off and that she increasingly turned to Miss Folsom as a surrogate mother.[24] Even so, the welfare of her Cherokee people remained a constant concern. In a letter dated December 24, 1894, for example, Lottie declares,

> . . . Hampton was really more like home than any place I know of. I hope the Cherokees there are doing well. I don't know how many nor who they are, because I have never heard.

In this particular letter, almost ten pages long, Lottie might be a mother from anywhere in America as she describes the everyday events of her household: Two-year-old Cora (Miss Folsom's namesake) is talking and is full of cute sayings; baby Fred is learning to walk and will soon be talking, too; husband John has applied for a position that apparently comes with a larger house for his family, but he is being forced to compete with a white man whose brother—a physician—is using his influence to sway those in charge. Commenting on the latter issue, Lottie writes:

> I do hope John will get the place. We cannot live comfortably on thirty dollars per month and meet our expenses. Of course if we were to live like Indians perhaps we could get along. But we don't wish to live that way. (SF, HUA)

Not only does Lottie sound like a typical American housewife, but, at first glance, the above lines suggest that Lottie has also developed a patronizing attitude toward the Indians among whom she is living. However receptive she may have been to the cultural values and practices of white America, however, Lottie Smith Pattee was still Cherokee, and because of her status as an Indian woman, she was forced to take an indirect approach to a problem all too common among Indian teachers and missionaries: receiving unequal pay for their labor. As French and Hornbuckle point out, the avoidance of overt hostilities regarding interpersonal matters and an emphasis on nonaggressiveness are traits of what is commonly known as the Cherokee "Harmony Ethic."[25] However, John Pattee's competitor belonged to a culture with no such constraints on aggressive interference. Therefore, Lottie resorts to a well-honed politeness strategy in requesting Miss Folsom's intervention.

In their pivotal work on politeness theory, Brown and Levinson indicate how various social and contextual factors prescribe a speaker's linguistic strategies when performing face-threatening acts, or FTAs. "Face" involves a speaker's desire to have her wants unimpeded (positive face) and her desire to make her wishes desirable to others (negative face) (62). The strategy selected by a speaker when face is threatened is determined by the "weightiness" of the FTA, which may be calculated by assessing the social distance between the participants, the relative power between them, and the rating of the imposition in the particular culture. In Lottie's case, the FTA is a request for the hearer (Miss Folsom) to use her influence against that of the white man's physician-brother in securing a promotion for the speaker's (Lottie's) husband. For Lottie, the situation is complicated by the fact that the two cultures involved (Cherokee and Anglo-American) would rate the imposition of the FTA quite differently. However, she demonstrates rhetorical sensitivity and skill in negotiating the cross-cultural exchange when she adopts what Brown and Levinson term an *off-record* strategy—hinting, which allows the hearer to feel generous for "deciding" (rather than agreeing) to help the original speaker—and when she attends to Miss Folsom's positive face at the expense of her own (71). That is, while seemingly denigrating her own people, Lottie is actually demonstrating an awareness of Miss Folsom's need for "positive consistent self-image" (Brown and Levinson 61). As elsewhere, Lottie is keenly aware of her white audience's need to feel benevolent and superior toward Indians. Her ad hoc dissociation from her people, an apparent affront to her own positive face, may be in reality a sophisticated linguistic strategy of politeness in order to secure their needs.

Although the "politeness theory" of Brown and Levinson may seem somewhat impenetrable to those of us less familiar with the language of social scientists, the ideas are succinctly expressed in the words of Anishinaabe elder Art Solomon: "We can only make ourselves understood if others are willing to listen" (Ruffo 120). And, as Lottie Smith demonstrates, others were often not inclined to listen unless the Indian self was effaced in favor of the white auditor.

The economic difficulties faced by Lottie and John were (are) widespread among Indians in professional positions.[26] As early as the eighteenth century, the Mohegan missionary Samson Occum had protested that white missionaries were earning as much in one year as he had been paid for twelve years of service. "I Can't Conceive how these gentlemen would have me Live," Occum wrote, ". . . but I *must Say*, 'I believe it is because I am a poor Indian'" ("Narrative" 946–47). When one considers the salaries of other employees of Indian agencies in South Dakota during the late 1800s, it seems little wonder that Lottie Pattee should insist that she and her husband do not wish to "live like Indians." Samuel Armstrong, for example, became alarmed in 1883 when some of the government's best agents began leaving the service, complaining that their salaries, ranging from $1,200 to $2,200 per year, were inadequate (Lindsey 61). Contrasted with those figures, the $360 per year the Pattees received from the agency was indeed a paltry sum, and Lottie, like Samson Occum before her, must have found it difficult to remain silent.

Living in poverty, hundreds of miles from friends and family, eventually began taking its toll on Lottie. In February 1899, she wrote to the editors of the *Southern Workman*:

> I wish I could see Hampton again. It is the only true home I have ever had. I wish you could see our family now. They are all bright pretty babies if I do say it. Fred does not care much for school and makes all kind of excuses to keep out, but Cora is a regular little scholar. (SF, HUA)

Later that year, the Pattees were transferred to the Chemawa School in Salem, Oregon, where John served as a teacher and Lottie became the school matron. Chemawa, like other nineteenth-century boarding schools, enforced rigid military-style rules. Nora Dauenhauer (Tlingit), whose father was one of the school's runaway students during the late 1800s, recalls his stories about Chemawa:

> He said the most terrible [experience] was when they remembered their Indian foods back at home as they passed from bunk to bunk raw potatoes they had swiped to eat after lights-out. . . . Even wearing the clothing issued to the students was difficult. In fear the students might steal something or put their hands in their pockets, they were given pants without pockets. . . . He was very sad when he told me about one of the boys from his hometown [in Alaska], and of how he was whipped in sewer and toilet water and how the schoolteachers or guards dunked his head under and held it there for a few moments. . . . My father remembered how lonely he, too, felt when the youngest students cried for home and their parents and were punished and sent to bed without food. (*Life* 29–30)

Lottie must have observed these abusive practices, day after day; not until she moved away from Oregon, however, did she register in letters her loathing of the Chemawa superintendent (see *Life* 174). Instead, she restricted her "news" to the ordinary, everyday events of her family and household. In a letter dated January 3, 1900, Lottie thanks Miss Folsom for Christmas gifts she has recently sent their family and brings her up to date on family news. "We had Cora vaccinated and it made her very sick," Lottie writes. "I do not know whether to have the other two vaccinated or not." Also, she apparently finds Oregon weather depressing, for she comments that Cora "is up and able to be out of doors when we have a bright day, which is not often." Finally, Lottie mentions that her job as a teacher has its disquieting moments, but she seems to attribute her stress wholly to the disgusting habits of her tobacco-chewing students. "I am getting along nicely with my work," she tells Miss Folsom. "Only at times I get discouraged and wonder what is the use of cleaning up day after day and still keep on cleaning. Some of the boys are nice but oh! The tobacco spit all over the floors!" With the affection of a young woman for her mother, Lottie asks in this same letter:

> How are you dear "Ma." We think and speak of you very often. There is no one whom we would rather see than you now. John talks of going to Hampton to take a course in Manual Training, but if he does he will have to take the rest of us too. I live in hopes that some day I may go back there and let my little ones get a start from there. I want them to come under the influence for good that is felt all around Hampton. The last Southern Workman made me homesick for the dear place where I spent so many happy days. . . . I think Cora will write you before long. With much love from your child
>
> Lottie *Smith* Pattee (SF, HUA)

Lottie's dream of returning with John and the children to Hampton was never realized. On August 13—just seven months after she had written the above letter—John died, very suddenly and unexpectedly, "while he was under the influence of chloroform" during surgery at the Salem Hospital, and Lottie was left to raise three small children alone (*SW,* October 1900: 587).

Now a thirty-year-old widow, Lottie looked to her friend Cora Folsom more than ever for direction and support. On June 16, 1901, she writes:

> I would have written to you as soon as I received your letter but the smallpox broke out in our school, and we did not write letters for a time . . . I have been waiting to see you and talk with you before I make any decision as to where I will go. I would like to go to Riverside, Cal. when they get the school built there . . . I want to talk with you. I can't write what I want to say . . . I cannot make up my mind to go home this summer. It will take two hundred dollars, and I don't know whether it will be that much good to me or not. I know it would do Ma a world of good to see us.
>
> I hope to hear soon that you are coming. There is no one I would rather see than you dear "Ma."
>
> Your child,
> Lottie

In an understated manner, reminiscent of young Jane Bushyhead's letter (quoted earlier in this chapter), Lottie details an incredible amount of stress in one letter—a smallpox epidemic in the school where she teaches, practical problems concerning where she and her three children will live, indecision about traveling to North Carolina for a visit with her dying mother, and insufficient funds to get there if she does decide to go—all this in addition to the grief she still carries from the death of her young husband, less than one year earlier.

During the summer of 1901, Lottie did visit her mother and family in North Carolina, but her heart still seemed to be at "dear old Hampton." In a letter posted September 11, 1901, after her return to Oregon, Lottie informs Miss Folsom, "Miss Reel is here and she told me about seeing you and her visit to dear Hampton.[27] Dear 'Ma,' it made me so homesick. I want to see you and Hampton once more." One encouraging result of her visit home to Cherokee earlier in the summer was that Lottie had been able to persuade her younger sister Rosa to enroll at Hampton. "I want to ask you to look after Rosa this Fall," she beseeches Miss Folsom. "Ma has decided to let her go to Hampton with Zona.[28] It will be a special favor to me if you can keep a motherly eye on her. You know she is young and has never been away from home before."

Finally, in this same letter, Lottie confides that she would like to get a transfer to Haskell Institute in Kansas, "because I think it is a far superior school to this" and "there the Indian children are a better class as a rule." Then she alludes to what may well have been her primary reason for seeking a transfer:

> The time has come, when it is all I can do to discipline Fred. Perhaps there I could put him in school and yet be with him or near him so that my little family will not be entirely separated. That is what I dread. (SF, HUA).

Like her Cherokee foremothers who attended the Brainerd Mission School during the early 1800s, Lottie was greatly concerned about anything that threatened to fracture her family, and in spite of her apparent love for Hampton, she was not willing to entrust missionaries and boarding school personnel with the care of her own children, especially her daughters. In fact, just a few days after posting the above letter to Miss Folsom, she wrote to her again, protesting one of the policies endorsed by Estelle Reel, superintendent of Indian Schools:

Miss Folsom, she says for me to put Cora in some school and Fred too, as a great many Superintendents would not want employees with children. O! I can't think of giving up my little girls. With Fred it is different. He needs a man to control him. But . . . I want to keep [Cora] in the same school with me and if possible to room with me. You know what vile stuff she would learn to put her in with a lot of girls. She may be no better than other children but I don't want her to learn all kinds of bad things . . . She is a bright little girl and I feel like this: if I separate the two girls they will grow up strangers to each other. I think that I could watch over them better than a stranger. What shall I do, dear "Ma?" I do not know what to do.

> With much love
> I am your loving child, Lottie
> (SF, HUA)

Obviously frustrated with trying to raise her son alone, Lottie seems far more willing to part with Fred than with her girls. It must be remembered, however, that only a few days earlier she was thinking of ways she could send her son to a good school without having to separate him from his family. In her own culture, Lottie's brothers would have assumed a strong avuncular role in the lives of her children, but in Oregon she apparently has no one to whom she can turn for help or consolation.[29] Thus, she would have been quite susceptible to the suggestions of Miss Reel and other American educators concerning the dangers of raising a young boy without the advantage of a male role model.[30]

Over the course of the next few months, Lottie's letters to Miss Folsom preserve a running account of her life as a widow, isolated from family and friends and trying to raise three small children on a salary of $480 per year. Denied the position she so desperately wanted at Haskell Institute, she resigns herself to "accept any transfer they may offer unless it should be in the Dakotas. I could never go there again" (Lottie Smith Pattee to Miss Folsom, October 15, 1901, SF, HUA).[31]

Two months later, however, all other trials seem to pale in the face of a new crisis—the threat of terminal illness in Lottie's own life. Fearing that "the time will not be long till I may pass on," she turns once again to her beloved Hampton "Ma," Cora Folsom. Prefacing her news with, "It is all part of some great plan of which only our Heavenly Father knows," Lottie tells Miss Folsom that she has discovered a "bunch" on her neck, which she fears "is that awful disease which takes off so many."[32] Perhaps in an attempt to alleviate her own anxieties, however, she reports that her youngest child, Baby Sophie, had also recently developed "two big bunches on her neck," and "by careful treatment we made them go away." Lottie ends her letter by reminding Miss Folsom, "I have lots of courage and am determined to do all, everything to get this out of my system" (December 30, 1901, SF, HUA).

She does not write again for an entire year—this time to announce that she has married "a dear good husband," Dr. E. S. Clark, and that they have moved to Whatcom, Washington, where they have bought "a cosey little home" and Dr. Clark has "bought one of the largest drug stores in this state."[33] Lottie further explains that they left Oregon to "get out of the Indian Service" and that her children are enrolled in the public school in Whatcom, where Cora "has made good progress, having been promoted twice this year." She reports that "Fred is also doing exceedingly well since coming here," and "as for me I have not been so well in several years as I am now." Adding to Lottie's happiness is her escape from what was apparently a very stressful situation at the Chemawa Indian School in Salem:

> Dear friend, I can't tell you how glad I am to be away from that school. Mr. Potter was very disagreeable and is my bitter enemy. But now I do not have to worry over anything that he can do or say. (December 17, 1902, SF, HUA)

The Clarks did not stay in Whatcom very long, for in a letter dated January 5, 1904, Lottie informs Miss Folsom of yet another move—this time, to Sumas, a small town located on the Canadian border. "Doctor did not like his work in Whatcom. . . . he can make more by practicing his profession here." Clearly, Lottie and her children are no longer enduring abject poverty, for she tells Miss Folsom:

> We have a nice cow and I make my own butter and still we have all the cream we can use. We have two nice ponies and a buckboard and buggy. So if you come I will take you all over the country and over into Canada. We can step across the line any day. (SF, HUA)

There is no indication that Lottie ever returned to working in Indian schools. In fact, in the last letter on file from her at Hampton—a letter addressed to Caroline Andrus, one of the institute's official correspondents with Indians—Lottie writes that she is helping her husband, Dr. Clark, "when he needs someone to give an anesthetic for him." Now a middle-aged woman whose children are grown and have families of their own, she closes her letter with, "I am very well and getting quite fleshy" (October 30, 1917).

This strong Cherokee woman spent her last days in the Masonic Home in Zenith, Washington, and at the age of ninety-five was still actively involved in teaching others. In a letter dated March 15, 1964, Lottie wrote to a niece in Cherokee, North Carolina:

> I have outlived all my sisters and brothers. Why? I do not know. But this I do know that I do have a feeling of love in my heart for everyone [there] . . . I am the oldest of the women [in the Masonic Home], but I am very much alive. My only trouble is my hearing and I do not see too well, but I have a Reading Group and there are 18 members. I am reading to them about Easter and what it means . . . I also read to our Nature Study group. So you see I am still carrying on. I love life with all its beauty.
>
> With love to you and yours I am
> Your Aunt Lottie, 95 years young

Lottie Smith Pattee Clark was not the only Eastern Cherokee girl to attend a boarding school, but she may have been the first to travel so far from home to pursue an education. Unlike the other women discussed in this chapter, she lived in isolation from her own people after marrying a Lakota man. The once-proud daughter of a Cherokee chief was reduced to worse poverty than she had ever suffered among her own people, and she was expected to adapt not only to Anglo-American culture but also to the ways of the Lakota people.

The writings of Lottie Smith—like those of her contemporaries Zitkala-Sa (Yankton Sioux writer-activist) and Susette La Flesche (Omaha journalist), as well as today's Indian women—dispel the popular notion that Indians who attended federal boarding schools rejected their Native heritage and adopted the culture of Euro-Americans in toto. Although Lottie Smith spent the rest of her life in the state of Washington, for example, she returned home as frequently as possible to visit her own people on the Qualla Boundary, and she continued to use the education she received at Hampton to encourage Indian people to take pride in their own cultural heritage. In other ways, Lottie exemplifies the accommodation many boarding school students embraced in order to adapt to what anthropologists term "acculturation stress." For some, observes Adams, this accommodation came in the form of "a grudging acceptance of the institutional pressure for compliance, the need to go through the motions and bide one's time until the ordeal was over—resistance in the guise of accommodation." Others, like Lottie, seemed to cooperate actively with the institution that was transforming them. Adams concludes:

> The response of accommodation could take any number of forms, ranging from complete identification with white ways to a pragmatic strategy of cultural adaptation. In any event, learning something about the white man's language and lifeways did not necessitate a wholesale abandonment of one's Indian self. Accommodation was not synonymous with surrender. (240)

As the words of her final letter indicate, Lottie Smith could no more surrender her Indian identity than she could forget her home in the Great Smoky Mountains. Unable to understand all the events of her long and eventful life, the stately Cherokee woman still knew one thing for certain: "I do have a feeling of love in my heart for everyone there [on the Qualla Boundary]."

Lottie Smith Clark (far right), age ninety-five, 1965. Courtesy Museum of the Cherokee Indian Archives.

Arizona Swayney (1875–1934)

Another Eastern Cherokee woman who distinguished herself at Hampton Institute was Arizona Swayney Blankenship. Born Arizona Nick, she was the eldest daughter of Big Cove resident Laura Nick, who eventually married John Swayney, a white farm laborer from Tennessee. By 1900, Laura Swayney had given birth to fourteen children, and Zona, as she was known to family and friends, had left the reservation and was enrolled at Hampton (Hill 216).

Like most of the Indian students who attended Hampton, Zona, who enrolled at the school in 1896, participated in the summer outing program that had been initiated by General Armstrong in 1878.[34] According to school documents, she worked for a Mrs. Nettleton in Stockbridge, Massachusetts, during the summers of 1895–96, earning $1.50 per week for "general housework." During the year 1897, she spent some fifteen weeks in the home of Mr. and Mrs. B. G. Boardman in Newport, Rhode Island, working for the same wages, but during the summer of 1898 Zona was forced to return home to North Carolina due to the declining health of her mother. In July 1898, the *Southern Workman* reported that "Zona rejoices that she is there rather than earning money at the North, for she hopes to be able to give her mother a summer of rest and relief, and to be able to leave her all right in the fall when she comes back for her senior year" (139).

The summer of 1899, however, found Zona back in Stockbridge, Massachusetts—this time in the home of a Mrs. Lincoln—and as late as 1902 she was still employed as a housekeeper, working for the Q. B. Scoville family in West Cornwall, Connecticut, where she received a salary of three dollars per week. Although Zona remarked that her work was "too hard" at the Scoville residence, she also described it as "very satisfactory." Her chief complaint was that she was forced to eat in the kitchen, instead of being allowed to take her meals with the Scoville family (Outing Record, SF, HUA).[35] Like many other outing students, Zona was learning the marginal terms upon which Indians would be accepted in American society—as common laborers and domestic servants—if whites had anything to say about it (Adams 163). What must have been more difficult for the young Cherokee student to perceive, however, was that federal boarding schools were not merely training Indian girls in subservience and submission to authority. As Tsianina Lomawaima observes, "The acute, piercing focus on Indian girls'

attire, comportment, posture, and hairstyle betray[ed] a deep-seated, racially defined perception of Indian people's corporal physical bodies as
'uncivilized'" (82). Hence, even as white educators publicly promoted "self-
help" programs for American Indians, they simultaneously attempted to
divest Indian students of every vestige of individuality and independence.

Like her friend Lottie Smith, Arizona Swayney was a stellar student
who became actively involved in extracurricular activities, as well as scholarly pursuits, while at Hampton. For example, she wrote articles for the
Indian newspaper, *Talks and Thoughts,* was often asked to speak during
special programs, and served as vice president of the Christian Endeavor
Society. Also, during her senior year Zona participated in a student-teaching
program at Whittier Elementary School, a school for black children in
Hampton. Of the latter experience she wrote, "At the Whittier School we
have an excellent chance to apply what we have learned [at Hampton], for
their children are taught along the line of industry as well as the acquisition
of knowledge through books" (*T&T,* Jan. 1901).[36]

For Zona, however, learning to use one's hands, as well as one's head,
had little to do with subservience or class status; rather, she viewed such
practical training as a means of revitalizing and perpetuating her own
Cherokee culture. One of the most devastating impacts boarding schools
had on Indian communities, in fact, was that students often returned home
demoralized and unable to bond with their families or elders; thus, elders
who had no one to receive their wisdom lost their reason for existence
(Fournier and Crey 62). Determined to counter this attack on cultural identity, and to preserve the traditions and dignity of the elders, Zona published
an article in *Talks and Thoughts* (June 1902) urging Indian students to take
up basket-making and other Native crafts:

> The study of basketry and pottery has been very interesting to me and
> there is no doubt but that similar native industries, on different reser-
> vations, would be as interesting to many Hampton students, if after
> their return home they would seek to learn about them. Even though
> one did not mean to make a business of this work it would encourage
> the old people to have the returned students show an interest in the
> native industries, and it would also help them to keep up these arts to
> have more pride in them, to do them better and with more care.

In the same article Zona noted that, at first, the Cherokee people could not
understand why she spent so much time on basketry after spending so many
years in school to get an education. "They laughed at me," she said,

"because I wanted to learn, but after seeing a very pretty basket which I made, and which was even better than my teacher's own work, they were quite anxious to learn basketry, too." Never one to waste words, she reminded her readers of the serious threat to their traditional way of life unless young Indians did their part to keep their cultures alive:

> There is only one woman at home who makes real nice baskets and only one man and one woman who can do the double weave and only one woman who can make pottery, so it seems high time for some of the younger people to try and do something toward preserving these arts on different reservations.

Ironically, federal policy shifts in the late 1890s gave rise to the teaching of hand weaving and basket making to Indian girls at Hampton Institute. Consequently, a school once dedicated to eradicating Indian culture became so interested in Zona's project that they began actively promoting her work. In August 1902, the *Indian Friend* announced:

> A Cherokee girl, graduate of Hampton Institute, has been studying at home the almost lost arts of her people, basketry and pottery. After encouraging the work among the Cherokees, she has returned to Hampton to teach these handicrafts among a larger, more influential circle of students. (SF, HUA)

In October 1902, Zona traveled to the beautiful Shawangunk Mountains in New York to attend the Lake Mohonk Conference of Friends of the Indian and to display baskets made by Hampton's Indian students. Reporting on that conference in the November issue of *Talks and Thoughts,* she recalls that "most of the time was given to the Indian question," but that various exhibits of Indian crafts also generated a great deal of interest, and "many orders were taken to be filled by the people there." Obviously encouraged by the support for Indians she sensed among Euro-Americans at the conference, Zona exults:

> The friends of the Indian at the Mohonk Conference are working in unity for one great cause, to uplift the Red man, and the Christ-like spirit was present in everything that was said or done. (HUA)

In 1905, she accepted a summer position at Dr. Charles Shepard's tea plantation in Summerville, South Carolina, teaching basketry, lace making,

Arizona Swayney, 1902. Courtesy of
Hampton University Archives.

beadwork, chair caning, and rug weaving to "the very poorest class of . . . children, both white and black." Dr. Shepard had launched an experiment several years earlier in which he employed "a small army of workers" to harvest tea—some of it selling for as much as ten dollars a pound. It was his desire that the black children who attended Pinehurst School, as well as poor white children enrolled at the St. Barnabas Mission School, might begin to earn money for themselves by making crafts to sell to the tourists. Many of the parents of these children, on the other hand, heartily disapproved of any form of industrial training, insisting that they were sending their children to school to learn reading, writing, and arithmetic, not basketry and rug weaving. "But after we had had one or two sales, and each child carried home the money for which her basket had sold," wrote Zona, "the parents were very much pleased and the mothers immediately became anxious to learn also" (*T&T,* November 1906).

For the next two years, Zona taught classes at Hampton, but in a letter dated April 29, 1908, Zona announces, "My name is to be changed in about two weeks, the exact date has not been set yet. I wish all my Hampton friends could be present" (SF, HUA). Although she provides no details concerning her prospective husband, family records show that she married Abraham Blankenship, a white man from Tennessee, and that they settled in the Cherokee community of Big Cove (known as Swayney to white residents), where they ran a store and post office.[37] In December 1909, Zona's brother Lorenzo wrote to Helen Townsend, housemother for the Indian girls at Hampton, informing her that he was teaching school for his sister because "she is very sick." Although at least one letter in Zona's student file suggests that her illness was related to difficulties in her marriage, the young bride never directly refers to her husband in any of her correspondence with Hampton friends (SF, HUA).[38]

On the other hand, she rarely fails to mention her children. For example, in a letter to Miss Andrus dated November 3, 1914, Zona writes, "I have four babies now—all little in a bunch. I am very happy with my babies—can't do much now but look after them. Yet I haven't forgotten my class motto, 'By example we lift as we climb'" (SF, HUA). In a letter to Miss Townsend (January 24, 1917), she dreams of sending all her children to Hampton someday. "I hope that they may have their wish fulfilled and that they will do well," she muses.

In an eight-page letter dated January 22, 1915, Zona thanks Miss Townsend for having sent Christmas gifts to her Cherokee students, provides an update on each of her own children, and writes glowingly of Dr. James Mooney and his family, who also sent Christmas gifts for the schoolchildren.[39] In closing, Zona states that "a consecration to the Lord *without a consecration to our neighbor* becomes an illusion or leads to fanaticism," adding, "It is this giving up of ourselves to the world . . . to love it even when it hates us, that constitutes for all really consecrated souls the true battle of life." Finally, she declares, "I wish to affirm anew my consecration to the Lord, not in my own strength but in the strength of Him who gave Himself for me," and she requests that the hymn "Take My Life and Let It Be" might be sung when her letter is read at the next meeting of the Christian Endeavor Society.[40]

Arizona Swayney Blankenship continued to write letters and postcards to her friends at Hampton until the Indian program was terminated in 1923.[41] Throughout her life, she maintained a strong interest in education, making sure not only that her own children were well educated, but also recruiting and writing letters of recommendation for several Cherokee students who wished to attend Hampton Institute. In 1933, the indomitable Zona suffered a paralytic stroke, and although she seemed to be recovering nicely, on March 8, 1934, a massive heart attack ended her life, at the age of fifty-nine. *The Smoky Mountain Indian Trail,* a local Cherokee newspaper, memorialized her in a front-page article on March 21, 1934:

> Mrs. Blankenship was one of the highly esteemed and honorable citizens of the Reservation. Her work and achievements among her people will long be remembered by her neighbors, friends, acquaintances, her relatives and loved ones.

Although Arizona Swayney Blankenship is remembered today primarily for her skill at basketry, her letters and speeches played the most vital role in preserving this aspect of Cherokee culture. Certainly she was cognizant of the federal government's policy of "kill the Indian and save the man"— a plan enthusiastically embraced by boarding schools like Carlisle and Hampton. Likewise, she was familiar with the contempt of many educators for Indian students who chose to "return to the blanket"—those who insisted on embracing traditional ways of living once they returned home to their respective tribes. Instead of passively abandoning the cultural practices of her Cherokee people, however, Zona chose to demonstrate the advantages of keeping artistic skills like basketry and pottery making alive. In so doing, she succeeded not only in renewing cultural pride among her Indian classmates at Hampton, but also in inspiring men like Dr. Charles Shepard of South Carolina to rethink the industrial training programs at their schools. Most important, Arizona Blankenship managed to instill in the Cherokee children she taught at Big Cove School a respect for the traditions of their elders—a legacy reflected yet today in the beautiful baskets and pottery sold by Cherokee artists in the museums and craft shops of Qualla Boundary.

Louisiana (Lula) Owl (1891–1985)

Several other Eastern Cherokee girls attended Hampton Institute, including Lottie Smith's sister Rosa and a niece, Stella Blythe. Some of these students were prolific letter writers, while others left only sparse records of their days at "dear old Hampton," but each of them clung proudly to her Cherokee heritage. One student who endeared herself not only to the faculty and students at Hampton, but also to her own people on the Qualla Boundary, was Louisiana Owl, better known as "Lula" to family and friends. The daughter of a Cherokee father and Catawba mother, Lula enrolled at Hampton in 1907 and became an accomplished writer, as well as a popular speaker.

Like Lottie Smith and Arizona Swayney, this young Cherokee woman quickly established herself as an outstanding student who took pride in her Indian heritage. During the summer of 1908, Lula embarked upon her first "outing" experience, working as a housekeeper and dairy worker for Mr. and Mrs. R. W. Skilton in Morris, Connecticut. Although Mrs. Skilton complained in her report to Hampton that "Lula could work quickly, but she spent a great deal of time fooling around," Lula expressed complete satisfaction with the Skiltons and requested that she be placed in their home the following summer. Instead, she was sent to Canaan, New York, where she cleaned rooms in a boarding house run by a Mrs. Finch. Her wages for four months were forty-seven dollars, plus nine dollars in tips, and Lula's only complaint was that she was forced to sleep in an attic storage space. According to her report, the room was "hot, with nothing but bare shingles" over it, leaked when it rained, and "everything was kept there." As if her living conditions were not irksome enough already, Lula was forced to share this congested space with another boarder, and except for a brief stint in 1911 as a housekeeper for Mrs. F. Ferry in Pittsfield, Massachusetts, she chose not to participate in the outing program again (Outing Record, SF, HUA).

For the next several summers, in fact, Lula taught summer school in Roddey, South Carolina, where her mother's people lived. Speaking before a crowd of two thousand people at the 1914 Hampton Institute Anniversary exercises, she proclaimed,

> I have a right to be proud of both [my parents'] tribes, although I do rank as a Cherokee instead of a Catawba. The fact that I am called Cherokee, instead of a Catawba, will perhaps seem strange to those who know anything at all about Indians and their customs, because it is customary for Indian children to go by their mother's tribe or nationality rather than by their father's. However, this custom is not always kept among the Cherokees; for if a Cherokee man married an Indian woman of another tribe and continued to live on the Cherokee reservation, their children would be enrolled as Cherokees and would be entitled to all Cherokee rights. The children of an Indian mother and a white father are also enrolled as Cherokees, but the children of white mothers and Indian fathers are not enrolled as Cherokees, and they are not entitled to Cherokee Indian rights—such as Indian money, land, and the privilege of attending Indian schools that are supported by the Government. (*SW*, September 1914: 484)

Lula's speech, which was published in its entirety by the *Southern Workman*, incorrectly implies that all Indian tribes share the same matrilineal system of kinship as the Cherokees; essentially, however, she is interested in defining Cherokee identity—a point of reference to which I will return in chapter 4 in my discussion of Hampton student Nancy Coleman.[42]

Another fascinating component of Lula's speech is her history of the nineteenth-century Mormon missionaries who came from Utah to live among her mother's people in South Carolina. Although her "mother's family is one of the families that do not believe in the Mormon faith," Lula clearly admires the Mormon elders who have, in some cases, laid down their very lives for the sake of the Catawba people.[43] Apparently undaunted by the large audience of Hampton graduates and benefactors who are, in general, representatives of mainline denominations staunchly opposed to the teachings of Mormonism, Lula speaks with a boldness and a liberty that reflect a far different spirit than the ultraconservative, missionary-censored letters written by schoolgirls at Brainerd a century earlier.

Not surprisingly, the young student who had taken first place in Hampton's essay contest just one year before was an equally skilled orator.[44] In closing her speech, Lula told her listeners how the Catawba children and their parents had been so disinterested in education that, until she went there to teach, their school terms had been only four months long. She had attempted to "awaken the interest of the people" through a series of programs and social gatherings, but these events were always poorly attended, for, as Lula puts it, "The majority of the Indians did not want me to take the school. They said that I was too young to manage the children." Finally, Lula decided to have the children use their artistic skills to design their own invitations to attend one of their programs, and to her surprise "these special written invitations did what a spoken 'All are cordially invited to attend' did not do; for almost every one who had received an invitation was present when we gave our entertainment."

As a result of Lula's innovative approaches to enlisting parental support, the school term was lengthened to nine months per year, a larger schoolhouse had to be built, and the tribe decided to hire two teachers instead of one. Lula's experience with the Catawbas was a stunning example of what the fifth-century philosopher Socrates referred to as good rhetoric: "The teacher who is raising the student toward transcendence plants seeds in the student's soul that will eventually flower and, in turn, reproduce themselves in other souls" (Bizzell and Herzberg 60). Hence, employing the reproductive metaphor of Socrates, Lula concludes her speech:

> Hampton makes it possible for every girl who goes out to be a helper in her home community. I am sure that I never should have been asked to take that school and certainly could not have been the helper that I tried to be if I had not had Hampton's training and its good reputation to back me up. (487)[45]

As several of Lula's letters indicate, however, she was just as concerned about how her personal actions would reflect upon Eastern Cherokee people as she was with "raising students toward transcendence." For example, in a letter to Helen Gould, one of Lula's scholarship providers, she confessed,

> When I first came here to school I felt ambitious and nothing seemed too hard to do, but I am ashamed to say that last year, I lost a part of my ambition, and try as hard as I would, I could not get it back. Last Summer I spent my vacation home among my native people, and they seem[ed] to expect so much of me, because I was a "Hamptonian," that I just couldn't fail them. This year . . . I am going to do my best not to disappoint my people. (November 5, 1912, SF, HUA).

Lula Owl was anything but a disappointment to her people. In spite of being temporarily incapacitated by an appendectomy in 1913, she completed her course work at Hampton, and after graduating on May 27, 1914, she entered nurses' training at the Chestnut Hill Hospital in Philadelphia. Her letters from Chestnut Hill provide a wealth of information pertaining to unusual medical cases, as well as a fascinating account of what it was like to be a student nurse in the early 1900s. On April 15, 1915, for example, Lula regretfully informed Caroline Andrus that she would not be able to attend Anniversary Week at Hampton due to her work schedule. "I am so disappointed," she wrote, "as I had saved my money and set my heart on coming. I spent most of the morning nearly in tears because I so wanted to come and too my patient sets me nearly crazy at times." Then follows an account of an elderly patient, Mrs. Hall, who suffers from senile dementia, and with whom Lula had been on twelve-hour duty for five weeks. "Guess I have to stay on to the end," Lula writes with resignation, making it clear to Miss Andrus that she does not share the doctor's prognosis of an imminent death in Mrs. Hall's case. Failing to understand what nursing skills she is supposed to be learning from this particular case, Lula questions the head nurse, whose cryptic answer is, "It teaches you patience and how to be tactful." "I have had to fight with myself a great many times [not to lose my temper]," Lula confesses, "but have controlled myself knowing that [Mrs. Hall] is not responsible for her speech or actions. She certainly has a vile tongue."

As a registered nurse myself, I find it impossible to conceive of any clinical program that would require one of its students to spend a total of more than three hundred hours on a single case.[46] Since Lula formally requested to be transferred to another case, she was obviously aware of the discrimination to which she was being subjected, but she wisely refrained from making any overt accusations to her mentor, Miss Andrus. Lula's unwavering sense of humor enabled her to endure even the most trying circumstance, and she concedes, "In spite of all our troubles [Mrs. Hall and I] are fond of each other. The minute I'm out of her sight she wants to know where 'Up a Tree' is. . . . She doesn't always remember Owl, but she knows I'm a bird up a tree," jokes Lula.

Although Lula's student file at Hampton does not provide any further details of her stay with Mrs. Hall, a letter written to Miss Andrus six months later (October 31, 1915) finds the young Cherokee nurse working night shift in the maternity department at Chestnut Hill, an assignment she has had for eight weeks. "I have almost full charge of the ward," she writes, "three private rooms and the delivery room and instruments. I take care of the patients and make all preparations for the delivery up until the last minute before the baby comes. It is always hard to know just when to call the night Supt. and doctor, but so far I have been able to keep my head." A recent delivery room experience, however had left Lula quite shaken:

> Last week we had an interesting and most pathetic delivery. The child was part monster and part human. It had three ears, teeth like this ᵥ**V~V**ᵥ, no nose nor eyes. From the lower jaw bone down to the feet it had a splendid healthy looking body, except that it was club-footed, its body was perfect. The head was the awfullest sight I have ever seen and hope to see. The doctors say it had no brains, anyway the top of its head was a large solid mass of bloody looking tissue with bits of fur here and there. Fortunately the mother did not see it, for as soon as the head appeared I threw a towel over it. At first we thought it was dead, but without any help it began to breathe and let out cry after cry. It was born about 4 o'clock a.m. & lived until 4 p.m. the next day.

As if having to assist with such a delivery were not trauma enough for twenty-four-year-old Lula, she was assigned duty as the baby's night nurse and was ordered to "feed it with a dropper every second hour." All night, the young nurse watched in horror as the baby "turned black in the face, or such face as it had," with each dropperful of milk she administered. What troubled her even more, however, was the horde of "doctors from everywhere [who] swarmed out here to see it." Some of these physicians "wanted to make a minute examination of it," she added, "but no amount of money could gain the father's consent." Lula's final comment on the case was "Thank goodness it's of the past."

Shifting topics immediately, she told Miss Andrus how much she liked her work, and how hard she was working for the obstetrical prize—a prize for which Lula said, "I am going to try hard but know I have no chance as the winners in my class have as good as been picked out already."[47]

Dated October 14, 1916, the last of the letters preserved in Lula's student file at Hampton is, like the majority of her correspondence, addressed to Caroline Andrus. "My graduating exercises are to be held this coming Tuesday," she announces. "How I wish that you could be here. It makes me feel quite lonely to know that not a soul really interested in me will be here for the exercises." Why none of Lula's former teachers and mentors at Hampton managed to be in Philadelphia for this momentous occasion is not clear. Much of the remainder of her letter, however, is a none too subtle indictment of Americans who seem obsessed with money and prestige. After discussing briefly her lifelong dream of working among the Southwestern Indians and her desire to transfer as soon as possible to Arizona, Lula plaintively asks Miss Andrus, "Can't you help me out? I don't know who the doctors are or how business of this sort is carried on." Lucrative "nursemaid" jobs were offered Lula, but she had no interest in such positions:

> A Mrs. Cassatt wants me to go to Havana, Cuba with her early in the spring but I refused and expect to make it a final answer, altho she offers such "tempting fruit"—and continues to beg me to go. She was my patient here for almost five weeks, but rest cures get on my nerves, especially when they are "make-believes." That is the disease of a number of our private patients. They think nothing of money that goes for $35 to $50, or $100 per week for rooms, two $25 nurses or one $35 nurse. It seems such a waste to me, and I don't enjoy being nurse on cases of the sort altho it is counted an honor. (SF, HUA)

In one of her letters, dated April 15, 1915, Lula also reflects on her lack of enthusiasm for what the other nurses classify as social "pleasure." "I gave up going out [evenings and weekends] as most of the places weren't to my taste," she tells Miss Andrus, and in spite of her colleagues' derisive ribbing about her being too full of "country ideas," Lula maintains that she prefers to rest during the few hours she has off work, for she has "discovered that work and pleasure don't get along together."

Like most of the Cherokee girls who attended boarding schools, Lula Owl may seem typically American in her speech, in her work ethic, and in her dreams and goals—and, in a sense, she is. As Richard Pratt lamented at a Denver conference in 1892, however, "The [Cherokees] have had tribal schools until it is asserted that they are civilized; yet they have no notion of joining us and becoming a part of the United States" ("Advantages of Mingling Indians" 265). Certainly, Lula was one of those Cherokees who had no intention of giving up her cultural heritage in exchange for promises of money or fame, nor of becoming so assimilated that she compromised her ability to work with more traditional Cherokees. Thus, she was able to claim an education at Hampton and to learn the ways of white doctors and hospitals in the sprawling city of Philadelphia without diluting for one moment her Cherokee identity.

Lula did eventually go West, where she spent several years working as a field and clinic nurse for the Bureau of Indian Affairs in Oklahoma—but

Lula Owl, Chestnut Hill Hospital, 1917.
Courtesy of Hampton University Archives.

not before distinguishing herself as an army nurse in World War I.[48] In 1965, she returned to her home in Cherokee, North Carolina, to retire. Nurse Lula did not actually retire until 1973, however, when she was eighty-two years old, for as John Finger points out, as the first Cherokee to hold a responsible health-care position on Qualla Boundary, she was "successful in dealing with Indians who otherwise would have refused treatment" (*Cherokee Americans* 66).[49]

In 1975, at the age of eighty-four, Lula Owl Gloyne, who took up bowling at seventy-nine, traveled to Charlotte, North Carolina, to participate in a bowling event. Her opponent was Kays Gary, a well-known columnist of the *Charlotte Observer* and a novice at bowling. In his tribute to Lula, Gary wrote, "I got scalped Saturday by a Cherokee lady with a bowling ball . . . I was afraid that even in my maiden effort I'd beat Lula and louse up a column, [but] Lula took care of my fears with the first ball at Parks Lanes. She rolled a strike." After relating several humorous incidents pertaining to Lula's bowling prowess, Gary gave this portrayal of his opponent:

> Impeccable in speech and gracious in manner, one senses Mrs. Gloyne is perhaps a bit piqued at being heralded for being 84. A grand dame she is but "I don't want people thinking I need assistance just because of my age," [she says] . . . She still lends her nursing skills in emergencies in Cherokee families but [according to Mrs. Gloyne], "I keep busy, too, teaching classes in chair-bottoming, basketweaving and mapmaking, all with vines." (French and Hornbuckle 219–20)

Lula Owl was only one year old when U.S. Commissioner of Indian Affairs Thomas J. Morgan made his famous "Plea for the Papoose" speech before a group of Indian sympathizers at Albany, New York, in 1892; as one of those "dusky babies" for whom the general professed to speak, however, she—like Lottie Smith and Arizona Swayney—was destined to disprove repeatedly his theories regarding the "helpless innocents" on Indian reservations who grow up in "ignorance, superstition, barbarism, and savagery." Morgan warned his New York audience that "the only possible way in which [Indians] can be saved from the awful doom that hangs over them is for the strong arm of the Nation to reach out, take them in their infancy and place them in its fostering schools; surrounding them in all that is good, and developing them into men and women instead of allowing them to grow up as barbarians and savages." In fact, if the "papoose" could speak, Morgan argued, he would cry out: "Our only hope is in your civilization, which we cannot adopt unless you give us your Bible, your spelling book, your plow and your ax. Grant us these and teach us how to use them, and then we shall be like you" (*SW,* April 1892: 59).

What Morgan apparently could not conceive of was an Indian who might cry out, "We do not wish to be like you." An unforeseen outcome of boarding school education was that Indian children would strengthen, not abandon, their culture by bonding with children of other Indian tribes. They learned bits of language and tribal customs from each other, and as a result of boarding school ties with other Indian students, observes Brenda Child (Red Lake Ojibwe), "summer celebrations on reservations became increasingly intertribal. New political alliances were forged. And for better or worse, the schools became part of [their] histories"—a relationship symbolized, suggests Child, by the star blanket (4).[56]

As discussed earlier in this chapter, culture is dynamic, always in a state of flux. Therefore, the notion that acculturation can only go one direction is a racist one, and generally assumes that American Indian cultures have been overpowered by Anglo cultures. Eastern Cherokee culture, for example, has both affected and been affected by European, African American, and intertribal influences. Still, as Craig Womack observes, Native cultures are always analyzed as if contact with other cultures somehow threatens "cultural purity." It is assumed that if Indians adopt new ways of thinking and being, they are no longer a culture (31).

Eastern Band Cherokees have been in contact with other cultures for hundreds of years, yet they have managed to maintain their language, worldview, and tribal government. Nurturing their children and maintaining a steadfast concern for future generations have always been central to Cherokee survival. Suzanne Fournier and Ernie Crey (Stó:lo) recognize that "it was their powerful cultural and spiritual traditions, founded on seemingly immutable bonds between children and extended families that enabled aboriginal nations to hold their ground" during their earliest encounters with Europeans, and not even the assimilation programs of federal boarding schools could eradicate those child-centered traditions (52). Each of the three Cherokee women discussed in this chapter demonstrates through her letters and/or speeches an ardent concern for the welfare of Indian communities, especially for the children. Lottie, for example, taught Indian children for several years. When Estelle Reel urged her to send her own children to boarding schools, Lottie refused to do so, declaring that she could "watch over them better than a stranger."

Zona worked with children, both on the tea plantations of South Carolina and on her own reservation, teaching them basketry, pottery, and other "lost arts" of the Cherokee people. Like Lottie, she made frequent mention of her own children, and she encouraged numerous Cherokee youths to pursue an education.

Lula combined her creative and oratorical skills to convince Catawba parents in South Carolina that she was capable of teaching their children, in spite of her youth, and when the Catawbas were lackadaisical about attending their children's school programs, Lula stimulated their interest by having each child make his or her own personal invitation.

The child-centered traditions of Cherokee women kept them rooted in their own culture, in spite of all attempts by boarding schools and government agents to assimilate them into white society. White middle- and upper-class women of the nineteenth century also increased their influence as mothers as they gained more control over their reproductive lives and the elevation of motherhood became a national ideal (Johnston, *Sexual Power* 53). However, Cherokee women had always enjoyed "an astonishing degree of sexual freedom" (Perdue, *The Cherokee* 180), and it is not inconceivable that some of the changes adopted by white women in their quest for "true womanhood" were partly a result of their contact with Indian women.[51]

Hampton and Carlisle designers had thought to abolish Indian culture. Instead, as the letters of Lottie, Zona, and Lula demonstrate, these students kept many of their Cherokee traditions alive by braiding other cultures with their own, and by using the power of the written and spoken word to remind their readers of the hope for any nation: the children.

Chapter 4 *A Time to Heal*

I learned your language when I was five years old.
I had to, regardless if I wanted to or not.
When I went to school we were told that we had to learn
one way or another;
If I didn't learn I had to go to the bathroom,
wash my mouth out with Ivory soap.
But I never did wash my Indian language out,
I still got it in my heart,
and I still carry on my Indian language.

—Edna Chekelelee,
"Cherokee Language"

When twenty-three-year-old Radmilla Cody won the annual Miss Navajo contest in 1997, her reign as the tribe's goodwill ambassador for 1998 not only ignited a discussion of what it means to be Indian but also exposed racial prejudices that threatened to divide the Navajo Nation. Cody, who was raised by her Navajo grandmother on an Arizona reservation, is fluent in the Diné language, and according to the *Albuquerque Journal*, she also knows how "to herd sheep, to weave rugs, to haul water and to cook over a kerosene stove" (Linthicum A11). As the daughter of a Navajo mother and an African American father, however, she was the first biracial woman to become Miss Navajo. Her African American features sparked the controversy. One Navajo man publicly protested that since "Miss Cody's appearance and physical characteristics are clearly black," she should focus on her African American heritage, and he warned that "tribal members who are of mixed race are a threat to the future of the tribe" (A11).

Questions pertaining to Indian identity are not restricted to the Navajos, nor is this a new issue in Indian Country. In fact, some of the most pressing concerns among American Indians today revolve around identity and tribal sovereignty; therefore, the oratory and literature discussed in this chapter will address the complexities of Indian identity, cultural preservation, and tribal sovereignty, and will explore some of the discourse strategies Eastern Cherokee women are using to facilitate healing and cultural restoration among their own people. Although the words of these women reflect an ongoing struggle with many of the same problems their ancestors were confronting during the nineteenth century, many scholars, as well as the media, continue to ignore contemporary issues and to speak of American Indians in the past tense. In the words of Sioux writer Charles Eastman (1858–1939), "I have not cared to pile up more dry bones, but to clothe them with flesh and blood" (xii). Hence, most of the women who have written the letters, speeches, and other literary works explored in the following pages are, at the time of this writing, still living. Furthermore, while none of them claims to speak for the Cherokee people as a whole, Shana Bushyhead, Jean Bushyhead Blanton, Edna Chekelelee, Marie Junaluska, Lynne Harlan, and Joyce Conseen Dugan are contemporary examples of what the poet Awiakta refers to as "a female phoenix":

> Not only do I rise
> from my own ashes,
> I have to carry them out! (*Selu* 135)

Issues of Identity among the Eastern Band Cherokees

Because of frequent intermarriage, many members of the Five Civilized Tribes were (and are) descendants of African Americans, as well as Euro-Americans, and, as Muskogee Creek writer Joy Harjo points out in her essay "Metamorphosis," racial prejudice is an ongoing problem, even among Indians. Describing her years as an Indian School student in Santa Fe in the late 1960s, Harjo writes, "To be Indian was difficult because of the demands of culture, of color, but to be of African blood was to carry a load that was nearly impossible" (16).

As early as 1914, Nancy Coleman, a triracial student from Cherokee, North Carolina, was forced to deal with the capricious nature of the Bureau of Indian Affairs in their enforcement of tribal enrollment procedures. After graduating from the Carlisle Indian School in Pennsylvania, Nancy, an enrolled member of the Eastern Band Cherokees, decided to further her education at Hampton. Strongly influenced by the Owl family to attend Hampton, Nancy immediately made application, and her student file is filled with letters of praise written by Carlisle faculty and staff members. For example, her outing employer, Emma Higgins, characterized the young Cherokee student as "a conscientious, good girl with more than average ability and industry and good disposition" (Higgins to president of Hampton, June 14, 1914). O. H. Lipps, supervisor of students at Carlisle, wrote the following to the principal at Hampton, H. B. Frissell:

> The girl's ambition is to become a teacher and I have taken the liberty to write to you in her behalf because I believe that the record she made here warrants me in stating that anything that can be done for her will be appreciated and that it will be an effort in the right direction. (September 29, 1914)

In a letter to one of her sponsors at Hampton, dated February 3, 1915, Nancy spoke of her lifelong dream of going back to "teach on the Cherokee Reservation among my people who need some good teachers." Pointing out the dearth of Indian teachers in Cherokee schools, Nancy added, "I think Indian boys and girls should have teachers among their own people who understand their peculiarities . . . I shall endeavor to study hard and graduate with the class of Nineteen Sixteen" (SF, HUA).

Ironically, it was Nancy's love for Hampton and for education that led to her eventual loss of tribal membership in the EBCI. In 1917, she persuaded her younger brother Calvin to apply for admission at Hampton; for reasons that remain unclear, James Henderson, Superintendent of Schools in Cherokee, informed Hampton officials that "Calvin's father is supposed to be of Indian and Negro blood and I am informed that his mother is a negress. The Colemans, although they claim to have Indian blood, are not recognized as Indians by the Cherokees, and do not associate with the Indians. So far as I know, their associates are niggers" (Henderson to Hampton officials, September 13, 1917).[1]

Angered by Henderson's comments, Nancy vehemently denied any black ancestry. Claiming her superiority to the black cook with whom she worked during an outing assignment, she insisted that she "had not one drop of negro blood" and was "all Indian and white" (Lindsey 207).

Nancy Coleman (left) with Cherokee friend Pearlie Wolfe, 1918. Courtesy of Hampton University Archives.

As historian George M. Fredrickson reminds us, "southern negropho-bia" was rampant in the early 1900s, and the notorious "one-drop" classifi-cation extended the "colored" category to individuals having even a minute degree of African blood.[2] Booker T. Washington, Hampton's most famous black graduate, had openly accepted "Separate but Equal" race relations in his "Atlanta Compromise Speech" of 1895, and the U.S. Supreme Court had put its stamp of approval on legalized racial segregation in the *Plessy v. Ferguson* decision of 1896 (275).[3] In spite of Henderson's lack of validation and blatant inaccuracies concerning the Coleman ancestry, therefore, he succeeded in depriving Nancy of any opportunity she might ever have to teach or to work for the Indian office, for by that time, it had "become gov-ernment policy not to employ Indians with black lineage" (Lindsey 207).

No amount of protest from Nancy was able to sway government offi-cials, and eventually she was forced to abandon her dream of teaching Cherokee children and to enroll in a nursing program for black and Indian students at Dixie Hospital in Hampton. Having lost her claim to member-ship in the Eastern Band Cherokees, Nancy gradually immersed herself in African American culture, and after graduating from Dixie Hospital in

1921, she married Ernest Thornton, a black graduate of Hampton, and moved to Northfield, Massachusetts. The last of Nancy's letters to be kept in her student file is dated January 24, 1928, and is addressed to a Miss Hiltz. She writes:

> My family of four children are growing nicely. The oldest will be six years old in May and will start school in September. He is very anxious to begin school. I hope his enthusiasm continues. The baby is a boy almost five months old. (SF, HUA)

What happened to the "above average" Indian girl of whom Hampton was once so proud? Did she eventually practice nursing? Was she accepted in the black community? Did she ever return home to the Cherokee reservation in North Carolina? For the present, these and other questions remain unanswered, for Nancy Coleman, stripped of her Cherokee status by a government official and forced to construct an entirely different identity and lifestyle, seems to have been erased from the pages of Cherokee history. That she refused to allow anyone else to define her, however, is evident in the complimentary close of her final letter to Hampton: "Sincerely yours, Nancy Thornton (Indian)."

The importance of identity as a major theme in contemporary North America is not difficult to trace, for although Native identity was not an issue at the time of contact, it quickly became a problem as invading people began constructing a national image inclined to "savor civilized order and savage freedom at the same time." This dialectic of simultaneous desire and repulsion, asserts Sioux scholar Philip Deloria, was a case of white Americans "wanting to have their cake and eat it too"; whereas "Euro-Americans had imprisoned themselves in the logical mind and the social order, Indians represented instinct and freedom," which spoke for "the spirit of the continent" (3). Today, the question of Indian identity, which has plagued both Native peoples and government officials since the birth of this nation, remains as troublesome as ever, it seems.

Nineteenth-century Friends of the Indian groups played a crucial role in the formation of today's ideas about who is an Indian.[4] Apparently unaware of the paradox of such measures, the Friends of the Indian proposed total assimilation of American Indians, yet "endorsed policies and practices which mandated that people first be identified as Indians." This group of intellectuals strongly endorsed the position of their most powerful national organization, the Indian Rights Association (IRA): "The solution of the problem lies in a natural and human absorption of the Indian into the common conditions of American life—annihilation for the Indian race, but a new life for the individual Indian" (Harmon 97). In American culture, argues Diana Fuss, whites have always seen race as a minority attribute; therefore, "it is easy enough for [them] to place under erasure something they *think* they never had to begin with" (93).

It would be unfair, however, to pretend that indigenous people have stood idly by, exerting no influence over the Indian images that have emerged in the American consciousness. Indeed, understanding the dilemma of Indian identity in North America today requires following what Philip Deloria refers to as the "interlocked historical trajectory" of Native people and Euro-Americans. Deloria observes that throughout

> . . . history, native people have been present at the margins, insinuating their way into Euro-American discourse, often attempting to nudge notions of Indianness in directions they found useful. As the nineteenth and twentieth centuries unfolded, increasing numbers of Indians participated in white people's Indian play, assisting, confirming, co-opting, challenging, and legitimating the performative tradition of aboriginal American identity. (8)

Feminist author and theorist bell hooks explains how this collusion with the oppressor occurs. Recalling the teaching methods of her sixth-grade history teacher during the 1950s, she writes:

> I am certain that the black female . . . who taught us to identify with the American government, who loved those students who could best recite the pledge of allegiance to the American flag, was not aware of the contradiction; that we should love this government that segregated us, that failed to send schools with all black students supplies that went to schools with only white pupils. Unknowingly she implanted in our psyches a seed of the racial imperialism that would keep us forever in bondage. (276)

In a similar fashion, many American Indians have been socialized to embrace a system that has exploited and stereotyped their culture, and some have gone so far as to engage in sacred ceremonies with non-Natives for profit. Often Indians who choose to facilitate the cultural appropriation of tribal dances, regalia, religious ceremonies, etc. perpetuate the very images their fellow Indians have denounced and have attempted to correct (Churchill 217).[5]

In spite of the complicity of some American Indians in sustaining stereotypical images, however, one cannot ignore the persistent and calculated role of the U.S. government in the escalating battles over such identity issues as blood-quantum. In 1887, for example, the General Allotment Act (also known as the Dawes Act) paved the way for the settlement of whites on Indian reservation lands and further facilitated the assimilation of American Indians into Anglo-American culture. Although the Dawes Act did not specifically refer to blood quantum, notes Daniel Littlefield, the issue emerged as a significant one in the wake of allotment, when Congress used it to determine which Indians were capable of handling their own land transactions: "competent" Indians could sell their land (usually to whites), while the "incompetents" were assigned guardians (usually whites) to oversee any land sales they made (personal correspondence, October 3, 2003). Ultimately, observes historian Wilcomb Washburn, the Dawes Act dealt "with all aspects of the relationship between white men and red: it determined how much land the red man would retain and how much the white man would acquire" (4).

Furthermore, tribal rolls were compiled by the U.S. government in a haphazard, often arbitrary fashion, leaving Indian communities with the thorny problem of deciding, generations later, who the "real" Indians are.[6] Increasingly, Indians were forced to prove their identity in order to acquire land, health care, or jobs, and in the face of rapidly depleting resources and an identity-based system of allotment, infighting became a common occurrence (DiNova 45).

According to anthropologist J. Anthony Paredes, the issue of federal recognition is central to the controversy over who is Indian.[7] As Paredes is quick to point out, however, this often leads to "outrageous claims and insinuations of duplicity, malfeasance, and racism" against those who review petitions for federal recognition (341). Furthermore, federally recognized groups such as the Eastern Band Cherokees are frequently criticized for their limited definition of "Indianness," and other groups—claiming kinship around the common bond of their "often highly romanticized, imagined cultural heritage"—are among their most vocal critics (Paredes 349).[8]

Satirizing the "Indianazi" tactics with which some tribes have responded to the identity issue, Spokane poet Gloria Bird proposes:

Bring out the tribally-owned bureaucrats to perform DNA testing to discover their true biological parentage . . . Empty their pockets of their belongings. They have no papers, no tribal ID, no tribal or federal recognition, no holes in their pockets? We place them under suspicion, their names on blacklists in tribal papers, sentence them to exposure and expatriation; have nothing to do with them, burn their books, do not read them . . . We are the self-appointed vigilantes of blood quantum. Call the Indianazi hotline, 1-800-NON-SKIN. (*River of History* 25)

More recently, the Indian Arts and Crafts Act (1990), which requires Native artists to prove their Indian ancestry in order to sell their crafts, has provoked even further dissension. "Ultimately," cautions Bird, "the go-for-the-jugular psychology of government agencies intent on colonizing the minds of the people rests on the policy of dividing and conquering, keeping us bickering among ourselves in order to distract us from the larger issues that affect our lives" ("Breaking" 27).

Regardless of their degree of Indian heritage, Native people are seldom thought of as "real Indians." For example, notes Cherokee scholar Jace Weaver, Time-Life publisher Henry Luce banned coverage of Native stories from his magazines in the 1950s and 1960s, believing that current Indians were "phonies." "Sadly," comments Weaver, "even modern-day Natives themselves have often fallen into the trap of accepting this belief. In cities, for example, they often feel forced to become the invented Indians of popular imagination, wearing long hair, beads, plastic ornaments, and imported leather, because not to play the invention game is to become utterly invisible" ("Ethnic" 28). Most Indians, however, have maintained a sense of humor about the whole issue of identity, as is evident in a quip by Jimmie Durham (Cherokee) at a conference in 1991: "The question of my 'identity' often comes up. I think I must be a mixed-blood. I claim to be male, although only one of my parents was male" (Jaimes 123).

Popular Culture and Cherokee Stereotypes

Jan Elliott, editor of *Indigenous Thought*, states, "Indians are the only minority group that the Indian lovers won't let out of the 19th Century. They love Indians as long as they can picture them riding around on ponies wearing beads and feathers, living in picturesque tee-pee villages and making long profound speeches" (Weaver, "Ethnic" 27). This fascination with Indians dates back further than the nineteenth century, though, and by tracing the historical trajectory of Cherokee stereotypes in popular culture, one can more readily understand the confusion over Indian identity that persists today. Cherokee orators and writers are still forced to contend with the same distorted images of their people as their ancestors confronted two centuries ago. In eighteenth-century England, for instance, the Cherokees were the best known tribe of American Indians, for delegations of chiefs had begun making visits to London as early as 1693 (Foreman, *Indians Abroad* 31). Hence, this southeastern tribe became the subject of numerous songs, dramas, and other literary works. In 1794, for example, Stephen Storace produced a comic opera, *The Cherokee*, which enjoyed eighteen performances during its first season at the Theatre Royal, Drury Lane. The words, written by a Mr. Cobb, are a far cry from the soft-spoken speech of the Eastern Cherokees, leading critic Roger Fiske to remark,

> It is a pity that Cobb never met any of these visitors. He had no idea how they behaved or spoke, [but] there was no good reason for his giving them such stilted dialogue. Malooko, the Cherokee chief, keeps making such remarks as "Lovely enchantress, if thou would'st pity move, show by thy feelings what thou would'st inspire," and "My lips are locked by policy's insidious bands." (529)[9]

In 1835, "The American Indian Girl," written by songwriter J. M. Smith, Jr., and composed by Charles E. Horn, became an instant hit among white middle-class audiences in the United States. Lamenting the loss of her "woodlands wild" and her unhappiness in "the white man's home," the ballad's young heroine sadly intones:

> . . . Give me back my forest shade,
> Where once I roam'd so blithe and gay,
> Where with my dusky mates I stray'd,
> In childhood's blest and happy day.
> (Ayers Collection, Newberry Library)

Such a "commodified identity" is analogous in some ways to black minstrelsy.[10] In her essay, "I Shop Therefore I Am," Susan Willis argues that the stereotypical blackface portrayed in minstrelsy shows allowed audiences to enjoy "flirting with the notion of actually seeing a black man perform on stage, when such was generally not allowed" (190). Eric Lott further describes minstrelsy as "a derisive celebration of the power of blacks," which is contained within the authority of the white male performer (Willis

190). In a similar fashion, popular art forms have served to refine, remake, and reinforce the mythical Indians of the dominant culture's imagination. Susan Scheckel cites a classic example of this mythologizing of Indians in her analysis of a nineteenth-century drama in which white actors impersonated Indians. On February 11, 1836, Scheckel reports, the *Washington Globe* advertised a special performance of George Curtis's play, *Pocahontas, or The Settlers of Virginia*. The announcement promised that during the second act of the play "Ten Cherokee Chiefs," who were in Washington for an official meeting, would appear onstage. John Ross (Principal Chief of the Cherokees) and his "merrie men," the advertisement proclaimed, "have most liberally offered their services, and will this evening appear and perform their real INDIAN WAR DANCE, exhibiting Hate, Triumph, Revenge, etc., and go through the CEREMONY OF SCALPING." In a subsequent letter to the *Globe,* Ross vehemently denied that he or any members of the Cherokee delegation had appeared onstage. Declared Ross, "We have been occupied with matters of graver import than to become allies of white men forming the dramatis personae. We have too high a regard for ourselves—too deep an interest in the welfare of our people, to be merry-making under our misfortunes" (February 15, 1836).[11] Scheckel concludes that "the deception— and its apparent success—reveals the depth of the American public's desire to insert the Cherokees into the national drama" (58–59).

As the twentieth century dawned, the theme of the picturesque "Cherokee princess" remained as popular as ever, and one of the biggest hit records of the 1930s was Ray Noble's "Cherokee." Originally written as part of an Indian Suite, a work dedicated to several different Indian tribes, Noble's song was made popular by such artists as Count Basie's band and the young trumpeter Billy May (Simon 48). Addressing his "Cherokee sweetheart/Child of the Prairie," the wistful lover in "Cherokee"—presumably a white male—croons:

> Sweet Indian maiden,
> Since first I met you,
> I can't forget you. . . .
> My sweet Indian maiden
> One day I'll hold you,
> In my arms fold you,
> Cherokee. (50–51)

Racial Uplift and the Cherokee Woman

There is a strong correlation between these early literary and musical portrayals of Native women and the stereotypical images of Indian women in popular culture today, and the antithesis of the erotic "Cherokee princess" is the objectified "Indian squaw." One of the nineteenth-century Friends of the Indian who perceived of Indian women as victimized "beasts of burden," totally at the mercy of their men, was Carl Schurz, a political refugee from Germany, and Secretary of the Interior during the 1880s. According to Schurz, Indian women were treated by their husbands "alternately with animal fondness, and with the cruel brutality of the slave-driver." It was his belief, therefore, that education was particularly important for Indian girls, for, in the words of Schurz, "If we want Indians to respect their women, we must lift up the Indian women to respect themselves" (20).

Schurz's premise that Indian women must first be taught to respect themselves if they are to gain the respect of others—or the concept of racial uplift—remained a widely accepted psychological principal in twentieth-century America.[12] What is disturbing about his philosophy, however, is that Schurz, like many white Americans today, seemed to believe that Indians—particularly Indian women—are incapable of lifting themselves up, that without the support and "superior" knowledge of those outside their communities, Indian people will surely destroy themselves.

An important aspect of "uplift" was (and is) accommodation to the dominant society. As black theologian Edward L. Wheeler points out, however, accommodation has tended to have a paradoxical effect. Describing the postbellum black church, Wheeler writes:

> Accommodation, which of course had a submissive tone, also had a subversive quality. On the one hand, uplift meant accommodation and surrender to the concepts, principles, and ideals of the dominant society. On the other, uplift was a denial of what white society meant by accommodation, for it spoke of a possibility to move beyond the limits prescribed by the dominant society. (xvii)

It is that interplay of accommodation and possibility that enables Cherokee women to contribute significantly to American society while simultaneously rebuilding the Cherokee cultural systems that have enabled them to survive hundreds of years of oppression and exploitation. This task is a daunting one, and Lee Maracle (Salish) expresses the sentiments of many Cherokee women when she laments:

> I sometimes feel like a foolish young grandmother armed with a tea-spoon, determined to remove three mountains from the path to liber-ation: the mountain of racism, the mountain of sexism and the moun-tain of nationalist oppression. (x)

Playing a major role in keeping their people focused on "the larger issues," Eastern Band Cherokee women are now insisting upon defining themselves and upon using their words as a means of renewing and sustain-ing cultural pride. Moreover, by resisting the negative images foisted upon them by outside forces, Eastern Band women are helping to garner support for tackling more pressing issues such as health care, land shortages, and unemployment, on the Qualla Boundary, home of the EBC.

Eastern Cherokee women are keenly aware of racial oppression and of the difficulties they face in making their voices heard outside their local community. Nevertheless, tribal leaders refuse to invest all their resources fighting a system that often leaves them feeling unable to "win," regardless of what they do. To illustrate the concept of oppression—of caging certain people in, with all avenues, in every direction, either blocked or booby-trapped—Marilyn Frye uses the analogy of a bird cage:

> If you look very closely at just one wire in the cage, you cannot see the other wires. If your conception of what is before you is determined by this myopic focus, you could look at that one wire, up and down the length of it, and be unable to see why a bird would not just fly around the wire any time it wanted to go somewhere. . . . There is no physical property of any one wire, *nothing* that the closest scrutiny could dis-cover, that will reveal how a bird could be inhibited or harmed by it except in the most accidental way. It is only when you step back, stop looking at the wires one by one, microscopically, and take a macro-scopic view of the whole cage, that you can see why the bird does not go anywhere. . . . It is perfectly obvious that the bird is surrounded by a network of systematically related barriers, no one of which would be the least hindrance to its flight, but which, by their relations to each other, are as confining as the solid walls of a dungeon. (40)

Attempting to give non-Natives "a macroscopic view of the whole cage" is one of the challenges faced by the Cherokee women discussed in this chapter. Recognizing the significant role their own people must play in the matter of keeping the Cherokee culture alive is of equal importance. Each aspect of cultural reclamation—preserving the Cherokee language, maintaining tribal sovereignty, resolving social issues, and revitalizing ancient traditions—falls under the rubric of spiritual healing. Moreover, as Craig Womack reminds us, the spiritual and the political are always interrelated:

> Politics without spirituality is not only out of balance but potentially oppressive. Traditional spirituality, without a commitment to intellectual growth, can result in a state of affairs little better than the worst of tribal politics. We need to lift ourselves up spiritually and intellectually. And spirituality without politics appropriates belief systems without taking responsibility for human liberation. (53)

Each of the women discussed in the following pages has contributed significantly to the spiritual and intellectual uplift of the Eastern Band Cherokees. Their discourse strategies range from writing protest letters to speaking in the White House, but their purpose is unanimous: to effect healing among their people and to restore a sense of cultural pride among the Cherokees.

Maggie Wachacha (1892–1993)

Maggie Axe Wachacha, a member of the Wild Potato clan, was born and raised in Snowbird, a small full-blood community, located in Graham County, North Carolina, some fifty miles from the Qualla Boundary. Although she had little formal education (fourth grade), Wachacha was literate in both Cherokee and English and was highly respected for her skills as an herbalist and midwife, as well as for her work as a translator and speaker. Unfortunately, I was not able to interview Maggie Wachacha before her death, and secondary sources pertaining to her life are rather limited; it is important to make mention of her in this study, however, for she played a pivotal role in revitalizing the Cherokee language and renewing cultural traditions that many Eastern Cherokees had long forgotten.

In 1937, she became clerk for the Cherokee Tribal Council, a position she held for almost fifty years.[13] According to Wachacha, no English was spoken in the Council meetings when she was initially asked to take the job (Calonehuskie 48). Gradually, however, English replaced Cherokee in the meetings, and it became her primary task to transcribe the minutes of each meeting from spoken English into the written Cherokee syllabary. Although it is said that Wachacha seldom spoke in Council, when she did speak, everyone present listened attentively and respectfully.

Other than the minutes she recorded in Tribal Council meetings, Wachacha seems to have left behind no published works. Her work as a language instructor, medicinal healer, and preserver of culture, however, have led to Wachacha's being recognized both locally and nationally as an outstanding Cherokee woman. In March 1986, for instance, Wachacha was one of five women to receive a Distinguished Woman of North Carolina award, and in June of that same year, *Newsweek* magazine recognized her as one of its one hundred American heroes in its special collection "Sweet Land of Liberty" (Swan 14). Her most significant award, though, came from her own Cherokee people when they bestowed upon her the title "Beloved Woman" in 1985, making Maggie Wachacha the first woman since Nancy Ward to receive this honor.[14]

Edna Chekelelee (1930–95)

Traditional Cherokee storyteller Edna Chekelelee, like Maggie Wachacha, grew up in the community of Snowbird. Having spoken Cherokee all her life, Chekelelee was determined to keep the language alive, and she devoted her life to teaching traditional arts and crafts, as well as Cherokee songs and dances, to as many children as possible.

Chekelelee was best known, however, as a storyteller, and many of her stories contain lessons for non-Natives, as well as for her own people. For example, Chekelelee tells of traveling several years ago to Tahlequah, Oklahoma, where she sang in a large amphitheater. After her performance, a group of people met her offstage and asked if she would come to Kansas City the following evening and sing at their church. Chekelelee agreed to accommodate them, but when she arrived at the church where she was to sing, she heard someone in the crowd ask, "When are the Indian people coming?"

"Well, I'm Indian," Chekelelee responded. "I just got here."

After finding a bathroom inside the church building and changing into a leather dress, she came out, and once again she heard someone say, "We want the real Indians."

"You do?" Chekelelee asked. "Well, I'm full-blooded Indian, how much more Indian can I get?"

Finally, a boy in the crowd declared, "I want an Indian with the big beautiful feathers on," to which Chekelelee answered:

> Oh, you're not really looking for an Indian,
> you're looking for something else.
> I said I was a full-blooded Cherokee Indian,
> I didn't say I was a chicken.
>
> (Duncan 141–42)

Defying the popular image of a silent, stoical, wooden Indian, Chekelelee demonstrates a rich sense of humor that surprises many non-Indians. Humorous as Chekelelee's response may be, however, it addresses a serious issue that has continued to haunt Cherokee orators and writers for centuries now: the issue of acculturation/identity. In order for American Indians to be taken seriously, a speaker or writer must adapt both language and dress to the dominant, acceptable form of mainstream America; by so doing, however, (s)he is immediately dismissed as inauthentic.

The dilemma for Cherokee women is often compounded by such binary concepts as Walter Ong's dichotomy between orality and literacy.[15] According to Ong's view, suggests Joanne DiNova, Native writers, representing oral—and therefore, less evolved—cultures, are "caught forever trying to catch up in the evolutionary race, with their 'level of progress' being measured by their ability to parrot white writing styles and content" (50)[16].

The Snowbird community where Edna Chekelelee grew up, however, has maintained a unique position in which Cherokee people have been able to interact with two worlds outside their own—white and nontraditional Indian—without jeopardizing their Indian status. In her phenomenal study, *Snowbird Cherokees: People of Persistence,* Sharlotte Neely analyzes a gospel music event in which traditionalist Snowbird Cherokees "simultaneously act out two different roles." They invite their white neighbors and several non-Indian singing groups to this Christian gathering, symbolizing the "community's oneness with its neighboring white Appalachian communities and the rest of America" (144). On the other hand, Neely observes, the Cherokees use their native language extensively, in both conversation and song; some wear Indian-style clothing and eat bean bread (a traditional Cherokee food), and many act out "typical harmony-oriented behavior, as when despite repeated requests from the audience, the Snowbird Quartet

[does] not perform until every other group [has] sung." Even the name of the event, the Trail of Tears Singing, connotes a Cherokee gathering (143).

Like the rest of her community, Chekelelee demonstrates her ability to survive as a traditional Indian, despite having to adapt culturally to the non-Indian world, and as her stories suggest, dichotomies such as Ong's "orality and literacy" do not profoundly affect her own cultural worldview. In "Storytelling," for example, Chekelelee recalls that as a child she was shooed from the porch when the old people sat around talking.

> They'd say,
> "Go on, you don't need to listen to this mean talk with the elder people.
> It's mean talk. You don't need to hear it."

Chekelelee, however, would crawl back up on the porch, lie down behind the old folks' chairs, and listen to what they were saying. Perhaps that was where she got her start telling ancient Cherokee legends. At any rate, Chekelelee reminds her audience, the Cherokee oral tradition is not the same as reading a story from a book:

> Before I knew it, I was telling [legends and stories] in different schools
> and going around to different schools,
> and I just got back from a three-weeks' tour.
> And this lady said,
> "Now tell the story same as you told night before last;
> just try to work it in to what you told."
> I said,
> "I'm not teaching school.
> When you're teaching school, you've got pen and paper to
> remember the next day where you were."
> I said,
> "I can't do that when I'm telling legend stories.
> Every time I go somewhere, I have to tell a different story,
> and I don't know how many stories I got in my head.
> Each one never comes out the same story."
> And nobody never tells the same stories. (Duncan 136–37)

Like culture, Chekelelee reminds us, stories are dynamic, never static; thus, her "memory" of a certain story is closely connected to the particular occasion or group of people with whom she is sharing it. Also, even though "standard" English is the rhetorical strategy emphasized in American classrooms, Chekelelee uses the vernacular language of her mountain community. Insisting on her "Indian way" of storytelling and speaking, therefore, enables Chekelelee not only to preserve an important element of her Cherokee culture but also to exercise her "rhetorical sovereignty" in a non-Indian classroom.

Shana Bushyhead

One contemporary Cherokee woman, who has become actively involved in subverting stereotypical conceptions of Indians and learning more about her own culture, is twenty-six-year-old Shana Bushyhead, a descendant of Jane Bushyhead whose "Letter from a Cherokee Schoolgirl" was introduced in chapter 3. When I met Shana during the summer of 1998, she was working as an intern at the Museum of the Cherokee Indian on the Qualla Boundary, and although her parents had taught her much about her cultural heritage as she was growing up in Wisconsin, this was the first time she had experienced living on a reservation. Like many young Cherokee women, Shana Bushyhead is discovering a strong correlation between her growing sense of identity as an Indian woman and her desire to help stem some of the agencies of change that threaten to destroy the culture of her people. That she should reach adulthood before thinking very seriously about what it means to be Cherokee in the United States is not unique to Indians, of course, for culture, suggest Chaffee and Chu, "refers to what people think, without their particularly thinking about it. Only when it changes do most people become aware of their own culture" (210).

Upon reading Jane Bushyhead's letter for the first time, Shana remarked:

> What is most impressive about her letter is not simply the strength that is shown in her writing, but her compassion . . . Jane allowed herself to feel [her] emotions. . . . [It is this] compassion that allows us to become better human beings, not simply ignoring what pains us. (Aug. 4, 1998)

Shana's point is that Indian women are no more fatalistic than other human beings; they laugh and cry, get angry and practice patience, just like their non-Native counterparts. Therefore, she does not define a "strong

Shana Bushyhead at the Museum
of the Cherokee Indian, 1998.
Photo by the author.

woman" according to her ability to deal stoically with harsh situations and unpleasant circumstances; rather, her concept of strength is one that involves intelligence and compassion, as well as emotional stamina. For Shana, these qualities are best exemplified in the life of her aunt, Jean Bushyhead Blanton, a Cherokee woman whose cultural contributions are discussed below and to whom Shana refers as "my premier role model and the type of woman I want to become."

Shana, who graduated in 1999 from Illinois Wesleyan University with a degree in history and English, was the only Native American in her entire student body. Like her Cherokee foremothers who attended mission schools and boarding schools during the nineteenth century, however, she has chosen the path of adaptation rather than assimilation. One of her dreams is to become a museum curator and to make a difference in the way museum visitors view American Indians, for, according to Shana, one of the major obstacles facing Native people today is the persistent belief among main-stream Americans that Native culture is static. In an attempt to combat such misconceptions, she hopes to "use the museum industry as a medium" for demonstrating that the culture of her people is "an ever-changing one."

In *Imagined Communities,* Benedict Anderson cites the museum, along with the census and the map, as one of the institutions of power that "profoundly shaped the way in which the colonial state imagined its dominion—the nature of the human beings it ruled, the geography of its domain, and the legitimacy of its ancestry" (163–64). Therefore, argues Anderson, "museums, and the museumizing imagination, are both profoundly political," and since they are increasingly linked to tourism, they allow the state to "appear as the guardian of a generalized, but also local Tradition" (178, 181).

Shana Bushyhead represents a new generation of Cherokee women who hold degrees in anthropology, history, and museum studies—disciplines that have historically "studied the Indian"—and she is not content to allow museums to continue treating Indians as mere artifacts. She is computer literate and has access to a network of media systems that were unheard of in the world of Jane Bushyhead and other nineteenth-century Cherokee girls. Shana's primary concern for her people, however, remains the same as that of her ancestors: the survival and cultural persistence of the Cherokee community.

Jean Bushyhead Blanton

Without question, the most endangered facet of Cherokee culture is the language, and today's popular English First movement in the United States poses an even greater threat.[17] Until recently, only a handful of elders and tribal leaders seemed disturbed about the threatened demise of the Cherokee language. In 1991, however, Rev. Robert Bushyhead (Shana Bushyhead's grandfather), began a one-man crusade to preserve the Kituwah (gi-DOO-wa) language—one of five dialects still spoken among Cherokee people. Bound to a wheelchair and in failing health, Reverend Bushyhead was eventually forced to solicit help, and in 1993 he "handed the preservation project reins" over to his daughter, Jean Bushyhead Blanton. Blanton, a teacher at the Cherokee Elementary School, took a leave of absence to assist her father in what would prove to be a race against time to preserve the Cherokee language.[18] According to a recent interview in *Southern*

Living, Blanton, a "self-avowed workaholic," brings a special enthusiasm and energy to this project, for like her father, she believes that "the language is a gift [from] the Great Spirit" and that every effort should be made to retain this important legacy (Friday 17).

Blanton's father grew up in a home where Cherokee was the only language spoken, but when he was sent to a boarding school in the town of Cherokee at the age of eight, Robert Bushyhead was severely punished for using his native language. Thus, like many other Cherokees who passed through BIA schools, he did not teach his own children to speak the language, "lest they be punished as we were" (Duncan 143). Consequently, Blanton did not begin learning Kituwah herself until only recently. Prior to her father's death, she spent hours each day compiling a voice language dictionary, recording words as her father pronounced them, and using each word in a sample sentence so that Cherokee youth could learn their native language. In addition to this language preservation project, Blanton assisted her father in creating daily lesson plans for some eight hundred students in the Cherokee Elementary School, as well as recording oral histories from the few remaining Kituwah-speaking tribal elders.

According to Blanton, her elderly father taught her to appreciate her Cherokee heritage, as well as her status as a woman. She always referred to him as "the rock in my life." Although Blanton occasionally speaks at conferences and other special functions, her primary goal at present is to complete the language project. While her work may not be as highly visible as the letters, speeches, and journals of other Eastern Band women, the contributions of Jean Bushyhead Blanton to Cherokee culture will eventually prove invaluable. Like her father, she is a persuasive advocate for the beauty of the spoken word, for, as she puts it, "language is culture" (Friday 17).

Marie Junaluska

Another Cherokee woman who is contributing significantly to the preservation of the Kituwah dialect is Marie Junaluska, one of the few members of the younger generation who grew up speaking her native language. In 1997, Junaluska was elected to the Tribal Council, where she represents the Painttown Township (one of seven communities on the Qualla Boundary), and she has also worked as a language and culture teacher in the Cherokee schools. Although Junaluska is best known for her work as a translator, she is also called upon frequently to speak at public functions.[19] For example, in

March 1998, Junaluska was asked to represent Principal Chief Joyce Dugan and the Eastern Band Cherokees at Sundance Institute's screening of the movie *Smoke Signals* in Atlanta, Georgia.[20] After offering a prayer in the Cherokee language, Junaluska spoke briefly and presented handmade baskets to director Chris Eyre, screenwriter Sherman Alexie, and president of CNN/Turner Original Pictures, Pat Mitchell, declaring, "It's truly an honor to be here in [Chief Dugan's] place" (*COF,* April 29, 1998: 1).

On July 1998, the city of Knoxville, Tennessee, invited Junaluska to the dedication of a monument commemorating the signing of the Treaty of Holston between Gov. William Blount and several Cherokee representatives in 1791. Citing the Holston Treaty as an agreement that "signaled the beginning of the erosion of our land base and of the decline of our cultural traditions," Junaluska pointed out that it also resulted in the division of the Cherokee Nation into three distinct groups: the Eastern Band of Cherokees in western North Carolina, the Cherokee Nation in Oklahoma, and the United Keetoowah Band in Oklahoma.

Declaring the same message Arizona Swayney expounded a century ago, Junaluska reminded her audience,

> While many think cultural traditions would be easiest to preserve, it is my feeling that one must live cultural traditions in order to preserve them. This is not an easy task for our young ones who would rather play video games and see motion pictures than to learn the arduous task of basketweaving or wood carving. (*COF,* July 29, 1998: 1)

More recently, Junaluska has extended the cultural outreach of the EBCI to the Holy Land. In October 1999, a Cherokee couple, Osley and Hazel Saunooke, told Junaluska of seeing a collection of ceramic plaques displaying the Lord's Prayer in different languages during a tour of Jerusalem. The Saunookes suggested that a similar plaque in the Cherokee language would be a good public relations move; Junaluska designed the lettering for a plaque, submitted a resolution authorizing it to be placed in the Pater Noster church in Jerusalem, and waited to hear from church authorities in Jerusalem. Of 535 prayer plaques submitted, the one written in the Cherokee syllabary was selected, and Junaluska was chosen to travel to the Holy Land in October 2000 to make a formal presentation to the church (*COF,* April 26, 2000: 1).[21]

Junaluska's role as a speaker, as a tribal representative at special events, and as a preserver of the Kituwah language demonstrates an alliance between culture and rhetoric that mainstream universities are only beginning to acknowledge. Discussions of such a merger are not without controversy, however. From the perspective of John M. Sloop and Mark Olson, for instance, scholars should exercise caution in making the two terms interchangeable, for there is a danger, they argue, that "the strengths of both disciplines might be weakened as they are conflated; that is, we might well end up with an 'apoliticized' cultural studies and an overgeneralized 'analytical' rhetorical studies" (Rosteck 6).

For many Indian scholars, culture and rhetoric have always been as inseparable as are the land and the people; thus, argues Gloria Bird, "everything [in both disciplines] is motivated by a political agenda. Indeed, being Indian in the United States is inherently political" ("Breaking" 28). Junaluska's proposal, then, "that one must live cultural traditions in order to preserve them," demands that Cherokee culture be readily accessible to the people—all the people—who live on the Qualla Boundary, as opposed to merely preserving their culture in museums and books. In the words of Lynne Harlan, former Executive Director of Cultural Resources for the EBCI, one of the goals of Cultural Resources is to encourage every member of the tribe to learn Cherokee, so that eventually no one will feel like an outsider in the presence of others in the community who are fluent in their native language.[22]

In addition to the Kituwah Language Project, a series of Cherokee language CD-ROMS are being used to assist adults, as well as school children, in learning the Cherokee language, and a video featuring Mr. Wahyah (Wolf) is being used to introduce the language to children in Headstart and other childcare programs on the reservation. "They always said our language would never die," comments Harlan. "It hasn't. It seems to be on the brink of extinction but through our schools, headstart, and the ambition of our people, our language is making a comeback. Kinda like our football team. Funny how Cherokees always survive. No matter what" (personal interview, August 1998).

Language, however, is only one aspect of cultural preservation programs on the Qualla Boundary. Gaining the respect of non-Native communities for Cherokee culture is likewise essential in sustaining the traditions of the Ani-yun-wiya, and both Harlan and Junaluska devote many hours each year to what Aristotle called "ceremonial" rhetoric. Aristotle's concept of ceremonial rhetoric was decidedly restrictive according to Native American views of time and space, for according to the Greek philosopher, the ceremonial orator is primarily "concerned with the present, since all men praise or blame in view of the state of things existing at the time" (*Rhetoric*, I, 1358b). On the other hand, the following speech—a speech prepared by Chief Joyce Dugan, dedicating the Native Garden at Western Carolina University—demonstrates how past, present, and future fuse into one continuous circle in Cherokee thought:

> Dr. Dan Pitillo [professor of biology at West Carolina University] has involved tribal members of my staff in this project, so the accomplishment we celebrate today is not this single project, but the increased collaboration between our communities. . . . The Native Garden represents the continuation of our [Cherokee] tradition of cultivating knowledge about the natural world and also represents the growth of an effort to forge new partnerships in areas which do not lend themselves easily to collaboration. Indeed the number of Cherokee students here at Western should make this collaboration simple. . . . The Native Garden, ga ye hi ahwisvnv, is the continuation of the circle in which we live and learn. The Eastern Band of Cherokee Indians is proud to have been a part of its planning. This circle will continue to enrich our lives, and we hope this education process continues as long as this garden grows. (EBC Cultural Resources file)

The above speech does address "the state of things existing at the time"; unlike Aristotle's model, however, the Cherokee oration also evokes memories of the past, as well as hope for the future, by reminding the audience that the Native Garden at West Carolina University represents "the continuation of our tradition of cultivating knowledge about the natural world," as well as "the continuation of the circle in which we live and learn." Furthermore, it can be inferred from Chief Dugan's speech that although the university community may not always have kept its promise to respect the Cherokees and their natural environment, they can now make amends by assisting the Eastern Band in educating their youth—an argument style proposed by Aristotle in Topic 5 from his "Twenty-eight Valid Topics":

> Argue from circumstances of past time. What has been promised at one time must be performed at another, even though times and circumstances may have changed. (Lanham 167)

Although Principal Chief Dugan, an alumna of West Carolina University, was the invited speaker at the Native Garden dedication, she was unable to attend this event in person. Therefore, she commissioned Lynne Harlan to serve as scribe, recording the chief's prepared remarks in a formal composition, while Marie Junaluska was appointed official orator, delivering the speech before students and university dignitaries gathered at the university for the occasion. This collaborative effort is important to note, for it illustrates the cultural resilience of the same communal spirit that compelled Nancy Ward to dictate her final speech to a writer, who was, in turn, charged with delivering Ward's words to an accomplished orator for public performance (see chapter 1).

As Junaluska's teenage daughter Nina can testify, rhetorical skills and language instruction begin at home. In April 2001, the Junaluskas traveled to Santa Fe, New Mexico, where Nina joined some 185 American Indian students in celebrating their native languages at the Native Youth Language Fair. Speaking to a reporter after her daughter had performed two songs in Cherokee, Marie Junaluska said, "[Nina's] been bombarded with Cherokee since early childhood. She was hearing the songs as she grew up. It's passed down by our grandmother to my mother and then to us, and we're passing it on to my grandson" (Benke, "Fight for Language").

Just as generations of Cherokee women before her have fought for the survival of their nation, Junaluska is concerned today with preserving and protecting the sovereignty of her people. Addressing a group in 1998 at the Treaty of Holston monument dedication in East Tennessee, Junaluska said, "Our status as a sovereign nation is in jeopardy and if we lose this battle, it will signal the end of our Cherokee way of life. It is sovereignty which enables us to work to preserve our language and cultural traditions. It is sovereignty which enables us to teach our children the language in our schools, and it is sovereignty which enables us to hold the last remaining vestige of our traditional lands" (Cultural Resources file).

The discursive strategy used to imprint her message on the minds of her audience is one rhetoricians refer to as anaphora—the repetition of a word or phrase at the beginning of successive phrases or clauses. Junaluska's remarks build to a climax as she reminds her listeners of their role in preserving Cherokee sovereignty—and the rhetorical effect is equally powerful: "The Treaty of Holston set into motion our legal standing as a sovereign nation," she told her audience, "and for that fact alone, we continue to have the right to exist as a distinct people. While many of the original terms of this treaty were never upheld, it is incumbent upon everyone here today to acknowledge and support the right of the Cherokee people to remain a sovereign nation" (Cultural Resources file).

The dedication of the Treaty of Holston monument occurred under much different circumstances than did the Native Garden dedication mentioned above; yet, Junaluska's speech at the Holston ceremony employs the same style of argumentation as did Joyce Dugan's speech at the Native Garden ceremony: a circular fusion of past, present, and future.

Apologies by countries, churches, and government agencies for past offenses against North American Indians have become common in recent years. For instance, in September 2002, four local churches sponsored a Day of Healing and Reconciliation on the Qualla Boundary for the purpose of healing "intergenerational grief and trauma" (Ellison and Ostendorff). On June 6, 2003, a similar event was organized by the Western North Carolina Conference of the United Methodist Church at Lake Junaluska, a few miles from the Qualla Boundary. Marie Junaluska was a special guest of honor. Hailed as a historic moment, it was the first time in the history of the conference that a service honoring Native Americans was led solely by indigenous people on land that was once owned by the Cherokee people. Bishop Charlene Kammerer issued a statement of reconciliation in which she said,

> Councilwoman Junaluska, I stand before you in humility as I represent my people called United Methodist in western North Carolina . . . . I confess to you that we have not always honored your land. We have not always honored your people. . . . We in the church sometimes do not even see your people standing in our midst, your people who are faithful and life-long United Methodists. We seek reconciliation and healing in our relationships. (Hand, "Native")

It was in 1827 that Cherokee women were banned from serving on the Tribal Council—during the lifetime of Chief Junaluska, for whom Lake Junaluska is named.[23] How ironic that the person selected to represent the Eastern Band Cherokees on the occasion of the above apology should be not only a descendant of Chief Junaluska but also a female member of the Tribal Council!

Lynne Harlan

Just as Marie Junaluska has established herself as a gifted orator, Lynne Harlan has gained a reputation as consummate speaker and letter writer for the EBCI, using her discourse skills to build rapport with the non-Native community, as well as to protest injustice and discrimination against the

Cherokee people. Harlan, who lauds her grandmother Birdie Sixkiller as the person who has been most influential in her life, decided early in life that she wanted to become a teacher like her grandmother. After graduating from Cherokee High School, however, Harlan enrolled in the premed program at the University of Oklahoma, where she began preparing for a career in medicine. She states, "I did fine until I got to Physiology class and was forced to work on cadavers. I just couldn't handle cutting a human body, so I left the university, not really knowing what I wanted to do with my life" (personal interview, July 1999). Eventually, though, she returned to Qualla and in 1988, Harlan graduated from the University of North Carolina at Asheville with a degree in American history. Having spent the summer of 1987 as an intern at the Smithsonian Institute in Washington, D.C., she decided to accept a position there, following her graduation from college. Although Harlan's official title was Museum Technician/Collections Consultant, she was, as she puts it, "pigeon-holed into Indian stuff because I am Indian," and during the next several years, she served first as a curator of exhibits at the Institute of American Indian Arts in Santa Fe, New Mexico, and then as a consultant for the American Indian Ritual Object Repatriation Foundation at the National Museum of the American Indian in New York.[24]

When Harlan was hired as Director of Cultural Resources for the EBCI in 1996, the language preservation program became her top priority. Although she is still actively involved in that project, she is first and foremost committed to helping Cherokee people regain a vision of a cultural community whose primary concern is staying together—a vision many elders fear their youths have lost. Creek scholar Donald Fixico contends that Indian people, "unlike Anglo-Americans who perceive themselves as the center of the universe, traditionally have viewed themselves as minuscule members of a vast universe" (207). Harlan is even clearer when she says, "Life is not about *me,* but many of our young people have lost sight of that" (personal interview, August 8, 1999). The community Harlan envisions is one in which human survival depends upon the cooperation of everyone within the tribe. Traditionally, Indian people have measured success not by what they have done, but by their interpersonal relationships with other kinspeople and tribal members.

Hundreds of years of colonization, however, have weakened traditional kinship systems and have left many Indian people struggling to survive on their own, rather than in harmony with the universe. Consequently, attempts to implement programs that may require individuals to place the needs of the community above their own personal needs or desires often meet with resistance—a situation to which Harlan responds by parodying a phrase from the 1985 film *Mask*: "These things are *good* . . . living on the reservation and working for my people; these things are *a drag* . . . living on the reservation and working for my people" (personal interview, July 1999).[25]

Cherokee women have a long history of confronting injustice, but in many cases, disrespect and intrusiveness on the part of non-Native researchers has deterred Eastern Band women from publicizing their thoughts and actions. One nineteenth-century interloper who found Cherokee women perplexingly "unsociable" was Anne Newport Royall, a well-known journalist from Washington, D.C. In 1818, Royall traveled to Alabama to observe the Cherokees living there. She was not favorably impressed with what she found. The women, Royall said, were "ugly lumps of things" who had "no expression of countenance" (155). Furthermore, Royall complained, even though the Cherokees spoke English, "not one word could I get out of them, of any sort" (157). Disappointed in her efforts to "promote their civilization," the Washington journalist concluded that no plan to civilize them would succeed. In Royall's words, "It is very probable that the most effectual means have been resorted to by our government to overcome their prejudices. I mean our rifles" (158). Royall's support of Indian removal was implicit in her report, and during her visit she apparently learned nothing at all of the thoughts and feelings of Cherokee women.

Twentieth-century researchers often demonstrated a similar unwillingness to spend time listening to the concerns of Indians. During the 1960s, for example, anthropologist Harriet Kupferer, after studying the EBCI for several months, concluded that even though Eastern Cherokees "think Indians have been mistreated and that something should be done . . . they do not get excited about it or the prospects of rectifying any condition" (128).[26]

Lynne Harlan is one of many Cherokee women who defy the image of indifference and apathy Kupferer attributes to the EBC. In spite of deterrents from outside, as well as from within the Cherokee community, Harlan remains undaunted, and her epistolary practices range from promoting the preservation of cultural heritage trails in North Carolina to writing letters of protest to individuals and institutions who persist in violating the civil rights of American Indians.

One of the issues Harlan has addressed is the matter of Indian mascots in high schools and universities across the United States. For instance, in 1998, when Cherokee sports fans began voicing their displeasure over the Squaw mascot used by the girls' basketball team at Erwin High School in western North Carolina, Harlan not only wrote letters to the Buncombe County School Board but also met with members of the basketball team and their parents to explain why the term "squaw" is offensive to many American Indians.[27]

It is not enough, however, argues social theorist Craig Calhoun, simply to acknowledge cultural differences, for "the very rhetoric of difference . . . can be turned to the repression of differences" (xviii). "Too often," Calhoun charges, "self-proclaimed multiculturalists offer a sort of cheap celebration of the existence of difference without a serious grappling with the challenges posed both by difference in general and by specific differences" (xix). Instead of disparaging the team in any way, therefore, Harlan wisely recognized that the "Squaw" mascot of the Erwin High School girls' team was a form of what Cornel Pewewardy (Comanche/Kiowa) calls *dysconscious racism*—racism that "accepts dominant white norms and privileges, and has become numb to the racial antics and negative behaviors portrayed by Indian mascots" (1).[28] Thus, Harlan was able to respond to the issue of racism without invalidating the strong feelings of the young basketball players:

> That mascot is about 30 years old. Our culture in this part of the country is 10,000 years old. So I think that certainly we speak to a tradition from a more—how shall I say—a more heartfelt angle. We've been called Squaws for 500 years and we've never been proud to be called Squaws. We don't deride [the basketball team] for being proud . . . but we want them to know how we feel when we hear that word. ("Team Nickname Controversy")

Just as nineteenth-century Cherokee schoolgirls countered the negative stereotypes of their Christian sponsors by accentuating the positive aspects of Cherokee culture, Harlan, along with Chief Dugan and other tribal leaders, sought to educate the Erwin High School girls by inviting them on a "cultural tour" of the Qualla Boundary. Arranging for the girls' basketball team to visit Cherokee provided an opportunity for Harlan to engage in discourse that was most likely both to awaken an interest in Cherokee culture and to evoke feelings of empathy concerning the offensiveness of the term "squaw." Thus, she implemented a rhetorical strategy known as *pathos,* acknowledging the sensibility of eighteenth-century rhetorician Hugh Blair's observation that "it is necessary to observe that there is a great difference between showing the hearers that they ought to be moved, and actually moving them" (Bizzell and Herzberg 825).

According to Harlan, some of the girls either refused or were forbidden by their parents to visit the Qualla Boundary. Those who did accept the tribe's invitation, however, expressed a heightened understanding of Indians and of the offensiveness of the term "squaw" after touring the Museum of the Cherokee Indian, Oconaluftee Village, and other cultural sites on the reservation (personal interview, May 1999). On March 5, 1999, the Buncombe County School Board issued a statement expressing their surprise that the controversial term "has developed a derogatory connotation and is offensive to many Native Americans." Declaring that "adoption and use of the word 'Squaw' was intended to reflect honor and pride the Erwin athletes and community have in their school," the Board did, however, vote unanimously to pass a resolution to change their mascot name (*COF,* March 10, 1999: 1).

In her role as orator and writer, Harlan frequently finds herself in the crossfire of what Mary Louise Pratt defines as "contact zones"—"social spaces where cultures meet, clash, and grapple with each other, often in contexts of highly asymmetrical relations of power" (34). Shortly after speaking out on the mascot controversy, Harlan was asked to travel to Knoxville, Tennessee, for a public hearing on another familiar problem: the threatened desecration of a Cherokee burial site. In late 1998, the Eastern Cherokees learned that a burial mound at the University of Tennessee stood directly in the path of a proposed parkway linking the university's main campus with its agricultural facilities. The proposed four-lane road and an eight-hundred-foot-long bridge had been criticized by opponents as "a back-room political deal and a waste of millions of dollars," but in an open forum attended by some two hundred people, transportation officials argued that the new parkway would be "the best use of state money because it will address long-range traffic needs." Also speaking at the forum was University of Tennessee President Joe Johnson, who promised critics that the mound would definitely be protected. Accustomed to hearing such reassurances, and disappointed that the Bureau of Planning and Development had failed to consult with Indians about the mound, Chief Joyce Dugan wrote letters to the university president, requesting that the burial mound be preserved. For her part, Harlan "sat in the front row and reminded Tennessee Department of Transportation (TDOT) official and Joe Johnson of their legal responsibilities" (*Knoxville News Sentinel,* February 11, 1999).

Closely related to the battle to stop the desecration of Indian burial mounds are ongoing attempts to facilitate the repatriation of Cherokee artifacts currently in the possession of museums and private collectors. In early 1996, Harlan learned that Christie's auction house in New York was looking at a Cherokee mask for possible consignment. The consignor, as it turned out, was Continental Casualty Company, a company that had amassed a large collection of Indian art to be put up for auction. As the result of a series of phone calls, letters, and visits, the ceremonial mask—a Buffalo mask made by Cherokee traditionalist Will West Long during the early 1900s—was returned to the Eastern Band Cherokees on February 25, 1997, and Lynne Harlan was one of four leaders to accept the mask on behalf of the tribe (*AIRORF News and Notes*, 1).

Harlan, a contributing author of *Mending the Circle: A Native American Repatriation Guide,* published by the AIRORF, cautions American Indians who anticipate pursuing the repatriation of tribal artifacts:

> Working with collections is time consuming, dirty, and often uncomfortable, especially when conducted in poorly lit, crowded spaces. Collections are often stored in cramped, awkward conditions . . . Good planning can help to accommodate the spiritual needs of Native Peoples. Even though all ceremonial needs may not be known until the collections have been viewed and identified, preplanning will certainly make on-site decisions easier. (59–61)

Such advice may seem elementary to those who have historically assumed the privilege of making decisions for Indians, but these rituals of speaking are liberatory for Eastern Band Cherokees who have for hundreds of years been considered socially and intellectually inferior by mainstream standards. By instructing indigenous peoples themselves regarding the proper methods and protocol for recovering stolen and/or lost cultural artifacts, Harlan is reclaiming the power her Cherokee foremothers once possessed to speak for and to their own people.

In one sense, then—although such a claim is often contested—anything she writes is political. Finding a public forum for her views is not always easy, however, for Harlan's voice, like that of Nancy Ward, is often muted by outside forces. Philosopher Linda Alcoff offers a reason for this persistent marginalization of Indian women and their writing: "When writers from oppressed races and nationalities have insisted that all writing is political, the claim has been dismissed as foolish or grounded in resentment or simply ignored; when prestigious European philosophers say that all writing is political, that statement is praised as a new and original truth" (103).

In addition to contesting racist practices such as the use of Indian mascots, the desecration of Indian burial sites, and the dishonorable management of sacred artifacts, Lynne Harlan devotes much of her time and energy to encouraging people from the Qualla Boundary to become involved in local and national projects affecting the tribe. Through the efforts of the EBCI, for example, the National Park Service has agreed to consider including the North Carolina section of the infamous Trail of Tears along with the nationally recognized trail that stretches from Tennessee to Oklahoma. The National Park Service, however, has indicated that it has almost no funding for this project—a project that is almost certain to boost cultural heritage tourism on the reservation, but which is likewise too costly for the tribe to finance alone.[29] Hence, the Cherokees must rely upon outside sources to help raise the necessary funding. In an interview for a documentary filmed by University of North Carolina Television, Harlan cautioned tribal members:

> We can talk about the Trail of Tears until we are blue in the face, but if [other North Carolinians] don't see that effort from another entity who already has a respect for protecting important national treasures, we don't have any leverage for telling people how important it is in *their* history. This is not just Cherokee history, but the history of a region. (UNC-TV, August 17, 1999)

Preserving natural resources, like revitalizing the Cherokee language and protecting the rights of her people, is a priority with Lynne Harlan, and the discourse methods she uses are vital to the survival of her people.

Joyce Dugan

At the forefront of cultural preservation, and perhaps the best-known Cherokee orator since John Ross (Principal Chief at the time of Removal in 1838), is Joyce Conseen Dugan, the first woman ever to be elected Principal Chief of the EBCI. Before her election to office on September 7, 1995, Dugan was Director of Education on the Qualla Boundary, and, like many Cherokees of her generation, her interest in sustaining Cherokee culture stems in part from her adolescent boarding school experiences.[30] After graduating from high school, Dugan enrolled at Bacone Indian College in Oklahoma, but one year later she returned to the Qualla Boundary, where she began working as a teacher's assistant. Finding that she enjoyed teaching, the young woman entered Western Carolina University, where she graduated in 1975 with a bachelor's degree in education and in 1981 with a master's degree in special education.[31]

Shortly after her inauguration, Chief Dugan told a group of fifth graders at the Cherokee Elementary School that although many people had encouraged her to run for chief, she had never seriously considered doing so until a tribal member said to her, "Don't squall over Tribal Government if you refuse to run for chief" ("Chief Dugan Visits"). Following on the heels of the previous administration, which would leave her "having to clean up messes" for most of her four-year term, Dugan was elected by an overwhelming majority. According to a report in the *Cherokee One Feather,* most of her first year as chief was spent taking care of internal affairs (February 19, 1997, 1).[32]

On June 23, 1997, speaking to a group of students at Southern Illinois University, Dugan cited a strong desire to "put culture back into the Cherokee school system" as one of her primary incentives for running as chief. Having never been taught the Cherokee language or culture during her own childhood, Chief Dugan told the students at the university that she had a dream of teaching preschool children the Cherokee language, and that she would live up to her promise to bring the culture back to the people (Rendleman 1).[33]

As director of education, Dugan had already won the support of many parents by designing a process that took Cherokee schools out of the Bureau of Indian Affairs in Washington and placed the system under Cherokee control. It was, however, her strong emphasis upon cultural preservation that convinced the majority of Cherokee voters to elect Joyce Dugan to the office of Principal Chief (*Asheville Citizen-Times,* Sept. 9, 1995: A2).

Tribal Sovereignty Issues: Casinos, Caged Bears, and Capital Punishment

Closely related to issues of Cherokee identity and cultural preservation is the ongoing battle among indigenous peoples to retain tribal sovereignty—a struggle with which Cherokees have long been familiar. After Georgia declared nineteenth-century Indian laws in that state to be null and void, for instance, the Cherokees sued—and won. In 1830, Chief Justice John Marshall ruled that the Cherokees were "a distinct political society, separated from others, capable of managing their own affairs and governing themselves" (Egan, "Prosperity" 4). As Craig Womack points out, however, "tribal sovereignty was not invented by Chief Justice Marshall, nor extended throughout Indian country via federal Indian law . . . [It] is inherent as an intellectual idea in Native cultures, and the concept, as well as the practice, predates European contact" (51). Nevertheless, sovereignty remains a widely misunderstood concept among non–Native Americans and with the advent of casinos in the late 1980s, political leaders such as former Senator Slade Gorton (R-WA) are more insistent than ever that Indian sovereignty is unfair and unworkable.[34]

When the U.S. Supreme Court ruled in 1998 that some two hundred Native tribes and villages in the state of Alaska had forfeited their tribal powers with the signing of the 1971 Alaska Native Claims Settlement Act, Chief Dugan became understandably concerned about the repercussions such a decision might have on the rest of Indian Country.[35] Responding as Cherokee women have for hundreds of years, however, Dugan declared, "Adversity just makes us stronger; internal conflicts are quickly put aside when we face any kind of threat from outside" (personal interview, May 1999).

The right to make decisions affecting the lives of Eastern Band Cherokees is crucial to retaining tribal sovereignty. One of Chief Dugan's fiercest battles has been with state politicians, churches, and private individuals who adamantly oppose the operation of Harrah's Cherokee Smoky Mountains Casino on the Qualla Boundary. The casino, which opened on November 13, 1997, has been, in the words of Dugan, "a different animal," and the relationship between Harrah's and the Cherokees has not always been an amicable one. In an interview with the executive editor of the *Asheville Citizen-Times*, George Benge, Dugan commented on some of the cultural differences affecting the Eastern Band's affiliation with Harrah's:

> I'm sure it's been a rude awakening for them to operate in Indian country because we come at [gambling] a bit differently. By that I mean that everything we do is not always about money. We have cultural issues that often take precedence, issues that an outsider might not understand. They may never understand why we would need to take off for the fall festival, for example. That, if we have a great-aunt who passes away, why we would feel the need to be off for that time . . . Over the years we have become as a tribe very sensitive to

nuances. It's based on years of discrimination and . . . I think Harrah's has had to learn that. (October 22, 1998: A5)

Cultural misunderstandings are not the only obstacle the Cherokees face pertaining to the issue of gambling. On November 18, 1997, a guest column titled "Trouble Is What's Coming 'Round the Mountain," appeared in the *Asheville Citizen-Times*. The author, Christopher W. Derrick, a Lake Junaluska, North Carolina, attorney, was highly critical of the Cherokees' casino operation, charging that it had the power to "destroy lives and break down the fabric of [the] community through increased crime, bankruptcy and personal addiction." To bolster his argument, Derrick invoked the Gambler, a character from Navajo oral traditions who is said to have learned gambling from his father, the Sun, and who won—then lost—everything. According to Derrick, the Gambler became known to the Navajos as the "one who wins people" and was thus a character to be shunned (A5).

Dugan responded to Derrick's column with words contrived to erase any doubt concerning her stance on outside interference in the affairs of the EBCI. Excerpts from her half-page rebuttal reflect an indignation that is common among reservation leaders today:

> Indeed [trouble] must have been what my ancestors thought when the first Europeans came into Cherokee territory, and it remains a continuing thought echoed throughout our 500-year encounter with Europeans and Euro-Americans. I always find it interesting when non-Native people attempt to interpret American Indian traditional legends to fit their own objectives. If Derrick were truly interested in American Indian history and tradition, he would have informed you of the dismal conditions in which American Indian communities exist; he would have told you of our need for improved health care and better access to education; he would have told you of our years of attempts at economic development which have proved ineffective; and he would have told you of the legal basis which we now exercise in our new casino venture. Instead Derrick has chosen to cite, incorrectly, many studies in an attempt to illustrate his point of view. (Nov. 25, 1998: A9)

Dugan then proceeds to refute Derrick's antigambling arguments, one by one, and to counter with her own well-documented claims, supporting the positive aspects of gambling. She also points out Derrick's position as special counsel to a member of the National Gambling Impact Study Commission and wonders whether he "has a special agenda to mislead, or whether his work is just sloppy." Finally, Dugan concludes with a reminder to the public that when surrounding towns and counties decided to sell alcohol, the EBCI "respected their right to govern their own affairs," and she asks that the Cherokees be afforded the same respect. "Over 150 years ago, my people were removed from our land and homes so non-Native populations could prosper and grow," Dugan said. "Now we ask for the same opportunity" (A9).

As casinos have begun to give Indians more economic power, white customers have become increasingly resentful of "rich Indians."[36] This, quips anthropologist Elizabeth Bird, is "an ironic reversal of power—in the past, Whites sold alcohol to Indians, exploiting a potential weakness, whereas today, Indians sell slot machines to Whites exploiting their weakness for gambling" (5). Moreover, suggests Bird, white culture feels angry at Indians who do not fit the romantic mold and since gambling is not compatible with the mystical notions many non-Natives entertain concerning Cherokees, America's imagery condemns them (4).

In a hegemonic society accustomed to speaking for Indians, it is not surprising that so many visitors to the Qualla Boundary feel responsible for instructing Cherokees in "the Indian way." This practice of speaking for others, posits Linda Alcoff, is often "born of a desire for mastery, to privilege oneself as the one who more correctly understands the truth about another's situation or as the one who can champion a just cause and thus achieve glory and praise" (115–16). A striking example of this discursive hierarchy, according to Chief Dugan, can be found in the letters received each week from irate tourists who take exception to the caging of black bears on the reservation—a custom that was begun several years ago by white proprietors who operated tourist shops within the Qualla Boundary. Dugan agrees that bears should be allowed to roam free in their natural habitat, and she is not offended by the letters per se.[37] Underlying the ostensibly good intentions of most of these correspondents, however, is the implication that the Cherokees are not competent to manage their own affairs; thus, Dugan laments that she invests more time in answering "black bear letters" than she devotes to correspondence on any other issue. A typical letter from the chief includes the following responses:

Thank you for your concern regarding the caging of black bears on the Qualla Boundary in Cherokee, North Carolina. Our Tribal Council recently passed a resolution prohibiting the caging of these animals in the manner you described; however, that resolution did not prohibit this practice for bears which were currently in captivity. The discussion leading to this decision centered around whether the bears could manage life in the wild after being caged since infancy. The resolution states that as the bears currently in captivity die, they will not be replaced.

The tribe employs an animal control officer who is responsible for oversight of the animals currently in captivity. While I strongly share your concern, my ability to affect this dreadful situation is limited. I will be forwarding your letter to the owners of the bear zoo, along with my concern about the issues you have raised. (personal files, Joyce Dugan)

On the surface, these "black bear letters" may have little or nothing to do with cultural persistence. A quick comparison of the above letter with the letters of Nancy Ward or Katteuha, on the other hand, will reveal that Chief Dugan, like her Cherokee foremothers, clearly establishes herself as a leader among her people. Her message, while courteous, is unmistakable: The Cherokees are effectively running their own affairs.

Protests from casino opponents and bear lovers may result merely in contemptuous remarks from Cherokee residents who resent outside interference. Any hint of danger to one of their own *people,* on the other hand, is cause for concern to the entire community. For example, when quiet-spoken, well-respected Jeremiah Locust Sr. was charged with first degree murder in the killing of U.S. Park Service Ranger Joseph Kolodski on June 21, 1998, on the Blue Ridge Parkway, shockwaves of disbelief spread throughout the Qualla Boundary. Many Cherokees testified that such a crime was totally out of character for Locust, and tribal leaders worried that he would not receive a fair trial. Acting immediately on behalf of her people, Principal Chief Dugan, along with Vice Chief Bill Ledford and the Tribal Council, sent a letter to Attorney General Janet Reno and U.S. Attorney Mark Calloway requesting that the death penalty not be sought in the trial of Locust.[38] In her letter, Chief Dugan described Locust as an asset to the Cherokee community and declared:

> It is the goal of the Tribe to ensure that all its members, as well as all people within and near the Reservation community are treated fairly. . . . The death penalty is not an appropriate remedy in this particular matter, and we urge the United States Attorney not to seek [it] in this case. (*COF,* July 8, 1998, 1)

Arguing that this should not become a racial issue, the family of Joseph Kolodski joined with Cherokee leaders in requesting that the life of Jeremiah Locust be spared. On August 25, 1999, the U.S. Attorney's Office withdrew its request to seek the death penalty, and Federal Court Judge Lacy Thornburg sentenced Locust to life imprisonment without parole (*COF*, Sept. 1, 1999, 1).[39] Though no one defended what Locust had done, the Eastern Band Cherokees would not disown him either, for he was "family." Unable to change the course of events, many would learn to seek healing through their art, as did Lynne Harlan in her poetic tribute to Jeremiah Locust:

> he is an ordinary man
> quiet and calm
> he knows the mountains
> they are in his blood
>
> he sings loudly
> at the graveyard
> on Sunday afternoons
>
> he knows things he cannot talk about
> he's seen things he cannot forget
> those images linger
> on the back of his eyelids
> deep in his soul
>
> one moment of insanity
> one moment of terror
> one instant of choice
>
> a lifetime of anger
> he must face now
> no one will know
> or understand
> his moment of weakness
> his moment of ill reason
>
> he is alone now
> he lives only in our hearts
> he is painted as a villain
>
> no one knows his heart

Issues of Healing and Reclamation

In her inaugural speech on October 2, 1995, newly elected Principal Chief Joyce Dugan stressed the need for *healing* within the Cherokee community. She gave thanks to God, "who has the power over all, has always protected us, and will see us through the recent dark past."[40] The word "healing" often conjures up images of vision quests, sacred ceremonies, or mystical incantations when used in conjunction with American Indians; moreover, popular culture, the New Age movement, and, in some cases, Indians themselves, have perpetuated the notion that Indians have a monopoly on spirituality. "It is just a little narcissistic, however," argues First Nations writer Lee Maracle, "for Native people to say that we always were a spiritual people, as though others were not. Everyone has a spirit; whether or not she reconciles herself to her spirit or strives to understand it does not change the fact of its existence" (114).

In the case of the Eastern Band Cherokees, healing took on mental and physical dimensions, as well as spiritual, as Chief Dugan tried to balance economic development with the preservation of cultural and natural resources on the reservation. Using her skills as a speaker and writer, Chief Dugan approached the healing process by focusing on three major areas of reclamation: (1) the land, (2) health care, and (3) tribal research. Recalling, for instance, that the Cherokee Nation in Oklahoma has entrusted the EBCI with protecting the ancient Cherokee homeland "until the time they might return," Dugan began a move early in her tenure as Principal Chief to purchase properties that once belonged to her people. Like the nineteenth-century Beloved Woman Nancy Ward, Dugan believes that Cherokees must "hold onto the land" if they are to survive culturally and economically. One of her first recommendations upon taking office, therefore, was that the tribe purchase a plot of land originally known as Kituwah, or Mother Town, which consisted of 309 acres, including burial mounds that archaeologists believe date back to 5000 to 6000 BC.[41]

Using profits from the tribe's recent venture into casino gaming, the Tribal Council agreed to pay $2.1 million for the property, and on October 11, 1997, Chief Dugan, joined by leaders from the United Keetoowah Band of Cherokees and members of the Cherokee Nation of Oklahoma, publicly reclaimed Kituwah. Not everyone approved of the transaction, and tribal leaders were openly criticized for "throwing away the tribe's money."[42] Chief Dugan's response to her critics was gracious, but resolute, as she reiterated her responsibility as a leader to protect the native homeland of the Cherokee people. "You may have heard criticism of the decision to buy 'that graveyard that we can't do anything with,'" she said, "but if you had heard the speeches of the Cherokees in attendance [at the reclamation ceremony], you would have an understanding of what this place means to us as Cherokees. The significance of place is not something we have learned, for we have not lost our homes because of removal. We are indeed fortunate that our ancestors worked so hard to preserve this heritage for us."

Chief Dugan then reminded the people that in 1816 Kituwah leaders signed a resolution including the statement that "we must conclude that we are left to do the best we can for ourselves and must act accordingly." This statement, declared Chief Dugan, is one by which the Cherokee people must still abide, and "doing the best we can for ourselves," she maintained, "includes insuring that there is an adequate land base for our future" (*COF,* October 15, 1997, 1).

Had it not been for casino profits, the Eastern Band Cherokees would have been in no position to buy Kituwah, or any other property. In spite of the fact that revenue from gambling has more than tripled the tribe's budget, however, Chief Dugan was not optimistic about the future of gaming on the reservation.[43] On the contrary, she views casino earnings as "merely a chance for the tribe to play catch-up, to stoke a bonfire of tribal health, education, and cultural programs" (Loy 39).

Also high on Chief Dugan's list of priorities for her people was health care. The rate of diabetes in Cherokees, for example, has doubled since 1990, and among the 12,018 members of the Eastern Band, the prevalence is one in three. Chief Dugan, whose own mother died at the age of sixty-two from complications of diabetes, expresses concern that Cherokee people are not taking prevention measures seriously enough, and it is commonly believed that Indians are "inevitably doomed by it." Urging tribal members to begin educating their children about diabetes, the chief warned in a State of the Tribe Address, "If the current rate of diabetes continues, it is going to decimate the Tribe. There are more and more amputees, more and more people on dialysis . . . Somehow we have to get people to listen" (*COF,* January 28, 1998, 4).

When she received a call from the White House in August 1997 requesting that she join President Bill Clinton as a keynote speaker at the Diabetic Initiatives Press Conference to be held at Georgetown University Medical Center, Chief Dugan gladly traveled to Washington.[44] Using the occasion as an opportunity to emphasize the phenomenal toll diabetes is taking upon Eastern Band Cherokees, Chief Dugan implored the dignitaries gathered there to remember the Cherokees' historical *past,* in order to comprehend more fully the statistics of the *present* and their impact on Cherokee survival in the *future*. She expressed appreciation for President Clinton's initiative, which "will have a special component in it to address the staggering diabetes problem affecting American Indians," adding:

> I believe I can safely say that every family on my reservation is either directly or indirectly affected by diabetes. Nationally, one out of every five American Indians has diabetes. Within my tribe, one of every three tribal members suffers from some form of the disease. These statistics are even more alarming when you realize that 100 years ago, diabetes did not exist among Indian people. Fifty years ago, it was considered a rare find in our people. Today it is epidemic in Indian communities . . . While we recognize the problems and have made progress addressing them through our own initiatives, we have been constrained by the lack of funds needed to move forward . . . We are hopeful that through the grant mechanism President Clinton will announce, we will at long last receive funding for the Eastern Band of Cherokees' Diabetes Center, thereby ensuring a brighter and healthier future for our people. (*COF,* August 13, 1997, 7)

Chief Dugan also managed to speak personally with President Clinton about her concerns, evoking a time when Cherokee society was structured around women who were unafraid to go directly to the top of the American political hierarchy to obtain help for their people.[45] Unlike many of her Cherokee foremothers, however, Chief Dugan has lived to see her efforts at advocacy rewarded. In September 1998, for example, Senator Lauch Faircloth (R-NC) announced that he had successfully secured $1 million in federal funds to be used by the Eastern Band Cherokees toward constructing a Diabetes and Wellness Center. On August 27, 1999, Chief Dugan participated in a ribbon-cutting ceremony at the new Seven Clans Dialysis Center.[46]

A third aspect of cultural reclamation, which tribal leaders hope will enhance healing among their people, involves the enforcement of rigorous guidelines for academics and independent scholars wishing to research Eastern Band Cherokees. The Cherokees are not alone in feeling compelled to impose such regulations, for throughout Indian Country tribal leaders are now protesting research methods that, more often than not, leave their people feeling embarrassed, angry, and exploited. The EBCI, for instance, receives some twenty requests each month to research their history, culture, and people; yet, according to Lynne Harlan, the tribe has rarely received anything in return. "We do occasionally get a copy of the finished product," Harlan acknowledged, "but not the research notes, photos, or

Joyce Conseen Dugan, Ah-tsi-nv-e-sdi, 1999. Courtesy of Joyce Conseen Dugan.

other materials which would prove beneficial to the people" (personal interview, July 1998). The Executive Director of Cultural Resources—a position formerly held by Harlan—has the authority to deny requests that are not perceived to be of benefit to the tribe, but a panel of reviewers helps determine which requests will be honored. Also, the Eastern Cherokees now require that a background check be done at the expense of the potential researcher, and that each outside scholar pay a research fee. Once a researcher has been approved, he or she must agree in writing to provide a copy of all data, completed reports or publications, photos, and audio- or videotapes obtained in the course of research.

At the same time, ethnographers are having to confront the ethical dilemmas posed by their practice of questioning and researching, for as

Anthony Paredes suggests, "It was one thing to publish ethnographies about [Indians] half a century ago; it is another to study people who read what you write and are more willing to talk back" (2). Furthermore, contends Renato Rosaldo, "Social analysis must now grapple with the realization that its objects of analysis are also analyzing subjects who critically interrogate ethnographers—their writings, their ethics, and their politics" (21).[47]

In his last collection of poems and essays, *Eating Bitterness,* the late Anishinaabe elder Art Solomon challenged contemporary Indian orators and writers with the following admonition:

> When enough Native people feel good about themselves, about their beliefs, spirituality and culture, then we have hope for the future simply because we may express ourselves according to the way we are. (Ruffo 119)

Concerning Solomon's words, Ojibwe writer Armand Ruffo comments, "The message here is clear; the need for healing, the need for expression, go hand in hand with each other. To bring hope to young Native people so they too can express themselves and heal is a communal task" (119). This, then, is the ultimate challenge accepted by Chief Joyce Dugan and each of the Cherokee women discussed in this chapter: to reaffirm women's power in tribal matters and to inspire and encourage their youth to express themselves verbally and in writing. If the letters and speeches of Eastern Cherokee women do not accomplish the healing they hope for in this generation, they will not give up; Cherokee women have, for centuries, been "keepers of the culture," and as Oneida poet Roberta Hill writes, "Indians know how to wait."[48]

Lynne Harlan and her infant son, 1997.
Courtesy of Lynne Harlan.

Conclusion

And how do we keep our balance?
That I can tell you in one word:
Tradition!

Because of our traditions, we've kept our balance for many
years.
Here in Anatevka we have our traditions for everything:
How to eat, how to sleep, how to work, even how to wear
clothes. . . .

Because of our traditions, everyone here knows who he is
and what God expects him to do.

—Prologue, Fiddler on the Roof

In May 1999, in an attempt to reconnect with an ancient tradition, Makah
hunters in Washington state harpooned their first gray whale in seventy-
three years. According to the Makah belief system, the hunt is an expression of mutual respect between humans and whales, one in which the whale
gives itself willingly to the hunters. Despite evidence that the gray whale
population is thriving—recent estimates put their number at 25,000 and
growing—the legal killing of one gray whale aroused vehement protest
(Crater 10A; Landers C1). Opponents voiced their disdain for the Makahs
and their traditions by hurling such epithets as "whale killers" and "slaugh-
terers" at the Indians. Others demonstrated their anger by making threatening telephone calls to tribal leaders, refusing to serve the Makahs at several local businesses, or by hacking into the tribe's Web site and altering it
(Large D1; Solomon A20). One angry letter writer even intimated that the
white "tradition" of delivering smallpox-infected blankets to Indians be
revived.[1]

Behind the heated demonstrations and charged rhetoric, however, were two primary objections. First, some protestors lamented that the hunt constituted an act of brutality against the whale, which has become fetishized and commodified in Anglo-American culture. Such an act, to some protesters, was incompatible with romantic images of "Indianness." To others, it recalled dormant images of the Indian as savage. Senator Slade Gorton (R-WA) called the Makah whale hunt "extraordinarily foolish and an affront to the sensibilities of tens of millions of their fellow Americans"—a comment that provoked one journalist to quip, "Slade should know, being an expert in offending the sensibilities of millions of Americans" (Landers C1).

The second strand of protest involved the Makahs' reclamation of a cultural *tradition*. "Some traditions should die," declared Jennifer Robinson, writer for the *Montreal Gazette*. "It would be easier to sympathize with the Makah and their desire to relive traditional ways if the slaughter [of a gray whale] had been a bit more—well, traditional—but to try to relive that way of life with assault weapons, speed boats and cell phones?" (B2). Such opponents ridiculed the Makahs for invoking tribal "tradition" while wearing "American" apparel such as blue jeans and athletic shoes.

In both cases, the protests concerned a failure of the Makah hunters to adhere to white preconceptions of what it is to be Indian and what it is to be traditional. The vehemence of the reaction points to the proprietary interest with which many Americans continue to approach Indian identity, and the lingering expectation that actual Indians will adhere to the preconceived and static identity defined for them by others. The reaction is also characteristic of the frustration of a society that has simultaneously constructed an image of "authentic" Indians as the embodiment of primal humanity, uncorrupted by civilization, and of assimilated Indians as "powerful examples of the corrosive evil of modern society" (P. Deloria 105). The contradictions often involved in non-Native concerns for the environment, however, have not gone unnoticed by Native writers and poets. In her poem, "Genocide," Nora Marks Dauenhauer (Tlingit) offers one perspective:

> Picketing the Eskimo
> Whaling Commission,
> an over-fed English girl
> stands with a sign,
> "Let the Whales Live." (*Droning* 26)

Attempting to sustain their culture within the confines of similar double-bind situations has been one of the most formidable challenges faced by the

Eastern Band Cherokee women discussed in this study, for as Lee Maracle observes, "Culture is the great separator that decides which direction a person will go when faced with a fork in the road" (37). The Cherokee people, like other indigenous peoples of North America, have come to such "forks" repeatedly during the past five hundred years. Some have gone one direction and some another, but in spite of the turbulent changes that have taken place within their homeland, Eastern Cherokee women have held fast to the traditions that have defined them as a sovereign nation and that have kept their people together.

At the turn of the nineteenth century, Beloved Women like Nancy Ward and Katteuha were pleading with the Cherokees "not to part with any more of our lands," and, repeatedly, they found themselves reminding their male counterparts—both Indian and white—of the sacred position women occupy as the life-givers of a nation. As mothers, these women had considerable influence in political affairs, as well as in the cultural preservation of the Cherokee people, and occasionally they used that power in ways that are difficult for contemporary Americans to comprehend. As we saw in chapter 1, for example, the Beloved Woman Nancy Ward felt compelled to warn white settlers of an impending attack from her own warriors, hoping to avoid unnecessary bloodshed and the further depletion of the Cherokee population. In his historical chronicles, *The Winning of the West,* Theodore Roosevelt describes an instance in 1776 in which "the Watauga people [in East Tennessee] received timely warning from a friendly squaw, to whom the whites ever showed respect and gratitude" (1:283). That "friendly squaw" was none other than Nancy Ward; only four years later, however, both Arthur Campbell and John Sevier refused to listen to Ward's "overtures of peace from the chiefs," for "they wished first to demolish the Hiwassee towns." Although the lives of Nancy Ward and her family were spared by the troops of Campbell and Sevier in 1780, "all the country of the Overhill Cherokees was laid waste, a thousand cabins were burned, and fifty thousand bushels of corn destroyed. Twenty-nine [Cherokee] warriors were killed, and seventeen women and children captured" (Roosevelt 2:302–3).

As long as Nancy Ward was using her position as a Beloved Woman to save the lives of white settlers, she was a heroine—the "Pocahontas of Tennessee, the Constant Friend of the American Pioneer." The rhetorical pleas of Ward in behalf of her own people, on the other hand, were blatantly ignored by American military leaders. In the words of Linda Gordon, however, "to be less powerful is not to be powerless, or even to lose all the time" (K. Anderson 15). Like the Makahs of Neah Bay, therefore, Ward and

Katteuha maintained a sense of "power" by keeping alive the traditions of the Cherokees, even as they and their people began to acquire the cultural traits of the Euro-Americans who had invaded their homeland.[2]

Cherokee concepts of power have not traditionally been based on hegemony and dominance. On the other hand, political power and cultural sovereignty are viewed as inextricably linked, because the ultimate goal of both is to preserve a way of life. When missionaries entered Cherokee country in the early 1800s, indigenous women suddenly found their cultural sovereignty, as well as their political sovereignty, under attack. Cherokee women, whose voices had already been muted in the political arena, were suddenly confronted by a religion that instructed them to remain silent at home as well. "Embedded in this ideology," notes Ramon Gutierrez, "was the belief that God's earthly and natural design made men dominant over women and that therefore females should submit to male authority" (226).[3]

Furthermore, as Robert Connors points out, the discipline of rhetoric, as it had evolved from the classical period through the eighteenth century, belonged almost exclusively to males. Public speaking was about contest and struggle, and it "categorically refused entry to women" (27).

The tradition of letter-writing, on the other hand, had always been open to women who were literate; if women were to make their voices heard, argues Connors, this "quiet and nonpublic sphere would be their most likely forum" (33). Thus, one way young Cherokee females were able to sustain their cultural values, while adopting Christian teachings, was to write letters that proved them "civilized" in the eyes of Euro-Americans. Nineteenth-century theorists, notes Nan Johnson, recognized the letter as a form of composition with close ties to exposition, and they supported Hugh Blair's definition of epistolary writing as "one of the leading divisions of literature" (212).[4]

The letters written by Brainerd schoolgirls during the early 1800s, then, took on a significance far beyond that of a mere class assignment. These letters became a means of communicating with an outside world that threatened to displace the culture of the Cherokees and to remove them from their homeland; they served to counter popular stereotypes of "savage" Indians; and they demonstrated the effectiveness of Christian mission schools in ways that encouraged donors to continue funding educational programs among the Cherokee people.

On the other hand, the Brainerd letters also reflect the intratribal class struggles that characterized many nineteenth-century Cherokee communities. As Choctaw historian Devon Mihesuah suggests, this intratribal factionalism is a form of oppression that dovetails with racism: As Indians adopted new value systems, many with a high "level of acculturation," or with "white blood," viewed themselves as more enlightened than others (*Natives and Academics* 39). With the increasing emphasis upon social stratification within their tribe, it is not surprising that attitudes of condescension and moral superiority towards non-Christian, traditionalist Cherokees creep into the letters of the Brainerd schoolgirls.

Significantly, however, not one of the Brainerd girls denies her Indian heritage nor expresses any interest in leaving the Cherokee community with which she identifies. Conversely, several of the letter writers express pride in their Cherokee culture and seem eager to educate their non-Native readers concerning the customs and beliefs of their people. In this sense, then, the young girls at Brainerd Mission School played a strategic role in the cultural preservation of their people. They did not allow Christianity to destroy their culture, for as Lynne Harlan explains, "[Cherokees] have always believed in the Creator. We have made the Church fit our needs, and have learned to express our worship differently" (Cherokee Women's Conference 1998).

As early as 1824, David Brown, brother of Catharine Brown, and himself a graduate of Brainerd, proclaimed "the Christian religion the religion of the [Cherokee] nation." Furthermore, in a letter to the editor of the *Family Visitor,* Brown made special note of the fact that, among the Cherokees, "the female character is elevated and duly respected" (*ASP* 2:661). By the late 1800s, however, the political status of Cherokee women had diminished, even among their own people, for a patriarchal American society declared woman's place to be in the home, not in the sociopolitical arena. Boarding schools began recruiting young Indian women and training them in domesticity and in "appropriate" vocational fields such as nursing and teaching. Cherokee women, like other Indian boarding school students, were limited in what they could write in the letters they sent to patrons or mentors, so any resistance they may have felt was repressed or greatly subdued.[5] In David Adams's opinion, the girls gained one very important lesson from their domestic training and the boarding school outing program: "Students learned something about the marginal terms upon which they would be incorporated into frontier society—as common laborers and domestic servants—if whites had anything to say about it" (*Education* 163).

Domestic training was only one component of preparing these girls for manual labor, however. In her astute analysis of the Chilocco Indian School in Oklahoma, K. Tsianina Lomawaima (Creek) contends that the underlying federal agenda for educating Indian girls was to train them in subservience and submission to authority. Her questions insist on a closer examination of the practices of control, regimentation, and restriction of girls in federal boarding schools:

> Why did the girls have to labor so long and hard? Why did they have to wear uniforms? Why was every moment of their waking and sleeping hours monitored so carefully? Why were they strictly forbidden to step outside their own yards? (81)[6]

Surely, such intense surveillance impacted the content and tone of their letters, as well as the conduct of the Cherokee girls who were enrolled in these schools. Moreover, by the 1880s the U.S. government had decreed that English would be the language of the schools. In 1886, J. D. C. Atkins, Commissioner of Indian Affairs, boasted, "There is not an Indian pupil whose tuition and maintenance is paid for by the United States government who is permitted to study any other language than our own vernacular— the language of the greatest, most powerful, and enterprising nationalities beneath the sun" (Coleman 1993, 105).

Multifarious forces of colonization united to subvert their culture and individuality. Yet, young boarding school graduates like Lottie Smith, Arizona Swayney, and Lula Owl managed to transform the regulatory literacy of the boarding school into a kind of liberatory literacy, and to establish themselves as highly accomplished, self-confident women whose determination to help their own people could never be squelched.[7] For these young women, their people—not government officials in Washington, D.C.—comprised the center of the world, for as Creek poet Joy Harjo concludes, "anything that matters" is in the place of one's heritage:

> My house is the red earth; it could be the center of the world. I've heard New York, Paris, or Tokyo called the center of the world, but I say it is magnificently humble. You could drive by and miss it. Radio waves can obscure it. Words cannot construct it, for there are some sounds left to sacred wordless form. For instance, that fool crow, picking through trash near the corral, understands the center of the world as greasy scraps of fat. Just ask him. ("Secrets from the Center of the World" 2)

As has been noted several times in this work, neither the world nor culture is static, and, resist as they would, nineteenth-century Cherokees were ultimately forced to assimilate or perish. By the turn of the century, Friends of the Indian were appealing to the American public to help save the "Vanishing American" they had once been so eager to mold into the image of the white man. In March 1913, an editorial from the *Memphis Commercial Appeal* (reprinted in *The Red Man*) began with the plea "Give the Indian a chance!" The author of the editorial cited numerous Indian men who had distinguished themselves as politicians, priests or ministers, businessmen, and athletes.[8] Apparently oblivious to the paradoxical message he was sending to his reading audience, the anonymous editor expounded on the virtues of "the picturesque wards of the Government":

> These sturdy sons of the forest, handicapped by the blood of an ancestry that knew no restraint, have adapted themselves to the ways of civilization and are standing shoulder to shoulder with their white brothers on the firing line of the business and professional world. In the battle against tremendous odds, that stoicism which is one of their chief characteristics has proved a valuable asset, no rebuff being severe enough to stay their onward march to success. (277–78)

Not everyone shared the Memphis editor's views on the assimilation of Indians, however. Professor Frederick Starr, an anthropologist at the University of Chicago in 1900, believed the "American people are becoming Indians and will eventually revert to the aboriginal type." Starr, who theorized that racial differences are due to physical and climactic conditions, claimed to have "minutely examined and measured the features of more than five thousand children of Pennsylvania Dutch parentage," and to have found in most cases "a lengthening of the face and broadening of the cheek bones, in accordance with the characteristic features of the Indian races." In an article facetiously titled, "We're Turning Red," the *Bartlesville Magnet* (OK) quoted Professor Starr as saying:

> All who come to America must converge toward the Indian type. Some may resist the influence longer than others, but the result will be sure to follow in time. As the features change, the temperament will change also. Mind is correlated with body and it is to be expected that those who came here centuries ago, became Indians. The people of France recognize the Indian characteristics in the faces of Americans who visit Paris, and they readily distinguish between American and English. (1)

Both the idea of the "vanishing Indian" and the brand of race theory posited by Professor Starr seem rather ludicrous from the perspective of most twenty-first-century Americans. Ironically, however, more and more white Americans are claiming Indian heritage, while the descendants of nineteenth-century Cherokees—many of them multiheritage Indians— find themselves frequently reviled, by both Indians and whites, for "acting white."[9] According to a 1999 report released by the American Association of University Women (AAUW), for example, American Indian girls who claim academic interests and success often feel like traitors to their race. One Indian girl told interviewers, "You can't imagine how much I've been criticized for reading," and the report concluded that, based on this logic, "'achievement' becomes the property of white girls and a source of social censure for nonwhite learners" (*COF*, Sept. 22, 1999, 1).[10]

Like many feminist groups, the AAUW has been inclined until only recently to focus on gender oppression and to overlook racial issues.[11] Because the struggle to survive has always been a far more forceful issue than either gender oppression, racism, or individual attainment among Eastern Cherokee women, Chief Dugan says that she entered into the race for Principal Chief without giving much thought to the fact that she was a woman. Addressing a Women in Industry group in Kingsport, Tennessee, Dugan explains:

> I've learned a most valuable lesson from my own people and from those who have preceded me throughout our rich Cherokee history— that is, when we face adversity, we pick ourselves up and learn from it, and hopefully, grow stronger with that newfound wisdom. Now, I have a question for you: Are these attributes that can only be held by a man? Or a woman? No—and this is why I never made an issue of being a woman in a traditionally male position. (Cultural Resources file, May 22, 1998)

Engaging in what Europeans defined as strictly "male" occupations was not considered aberrant behavior for Cherokee women during the "political" careers of Nancy Ward and Katteuha; today, however, as numerous studies suggest, gender roles do influence voters, candidates, and society in general. In fact, some surveys show that voters hold female politicians to higher standards than male politicians. In a 2001 study, for example, the California Association for the National Organization for Women (CANOW) found that overall, in comparing the educational backgrounds of male and female senators, more than twice as many women hold advanced degrees as do men. Furthermore, women are usually expected to be more nurturing than men and to have had previous experience in a "caring" profession, such as teaching ("Different Voter Expectations" 3).

When Joyce Dugan ran for Principal Chief, she learned to accept "opposition from some Cherokee men who simply told her that they could not support a woman for chief" (Loy 39).[12] Moreover, she was not surprised that some of her most vocal critics were women, for she believes that traditionally, Cherokee women have been more outspoken than men. In general, however, she did not engage in gender debates, choosing rather to keep a simple plaque on her desk proclaiming, "The best man for the job is usually a woman."

Concerning racial issues, on the other hand, the Chief was more outspoken. When she was invited to take part in a roundtable discussion on race at the White House in January 1998, for example, Dugan expressed concerns over President Clinton's failure to appoint a Native American to his Initiative on Race Commission. Admitting that her tribe had "never sat down and discussed race relations," the Chief said, "We've never made a big issue of it. In fact, many have just come to accept [racism], and that's sad in and of itself" (*COF,* February 4, 1998: 1).

Philosophers Anthony Appiah and Amy Gutmann believe that *race* is "nothing more than a social construct masquerading as scientific fact." They argue, therefore, that we should talk about "color consciousness" instead of "race consciousness," and that American individuals should not view their own or their fellow citizens' identities as being "too tightly scripted" by race (14–15). Appiah, in fact, argues that the only race in the United States is the "human race" (32). Both Appiah and Gutmann acknowledge, however, that individuals who are grouped together on the basis of race tend to share a common *culture,* based on a self-consciousness about group membership and values. In his introduction to Appiah and Gutmann's collaborative work, *Color Conscious,* David Wilkins contends, "White Americans have never had this kind of self-awareness. With the exception of white supremacists and the most committed white multiculturalists, white Americans rarely see themselves as 'raced' at all . . . For most whites, therefore, their culture is 'American culture,' or, even more unselfconsciously, simply the way things are." Wilkins further asserts that while it is unlikely that Asian and Hispanic peoples "share a common culture in any morally significant way," black Americans have had a very different experience. "Unlike whites, blacks cannot forget for one minute that they have a race; a race that links each individual black to the fate of every other black" (Appiah 21–22).

Like most American scholars, Appiah and Gutmann seem to view race and culture strictly as a black/white issue.[13] Furthermore, in a work that purports to "explore the racial dilemmas facing our nation," no mention whatsoever is made of the indigenous inhabitants of the United States. Native Americans, too, find it difficult to forget that they are a distinctive "race," or that hundreds of years of oppression and exploitation have linked "each individual [Indian] to the fate of every other [Indian]." Describing Indian hating as "America's oldest racism," Mario Gonzalez and Elizabeth Cook-Lynn write:

> Like all people confronted with oppressive government and racist colonialism, [Indians] are familiar with hatred. It begins with the hatred felt from others and the hatred felt for others, from outsiders, and, then, it sometimes turns into self-hatred, that is, internalized oppression, which eventually, and mercifully, can become the landscape of resistance. (87–88)

Most scholars, suggests Karen Anderson, "tend to equate resistance to white authority with the preservation of culture" (25). Resistance, however, is not always combative. "Knowledge promotes acceptance," declares Joyce Dugan, and one way Cherokee women have attempted to sustain their culture has been to promote interest among non-Natives in Cherokee history, language, and tribal traditions. Until the grand opening of Harrah's Casino on the Qualla Boundary in 1997, many Americans were oblivious to the existence of the EBCI. With the advent of the casino came new opportunities to educate travelers from all over the world about Cherokees, and reservation museums and cultural centers have experienced an overwhelming surge of interest in the culture of their people.

Unfortunately, the opening of the casino also provoked negative reactions from non-Natives: tribal members began experiencing increased racism from businesses and private individuals who resented "rich Indians who don't have to pay taxes."[14] Recalling the popular saying of Andrew Jackson's time, "The only good Indian is a dead Indian," Dugan notes that today's society seems to believe that "the only good Indian is a *poor* Indian" (*COF,* February 4, 1998, 1).

While serving as Principal Chief, Dugan often urged the tribe to consider how their economic assets can best benefit the entire community, not just a handful of individuals, and, as a leader strongly committed to protecting and preserving the cultural heritage of her people, she admonished them to hold onto those things "which distinguish us as Cherokees." Dugan's efforts to educate the public concerning the issues affecting the EBCI led her to become involved in local, state, and federal organizations. In an advertisement during her campaign for reelection as Principal Chief in 1999, Dugan advised tribal members:

> Long gone are the days when we could consider ourselves separate from the region and state that surrounds us. We must continue to build political in-roads with both the State of North Carolina and the Federal Government in order to protect our recently acquired economic assets. Never before has our Tribe been faced with so many opportunities. We must use these opportunities to address the concerns that have plagued our People for over 200 years. We must take the initiative and prepare ourselves for the challenges that face us at present and in the near future. (*COF*, May 19, 1999, 11)

As the first female in the history of the Eastern Band Cherokees to be elected Principal Chief, Joyce Dugan was called upon to deal with a system Joy Harjo (Creek) has called the "overculture." It is a system, says Harjo, in which "human worth is determined by money, material wealth, color of skin, religion and other capricious factors that do not tell the true value of a soul . . . an insane system. Those who profit from this system have also determined, by rationale and plundering, that the earth also has no soul, neither do the creatures, plants or other life forms matter. There is no culture rooted here from the heart, or the need to sing" (*Map* 17).

One of the consequences of this "overculture" is intratribal conflict, and like Nanye'hi, the Beloved Woman of the eighteenth century, Chief Dugan found it impossible to please all the people all the time. As the 1999 election of Principal Chief of the EBCI drew nearer, accusations and rumors pertaining to Chief Dugan and her administration escalated. Rumors persisted concerning the potential closing of the Cherokee Hospital and loss of medical benefits, especially for the elderly. Letters to the editor of the local newspaper charged that "the Council and Chief's office have almost squandered our hospital away without notice" and chastised Chief Dugan for having closed "work sessions." One writer suggested that people were so fearful of retaliation that they refused "to speak out against the current administration" (*COF*, September 1, 1999, 2). Former Chief Jonathan "Ed" Taylor ran half-page advertisements in the *Cherokee One Feather* advising tribal members to vote against a proposed Constitution supported by Chief Dugan. Taylor warned that the new document would allow tribal leaders to bring litigation against enrolled members, but "the enrolled members can't sue them." This situation, he declared would leave the enrolled member "with NO RIGHTS AT ALL!!" (Aug. 25, 1999: 11).[15]

Avoiding the temptation to engage in mudslinging herself, Chief Dugan attempted to run a campaign based on issues most crucial to the cultural survival of her people. After defeating six male candidates in the 1999 primary for Principal Chief, however, incumbent Joyce Dugan lost to Leon Jones, former Council representative and Chief Magistrate for the EBCI, in the final election on September 2, 1999.[16] Although disappointed over her loss, Dugan expressed satisfaction with having "done a good job" during her four years as Principal Chief of the EBCI; at the same time, she admitted to feeling "somewhat relieved" to be leaving a job that had made incredible demands on her time and which had thrust her into the spotlight of public scrutiny for four years of her life (COF, Sept. 8, 1999: 1).

Some may interpret Chief Dugan's defeat as a loss of power for Cherokee women. In a 1998 commencement speech at Western Carolina University, however, Dugan summed up her own philosophy: "When you fail to meet one challenge, either revise it, discard it, or try another way to meet it" (Cultural Resources file). Dugan's primary goal is to preserve and protect the cultural heritage of her people, and losing her bid for reelection as Principal Chief did not thwart the attainment of that goal. Today, as Director of External Relations and Career Development for Harrah's Cherokee Casino and Hotel, Joyce Dugan is still promoting Eastern Cherokee culture and history. In 2002, Dugan and Lynne Harlan, now a public relations assistant at Harrah's, coauthored The Cherokee, a sketch of Cherokee history, culture, and traditions, accompanied by beautiful photographs of the land and people of Qualla Boundary. The spirit of Joyce Dugan and Lynne Harlan, as well as that of all the Cherokee women about whom I've written in this work, is captured in the cover-page inscription of The Cherokee: "[We do] not wish to present tragedies or hardships, but rather, a story of pride and hope for a stronger future."

As I have attempted to demonstrate throughout this study, the context in which actions occur is critical to interpreting their meanings. The nineteenth century, for instance, brought immense changes to Indian lifestyles. As a result of acculturative forces, boarding schools—"forbidding arenas for cultural conflict in the early 1800s"—had become, by the turn of the century, an integral part of the Indian experience. "To be Indian in white America," writes David Adams, "meant being carried off to a faraway place where the white man cut off your hair, put you in a uniform, and told you that your ancestors were savages" (*Education for Extinction* 263). Long years of separation from their families and being forbidden to speak their native languages eroded family bonds and ancient tribal traditions (Ruoff 4).

Policymakers and school authorities eventually discovered, however, that the acculturation process does not always involve the complete abandonment of one belief system for another; it can also be "a selective process of sorting some things out for adoption and others for rejection" (Adams 266). Some of the Cherokee females discussed in this work exhibited patterns of resistance, while others cooperated with the assimilationists, but insisted on doing so on their own terms. Consequently, as LaVonne Ruoff points out, "although individual Indians today vary in the extent to which they follow tribal traditions, their worldviews and values continue to reflect those of their ancestors" (2).

Qualla Boundary today, with its gift shops and casino lights, traffic congestion and crowded sidewalks, represents a very different "culture" than Nanye'hi and Katteuha experienced in the eighteenth century; the Cherokee girls who attended Brainerd Mission School would undoubtedly be shocked to find Cherokee children of today studying textbooks written in their own language and performing dances that missionary teachers once condemned as "pagan"; and the young women who attended Hampton Institute might be just as surprised at the number of Cherokee women today studying at prestigious universities and enjoying careers as attorneys, engineers, physicians, and professors. Yet, the strategy utilized by modern-day Cherokee women for confronting racism and preserving the culture of their people is essentially the same strategy employed by their foremothers discussed in this work: using letters and speeches to educate the public about Eastern Band Cherokees. Contemporary women, like their Cherokee foremothers, often meet with discouragement and disappointment as they seek to foster a spirit of self-determination and hope among their people. Many female orators and writers share the sentiments expressed by Janice Gould (Maidu) in her poem "We Exist":

> Indians must be the loneliest people on Earth–
> lonely from our histories,
> our losses,
> even those things we cannot name
> which are inside us.

> Our writers try to counteract the history
> that says we are a dead, a conquered People.
> But our words are like a shout in a blizzard. (33)

Contending, nevertheless, that even the words of the unheard are of value, First Nations writer Lee Maracle observes:

> The result of being colonized is the internalization of the need to remain invisible. The colonizers erase you, not easily, but with shame and brutality. Eventually you want to stay that way. Being a writer is getting up there and writing yourself onto everyone's blackboard. (8)

Writing themselves on to everyone's blackboard—making their voices heard and comprehended—has been the challenge of Eastern Cherokee women for more than three centuries. "Progress" and change continue to threaten the survival of a culture they cherish, and the voices of Cherokee women often seem like a "shout in a blizzard." Yet they persist in writing and speaking, believing—as *Tsa-la-gi* women always have—that "as long as fire burns and the people dance, the Cherokees will continue" (*Cherokee, "The Principal People"*).[17]

Appendix A:

Eastern Band Cherokee Females Attending Hampton Institute, 1878–1923

Dates listed in parentheses are the dates of attendance at Hampton.

Blythe, Stella (1905–9)

Coleman, Nancy (1914–18)

Crowe, Sally (1895–98)

Dunlap, Alice (1901–3)

Lee, Julia (1895–1900)

Lee, Nancy (1895–97)

Lee, Nora (1897–1900)

Owl, Agnes (1910–12)

Owl, Louisiana (Lula) (1907–14)

Saunooke, Nancy (1895–1901)

Smith, Lottie (1890–91)

Smith, Rosa Lena (1901–2)

Swayney, Arizona (1896–1903)

Taylor, Lizzie (1897–99)

Welch, Lucinda Grace (1910–12)

Wolf, Margaret Pearlie (1903–6)

Wolf, Tinola (1895–96)

Appendix B:

Eastern Band Cherokee Females Attending Carlisle Indian School, 1879–1918

Arch, Jennie

Beck, Diana

Beck, Ella

Beck, Mamie

Beck, May

Beck, Rose

Beck, Stacy N.

Bird, Lizzie

Blythe, Stella

Bradley, Margaret

Catolst, Etta

Coleman, Nancy

Crow, Alice Bigwitch

Crowe, Dora Dell

Crowe, Minnie

Crowe, Nana Anona

Cucumber, Gena

Davis, Anita

French, Maud

George, Annie

Gilstrap, Anna

Gilstrap, Mamie

Gray Beard, Sallie

Green, Willie Lucy

Hill, Minda

Hornbuckle, Maggie

Jackson, Sarah

Larch, Olive

Little John, Agnes

Long, Rachel

Miller, Iva

Nick, Bessie E. Ganola

Owl, Agnes

Owl, Kamie

Owl, Martha Jane

Oxendine, Lacy

Powell, Sarah

Reed, Lucinda (Cindy)

Reed, Margaret Goleach

Saunooke, Dora

Saunooke, Isabel

Saunooke, Malinda

Saunooke, Nannie

Sequoyah, Lizzie

Sequoyah, Luzena

Smith, Lottie

Smith, Mary Ann

Swaney, Calcina

Swayney, Luzena

Tramper, Lottie C.

Tubbs, Laura

Wahyahnetah, Margaret
(Maggie)

Washington, Rachel

Welch, Charlotte
(Lottie)

Welch, Cornetta

Welch, Lucinda

Welch, Lucinda Grace

Welch, Lucinda M.

Welsh, Mary

Wolf, Callie

Wolfe, Amanda

Wolfe, Mary

Wolfe, Pearl

Woodell, Margaret

Notes

Preface

1. J. S. Brown, A. Collins, and P. Duguid, "Situated Cognition and the Culture of Learning," *Educational Researcher* 17.1 (1989): 32–42; A. Hennessy, "Situated Cognition and Cognitive Apprenticeship," *Studies in Science Education* 22 (1993): 1–41; J. Lave and E. Wenger, *Situated Learning and Legitimate Peripheral Participation* (Cambridge, UK: Cambridge Univ. Press, 1991).

Introduction

1. Included in the papers were messages to the Cherokees from Indian Superintendent John Stuart, Lord Dunmore, Patrick Henry, and other British and American officials. When American forces burned Chota on December 28, 1780, they turned the Cherokee archives over to Col. Arthur Campbell, who subsequently wrote to Thomas Jefferson, then governor of Virginia. Jefferson forwarded a copy of Campbell's letter to John Hanson, president of the Continental Congress, and in 1781 the entire depository was sent to Philadelphia. Today, the "Archives of the Cherokees" are part of the Papers of the Continental Congress (see Alden 240–42 for a more detailed description of the archives).

2. For an informative history of the peaks and troughs of Indian loan-word borrowing in North America, see Cutler.

3. From 1817 to 1819, a white attorney named William Holland Thomas—the adopted son of Chief Yonaguska—negotiated with the federal government for the purchase of land, outside the boundaries of the Cherokee Nation, to be sold to Cherokees. According to the Treaty of 1819, Cherokees living within ceded territory could register for lots of 640 acres and become citizens of North Carolina. Because they were not living on tribal lands, this group of Cherokees did not have to go west during the Removal of the 1830s.

4. In April 1984, for the first time in 147 years, the chiefs and councils of the Eastern Band Cherokees and the Western Cherokee Nation brought

their people together to discuss mutual concerns at Red Clay, Tennessee, site of the final council meeting prior to removal in 1838. More than twenty thousand people attended the two-day reunion, and the two councils have maintained close ties since.

5. In 1895, a federal court ruled that the Eastern Cherokees were wards, not citizens. Democratic politicians (a majority in North Carolina), angered by the Republican votes cast in past elections by the Cherokees, decided that the Indians could no longer vote; the Cherokees were unable to vote in the elections of 1900 and did not regain that right until 1930 (see Perdue, *The Cherokee* 83–91).

6. As Devon Mihesuah points out, while several white scholars are attempting revisionist histories ("New Indian History"), which include commentaries on American Indians, rarely do these historians include Indian voices or utilize Indian informants. Furthermore, many scholars agree with anthropologist Edwin Ardener's opinion that oral histories are unreliable as source material because "the memory of [past] events has been totally restructured." Merely offering mundane descriptions of what happened in the past is nothing more than the "Old Indian History," says Mihesuah (*Natives* 2).

7. Two of the new Indian histories that have drawn fire from Indian scholars are Richard White's *The Middle Ground: Indians, Empires, and Republics in the Great Lakes Region, 1650–1815* (New York: Cambridge Univ. Press, 1991) and Ramon A. Gutierrez's *When Jesus Came, the Corn Mothers Went Away: Marriage, Sexuality and Power in New Mexico, 1500–1846* (Stanford, CA: Stanford Univ. Press, 1990); see also Susan Miller (Seminole), "Licensed Trafficking and Ethnogenetic Engineering," *Natives and Academics,* ed. Devon A. Mihesuah (Lincoln: Univ. of Nebraska Press, 1998), 100–110. In the essay review "Comfortable Fictions and the Struggle for Turf" (*Natives and Academics* 65–83), Vine Deloria Jr. (Standing Rock Sioux) takes on James Clifton's *The Invented Indian* (1990), a collection of essays by anthropologists and other social scientists who, according to Deloria, "are known within Indian circles but known as bitter people eager to criticize Indians at the drop of a hat." The fault most Native scholars find with non-Native "experts" on Indian history/culture is not that they are deliberately misrepresenting Indians but that they are writing outside their own experience; because they seldom consult with members of the specific tribes about which they write, these scholars often cause further problems for American Indians by reinforcing damaging stereotypes and perpetuating cultural imperialism.

8. *COF,* Sept. 25, 1996, 2.

9. *COF,* Oct. 2, 1996, 2.

10. The central claim of Lepore's book *The Name of War: King Philip's War and the Origins of American Identity* (New York: Alfred A. Knopf, 1998) is that "wounds and words—the injuries and their interpretation—cannot be separated."

11. As Devon Mihesuah points out in *American Indians: Stereotypes and Realities* (Atlanta: Clarity Press, 1996), even though Indian women were banned from meetings with Euro-Americans, they continued to exert "a powerful influence by advising their husbands in private; the men then took 'their' opinions to council" (63).

12. *Presidential Papers Microfilm: Andrew Jackson,* Washington, 1961, series 1, reel 22.

13. Anthologies of American literature have not done much better at recognizing the value of Indian writing—particularly that of Native women. For example, Prentice Hall does not mention a single Indian woman author in volume 1 of its 2000 edition and only two Native females in volume 2; *The Bedford Introduction to Literature* (2000) includes the work of only two Indian women in its ambitious 2,000-page volume; *The Norton Anthology* (1998) mentions only one Indian woman in volume 1 (1620–1865) but includes the work of five Native women authors in volume 2 (1865–present); and *The Heath Anthology,* which listed only one Indian woman among some 140 authors published in its 1994 edition, included five works by Native women in its 2002 edition.

14. In the foreword of each volume of the Schomburg Library of Nineteenth-Century Black Women Writers, Henry Louis Gates describes a similar skepticism regarding African American writers—a phenomenon Gates attributes to persistent questions in the Euro-American mind concerning the ability of people of color to master "the arts and sciences."

15. This phrase is borrowed from Sarah H. Hill's introduction to her phenomenal study of Cherokee women and their adaptation to cultural transformations in their world; *Weaving New Worlds: Southeastern Cherokee Women and Their Basketry* (Chapel Hill: Univ. of North Carolina Press, 1997).

16. This trend seems to be shifting, as evidenced by several recent publications: Hill, *Weaving New Worlds*; Sara Gwenyth Parker, "The Transformation of Cherokee Appalachia" (Diss., Univ. of California at Berkeley, 1991); and Theda Perdue, *Cherokee Women: Gender and Culture Change, 1700–1835* (Lincoln: Univ. of Nebraska Press, 1998).

17. For an excellent history of a small group of Cherokee families who established postremoval settlements in and around the Ducktown Basin in Polk County, Tennessee, see Betty J. Duggan's "Being Cherokee in a White World: The Ethnic Persistence of a Post-Removal American Indian Enclave" (Diss., Univ. of Tennessee, 1998).

18. The Lumbees, with some 40,000 enrolled members, are the largest tribe in the Southeast, but to date they have obtained only state recognition, not federal.

19. Alfonso Ortiz, "Cultural Meanings of Corn in Aboriginal North America," *Northeast Indian Quarterly* (Spring/Summer 1989): 64.

20. Nancy Ward died in 1822 at her home on the Ocoee River in Polk County, Tennessee. An interesting account of her death can be found in the manuscript "Some Recollections of Jack Hilderbrand as Dictated to Jack Williams, Esq., and M. O. Cate, at the Home of Hilderbrand, in the Summer of 1903" (Cleveland Public Library, Cleveland, TN).

21. For a comprehensive discussion of the impact of changing gender constructions on Cherokee culture, see Theda Perdue's *Cherokee Women*.

22. In the spring of 1772, Phillis Wheatley was brought before a group of eighteen of "the most respectable characters in Boston" to defend her claim to having written a collection of poems she wished to publish. After interrogating the young girl, this group of distinguished men signed a two-paragraph "Attestation" that prefaces Wheatley's book, and without which it would have been almost impossible to secure a publisher. In a similar fashion, nineteenth-century Cherokee leaders were frequently charged with having their letters/speeches written by white men.

23. I use the term "enabler" here, not in the negative sense commonly associated with enablers in contemporary discussions of codependency, but to denote an encourager, or one who empowers her people.

24. *COF,* Oct. 4, 1995, 1.

25. For a cogent discussion on the importance of "the defined self," see Audre Lorde, *Sister Outsider* (Freedom, CA: Crossing Press, 1984), 45.

Chapter 1

1. In 1923, the Chattanooga chapter of the Daughters of the American Revolution honored Nancy Ward (Nanye'hi) by marking her grave with a fence, and in 1990 the Polk County Historical Society erected a roadside marker to inform passersby of the Beloved Woman's burial site.

2. Shamblin does not document his claim that Nancy Ward's ashes are in her grave. Since Cherokees have not traditionally cremated their dead, and since other historians indicate that her body was buried there, Shamblin's information is questionable.

3. Although the theme of the "vanishing Indian" was most prevalent in late-nineteenth-century writings, the concept of romanticized Indians disappearing as civilization advances evolved much earlier. For example, during the 1820s and 1830s, the vanishing Indian was a primary motif in the novels of Lydia Maria Child, James Fenimore Cooper, Catherine Sedgwick, and a

host of other American authors, as well as in the art of such men as Karl Bodmer, George Catlin, and Alfred Jacob Miller. The early 1900s witnessed a resurgence of this theme, as evidenced in the Vanishing American paintings of Edward Curtis, Zane Grey's novel *The Vanishing American,* and a Hollywood movie by the same title that was based on Grey's novel.

4. According to the *Oxford English Dictionary,* the earliest known use of the term *paleface* was by G. A. McCall in *Letters from Frontiers* (1822): "[At a masquerade ball, a man dressed as] an Indian chief . . . thus accosted him,—'Ah, Paleface! what brings you here?'" James Fenimore Cooper either coined or gave currency to "happy hunting ground," and Washington Irving added to its literary aura (see Cutler 132).

5. The terms "War Woman" and "Beloved Woman" are commonly used interchangeably and may have applied to the same women. Perdue suggests that "beloved women were elderly, while War Women were of indeterminate age," and that, once a woman passed menopause, her title probably changed from "War Woman" to "Beloved Woman" (*Cherokee Women* 39). Sara Parker, on the other hand, argues that the War Women and the Beloveds were two distinct organizations, fulfilling distinctly different roles (see "The Transformation of Cherokee Appalachia" 122). Nanye'hi apparently held dual posts.

6. The eighteenth-century trader James Adair, unaccustomed to a society in which women shared the same rights as men, coined this phrase. Describing the "Cheerakes" in his *History of the American Indians* (1775), Adair writes, "They have been a considerable while under petticoat-government and allow their women full liberty to plant their brows with horns as oft as they please, without fear of punishment" (232).

7. "America" is used here to designate the United States, or the territories that were to become part of the United States; "Americans," in the context of this chapter, refers to the English-speaking people of European descent who settled in these territories.

8. In 1788 a group of frontier fighters, led by men like John Sevier and claiming that the Upper Towns were aiding and abetting the more militant Chickamauga Cherokees in the Lower Towns, murdered a group of Upper Town chiefs led by Onitositaii (Old Tassel) who came to bargain with them under a flag of truce (William McLoughlin, *Cherokee Renascence in the New Republic* [Princeton: Princeton Univ. Press, 1986], 23).

9. According to Old Tassel's testimony, Col. Richard Henderson forged a deed to Cherokee lands—a charge the commissioners never denied. Upon being informed that Henderson, along with other men involved in this fraud, had all died, Old Tassel retorted, "I know they are dead, and I am sorry for it, and I suppose it is too late to recover [the land]. If Henderson were living, I should have the pleasure of telling him he was a liar" (*ASP* 1:42).

10. According to historical accounts, Nanye'hi, the mother of two small children, accompanied her first husband, Kingfisher, to the 1755 Battle of Taliwa (near present-day Canton, Georgia). While chewing lead bullets for her husband's rifle, Nanye'hi saw her husband killed by a deadly Creek bullet. Picking up Kingfisher's rifle, she joined the battle herself, reportedly rallying the Cherokees to an overwhelming victory and earning the title War Woman. She was not, however, the only woman honored in this manner. Another eighteenth-century Cherokee, Cuhtahlatah (Wild Hemp), led Cherokee warriors to victory in a similar fashion after her husband was killed in battle; she was designated a War Woman, as were numerous other Cherokee female warriors (see Parker, *Transformation* chap. 4).

11. The acceptance of beads (usually cut from the shell of a clam or conch and often referred to as *wampum*) by the commissioners rendered the treaty binding; smoking the Cherokees' gift of tobacco symbolized a commitment to maintaining the peace between their two nations.

12. Although the Treaty of Hopewell guaranteed the Cherokees governmental protection from encroaching frontiersmen and their families, Congress proved inadequate for dealing with such conflicts. Subsequently, Cherokees took matters into their own hands, killing several white trespassers, thus being forced by a second treaty—the Treaty of Coyatee—to surrender even more land.

13. Quoting from eighteenth-century South Carolina Council minutes, John Phillip Reid, in *A Law of Blood* (New York: New York Univ. Press, 1970), notes that Ward's uncle, Attakullakulla (Little Carpenter) startled Charles Town council members during a 1757 meeting by asking why they were all males. After being informed that it was Cherokee custom to admit females to their councils, "it took [Governor] Lyttelton two or three days," adds Reid, "to come up with the rather lame answer that 'the White Men do place a Confidence in their Women and share their Counsels with them when they know their Hearts to be good'" (69).

14. For a lucid and well-documented discussion of various Cherokee Beloved Women and War Women, see Parker 117–49.

15. By means of what is known in Indian Country as the "moccasin telegraph," Indians were able to stay abreast of what was happening in various parts of the continent. Although, as Ronald Wright points out in his superb work *Stolen Continents* (New York: Viking Press, 1992), historians have tried to deny or diminish the Iroquois impact on the American Constitution, Benjamin Franklin had taken careful notes when Canasatego spoke at the Treaty of Lancaster. In 1751, Franklin wrote, "It would be a very strange thing if Six Nations of ignorant savages should be capable of forming a scheme for a union, and be able to execute it in such a manner as that it has subsisted ages, and appears indissoluble; and yet that a like union should be impracticable for ten or a dozen English Colonies" (116).

16. Cherokee scholar Alan Kilpatrick expounds upon this worldview in his prediction that "traditionalist Cherokees will continue to behave in accordance with their views of the sacred world, a realm where only ancient powers can purify and protect the human spirit from the dark, unseen forces that diminish us all" (*The Night* 144). Also, see Jack Frederick Kilpatrick and Anna Gritts Kilpatrick, *Walk in Your Soul: Love Incantations of the Oklahoma Cherokees* (Dallas: Southern Methodist Univ. Press, 1965).

17. During the seventeenth century, colonial governors were so intolerant of Englishmen running off to live among the Indians that, in 1612, Gov. Thomas Dale of Jamestown had them hunted down and executed. Franklin complained that, although no Indian could ever be persuaded to live willingly among whites, white individuals who lived awhile among Indians "become disgusted with our manner of life . . . and take the first good Opportunity of escaping again into the Woods, from whence there is no reclaiming them" (Stannard 104).

18. The socio-religious beliefs of Cherokee women pertaining to their connection to "the female life-forces of the universe" are not to be confused with the essentialist vision of women's intrinsic connection to the earth espoused by many non-Indian New Age followers (See Philip Deloria's "Counterculture Indians and the New Age," *Playing Indian*, 154–80).

19. In "The Cult of True Womanhood," Barbara Welter lists four cardinal virtues of the ideal nineteenth-century woman: piety, purity, submissiveness, and domesticity. Elizabeth Fox-Genovese argues, however, that Welter's true womanhood ideology "constituted a prescription for, rather than a description of, behavior (*Feminism without Illusions* 35), and in "The Sentimentalists: Promise and Betrayal in the Home," *Signs* 4 (Spring 1979): 434–46, an article summarizing the main positions in the debate over the significance of sentimental fiction, Mary Kelley extends the discussion to women's writing.

20. Other Indian captivity narratives include Kathryn Derounian-Stodola's *Women's Indian Captivity Narratives* (New York: Penguin, 1998); Frederick Drimmer's *Captured by the Indians: 15 Firsthand Accounts, 1750–1870* (Mineola, NY: Dover, 1985); Mary Rowlandson, *The Sovereignty and Goodness of God, Together with the Faithfulness of His Promises Displayed; Being a Narrative of the Captivity and Restauration of Mrs. Mary Rowlandson* (1682); John Williams, *The Redeemed Captive, Returned to Zion* (1707); Charles H. Lincoln, *Narratives of the Indian Wars, 1675–1699* (1913; reprinted by Barnes and Noble, 1959).

21. The general rule, according to Reid, was that prisoners legally belonged to their captors; however, Cherokee custom dictated that women who had lost a family member to war or disease be given the option of acquiring a captive to replace the deceased. Therefore, in the case of Menzies, Reid contends, it was not his rejection by the woman who had

a legal right to decide his fate, but the fact that no one was willing to adopt him, which sent the captive surgeon to the stake (*A Law of Blood* 191).

22. Marrant reports that he spent "ten weeks and three days" helping the Cherokee hunter kill and skin deer (20).

23. Marrant incorporates each of the four dominant forms of Puritanical persuasion, as outlined by Donald Pease in his captivity narrative: jeremiad, typology, sermon, meditation. For an intriguing discussion of Marrant's reworking of the trope of the Talking Book in the slave narrative of James Albert Ukawsaw Gronniosaw (1774), see Henry Louis Gates Jr., *The Signifying Monkey: A Theory of African-American Literary Criticism* (Oxford: Oxford Univ. Press, 1988), 142–46.

24. Marrant gives no indication that he was ever a captive of the Cherokee hunter who befriended him, only that he was strongly encouraged by the man to return with him to his village. It was apparently his value as a replacement for a Cherokee male (lost to disease or war), therefore, which led the other men to "capture" the young boy upon his arrival in their midst.

25. For a comprehensive discussion of Cherokee concepts of slavery, see Theda Perdue, *Slavery and the Evolution of Cherokee Society* (Knoxville: Univ. of Tennessee Press, 1979).

26. Robert Conley, in his fictional masterpiece *War Woman* (New York: St. Martin's Press, 1997), provides an insightful analysis of the problems that arise when greed and the lust for power disrupt traditional principles of balance and order in Cherokee society.

27. The rallying cry of Nancy Ward's cousin, Dragging Canoe, and his hundreds of young supporters was "We are not yet conquered!" (Pat Alderman, *Nancy Ward: Cherokee Chieftainess and Dragging Canoe: Cherokee-Chickamauga War Chief* [Johnson City, TN: Overmountain Press, 1978], 73).

28. According to Alderman, "Before the Meet began, the commissioners had planned to seek all the land north of the Little Tennessee River" (65).

29. In 1801, just days prior to a proposed meeting with the U.S. commissioners, a Cherokee woman, carrying her three-month-old infant, was murdered on her way to sell "the products of her industry" in Knoxville, Tennessee. Angered over the commissioners' report that the perpetrator (a white man) had "escaped from the country," the chiefs announced that they would not meet with the Americans until they "had the murderer in custody, and would execute him in their presence" (Hawkins 374).

30. In the eighteenth century the Cherokees had no centralized political system; rather, each town was self-sufficient and self-governing. Public ridicule, disdain, or ostracism were the only forces employed by the Cherokees to keep down dissidence; thus, the councils did not exercise coercive power over individuals, for custom and public opinion sufficed to maintain order.

The title of Beloved Woman, while it did not bestow special political power upon Nanye'hi in the Euro-American sense, was nevertheless a position of reverential power among the Cherokees, based, firstly, on her ability to bear children, and, secondly, on her wisdom and age (McLoughlin, *Cherokee Renascence* 10–12; Perdue, *Cherokee Women* 101).

31. According to Sara Parker, the speeches of Nanye'hi were interpreted and recorded by James McCormick, a longtime resident in the Cherokee Nation, and were preserved by trader Joseph Martin (Nanye'hi's son-in-law) among his private papers (145).

32. Reid clarifies the rights and privileges of women in the matrilineal clan system of the Cherokees (*A Law of Blood* 35–48).

33. Ward's great-grandson, Jack Hilderbrand, makes an interesting claim that historians and biographers seem reluctant to address. He states, in sworn testimony, that Nancy Ward, whose father was a Delaware, was 2 years old when the Delawares made their famous treaty with William Penn in 1682, and that she was 140 years old at the time of her death ("Recollections").

34. Whirlwind, believed by many in her village to be a witch, often endured insults, contentions, and even threats on her life as she led her Cherokee people through the terrifying days of their first encounters with encroaching European settlers. Conley's *War Woman* analyzes and clarifies the status of Cherokee women in a manner that not only sheds light on the role Nancy Ward played as Beloved Woman but also provides fascinating insight into the joys and sorrows she must have experienced as a female leader.

35. Lt. Henry Timberlake, who took up residence among the Cherokees shortly after Fort Loudon was abandoned in 1760, reported that Cherokee women who were married to white soldiers at the fort continued to bring food to their husbands, in direct defiance of War Chief Willinawaw. According to Timberlake, the white soldiers had been "blocked up" at Fort Loudon in order to be starved into surrendering to the Cherokees. Although Willinawaw threatened death to any Cherokee who aided the enemy, the women "laughing at his threats, boldly told [Willinawaw], they would succour their husbands every day, and were sure, that, if he killed them, their relations would make his death atone for theirs" (89–90).

Chapter 2

1. I wish to give credit to Marilou Awiakta for introducing, as early as 1981, the connection between Einstein's theory of relativity and the Cherokee concept of time in her essay "Amazons in Appalachia," *Selu* 92.

2. It is important to note that Selu and Kana'ti, though often referred to as "superior beings," were not Cherokee deities. On the contrary, argues

Sickatower, one of John Howard Payne's aged informants, "We old Indians believed in the one Creator who governs the affairs of the Universe and whose place is in the center of the sky, directly overhead" (JHP 2:50). Also, in a letter to Payne, Principal Chief John Ross states that the Cherokees have traditionally been believers in "Three Beings—always one in mind and in all their works." This trinity of Beings, contends Chief Ross, "created all things, are always present, know all things, and direct when and how all are to die." Furthermore, according to informant Andrew Sanders (whose Cherokee name is Snake), these teachings "have not been received from white men, [but by] Antiquarians who . . . are men of integrity and universally declare that they were handed down from their fathers . . . who have been almost entirely secluded from whites" (4:2–3).

3. Sociologist Wilma Dunaway argues that although most Cherokee women resisted cultural and political change, male leaders of the Cherokee Nation envisioned a future that embraced acculturation (see Dunaway's "Rethinking Cherokee Acculturation").

4. According to Brainerd missionary Jeremiah Evarts, Catharine Brown's parents were "half-breeds, who have never learnt to speak English." Her brother David and her half-brother Edward also attended the Brainerd Mission School.

5. Some months after Catharine had been admitted to Brainerd Mission School, the missionaries learned that U.S. soldiers encamped near the Brown home during the war with the Creeks had constantly preyed upon the young girl, but that she, "at the peril of her health and body, successfully escaped the society of the immoral soldiers" by fleeing from her home and hiding out in the forest (Walker 177).

6. Although the ABCFM preferred that their missionaries be married, Daniel Butrick was with the mission almost ten years before finally marrying Elizabeth Proctor, a young woman from his native Massachusetts. Butrick, who disagreed with some of the ethnocentric and elitist attitudes of Cyrus Kingsbury (founder of Brainerd Mission), made an effort to learn the language and customs of the Cherokee people and was a great favorite among them. When the Cherokees were forcibly removed west in 1838, Butrick and his family went with them.

7. For an overview of Cherokee religion and the significance of such elements as fire and water in traditional worship, see D. H. Corkran's "The Nature of the Cherokee Supreme Being."

8. Some 600 to 800 Cherokees lived at Creek Path until about 1830, when removal of Indians to lands west of the Mississippi caused a rapid decline in the population (see Mary Higginbotham's "Creek Path Mission," *JCS* [Fall 1976]: 72–86). Another Cherokee student at the Brainerd Mission School, John Arch, had already been placed in charge of a school for boys

at Creek Path, and for a while, in July 1820, he and Catharine Brown were entrusted with running the Creek Path Mission while missionary Daniel Butrick was away on business. Five years later, both Catharine and John were dead as a result of tuberculosis.

9. Article III, Section 4 of the Cherokee Constitution declared that "no person who is of negro or mulatto parentage . . . shall be eligible to hold any office of profit, honor or trust under this Government," and Article III, Section 7 banned blacks from voting. In 1841, an act prohibiting "the teaching of negroes to read and write" was passed by the Cherokee Nation.

10. On the other hand, Walker's insistence that it was "the looseness of manners of so many Indian squaws observed by the missionaries" that led them to misjudge the moral character of Catharine when she enrolled at Brainerd reveals his own misunderstanding of Cherokee culture and of the sexual autonomy accorded Cherokee women. For an insightful analysis of the conflict between Christianity and Cherokee values pertaining to the sexual behavior of women, see Theda Perdue's chapter, "Selu Meets Eve," in *Cherokee Women* 159–84.

11. According to a note in the *Brainerd Journal,* Lydia married Milo Hoyt, son of prominent Brainerd missionary Ard Hoyt, in 1820. It is recorded in the "Catalogue," written by the missionaries in 1822, that "she makes a good wife and a respectable woman." Early in 1834, Milo and Lydia enrolled for emigration, arriving at Fort Smith, Arkansas, on May 16, 1834. Eventually, the couple separated and Milo moved to Ohio, while Lydia joined her father's family in Tahlequah, Indian Territory. She died July 10, 1862; reportedly she was "lifting a calf from a well and never recovered" (see Phillips 471).

12. For a discussion of the origin of Cherokee song compositions and their significance in the social life of the people, see Speck and Broom 13–16.

13. According to Robert Walker, Erastus and Sarah Coleman Dean— the ABCFM missionaries who left their son in the care of Nancy Reece and her family—were compelled to return north in July 1825, due to the failing health of Mrs. Dean. She died at Newburyport, Massachusetts, on May 21, 1826, apparently separated from her three-year-old son, Chester (see *Torchlights* 51 and the Oct. 13, 1822, entry in *Brainerd Journal*). I have been unable to find any record of the second child to whom Nancy refers in her letter.

14. Excerpt from a letter written by Cyrus Kingsbury, November 25, 1816, to Dr. Samuel Worcester, corresponding secretary of the American Board.

15. For example, nine-year-old Polly Wilson confides in a letter to Jeremiah Evarts, "Last year I was series about my soul but now I do not

think so much about it as I did then sometimes I feel that I must have a new heart before I die or I must go to hell and perish forever" (JHP 8:52); and in a note to a relative, Polly confesses, "Satan is trying to get our minds from God. I have felt as tho I love God but I am afraid I am decieving [*sic*] myself" (8:39). Another young girl, Ann Bush, writes to her sister, "You say that I must tell you my feelings. I have thought about my soul. I sometimes have felt afraid that God would leave this place" (8:38).

16. In her autobiography, *Where Courage Is Like a Wild Horse* (Lincoln: Univ. of Nebraska Press, 1997), Sharon Skolnick (Okee-Chee) describes a Sunday sermon at the Murrow Indian Orphanage (Muskogee, Oklahoma), where she and her sister were placed as young children:

> Let me tell you about hellfire, children. All of hell is paved with sulfur. Matches are made of sulfur. It is sulfur makes them leap into flame and pop and hiss and burn so hot. Imagine a world that is nothing but sulfur. The flowers are yellow, made of sulfur. They burn you when you smell them. The butterflies are yellow; when they brush your skin, they burn you. The birds are all yellow like canaries. Yes, made of sulfur. You will wear yellow clothes that burn your skin every minute. That is hell. And that is where bad little boys and girls who cannot listen to their elders are sure to end up. (20)

Fortunately, Mrs. Joseph, an Indian woman hired to be housemother to the orphan girls at Murrow, took time to comfort her frightened charges and to assure them that "Jesus loved the children more than anyone."

17. Both Jackson and Lumpkin resented the involvement of missionaries in protesting Indian removal. "Such phony philanthropists misled the Indians and advocated policies that guaranteed their destruction," argued Lumpkin, and he characterized the missionaries' letters and speeches as having "much more of the character of the politician and lawyer than that of an humble missionary" (Andrew 225).

18. *The Brainerd Journal* contains numerous references to the missionaries' attitudes concerning grief. On the occasion of George McDonald's funeral, for example, Cyrus Kingsbury reports, "There was not that order which we see in the Northern States but everything was decent & solemn" (Phillips and Phillips 30). The death of an eleven-month-old Cherokee baby due to dysentery evokes the following comments: "This day the remains of [the child] was deposited in the mission burying ground. Both the father and the mother behaved with great propriety on this trying occasion" (225). And when one of the Brainerd scholars, fourteen-year-old John Rackley, died quite suddenly, the journalist notes the arrival of the boy's grandmother at the school, "inexpressibly borne down with grief"; the following day's entry reads simply, "The remains of the deceased child were committed to the tomb" (247).

19. See Andrew 153–208.

20. One of the most controversial studies portraying Andrew Jackson as an Indian hater is political scientist Michael P. Rogin's psychoanalytic

work *Fathers and Children: Andrew Jackson and the Subjugation of the American Indian* (New York: Alfred A. Knopf, 1975). Ronald Takaki, author of *Iron Cages: Race and Culture in Nineteenth-Century America* (New York: Alfred A. Knopf, 1979), likewise depicts Jackson as a man filled with hatred for Indians, characterizing him as one who developed "a metaphysics for genocide." Francis Paul Prucha, on the other hand, argues in *The Great Father: The United States Government and the American Indian* (Lincoln: Univ. of Nebraska Press, 1984) that Jackson's concern for the well-being and advancement of the Indians was genuine, and Robert V. Remini, author of the three-volume history *Andrew Jackson* (New York: Harper and Row, 1977–84), revised an earlier argument (1963) that Jackson had "a remarkable talent for slaughtering Indians" to contend that Jackson was "most anxious to preserve Indian life and culture." For a more detailed discussion of these conflicting views, see Ronald N. Satz's essay "Rhetoric Versus Reality," in *Cherokee Removal: Before and After,* ed. William L. Anderson (Athens: Univ. of Georgia Press, 1991), 29–54.

Chapter 3

1. Gov. John Sevier, who had once referred to the "Little Cherokees" as "nits that make lice," also witnessed the children's performance and is said to have been moved to tears by the sight. Grasping Reverend Blackburn's hand and shaking it, Sevier said, "I have often stood unmoved amidst showers of bullets from the Indian rifles, but this effectually unmans me. I see civilization taking the ground of barbarism, and the praises of Jesus succeeding the war whoop of the savage" (Woodward 125).

2. Other scholars maintain that Blackburn gave up his mission work because of "impaired health and the growing needs of his family" (see Walter Posey, *The Presbyterian Church in the Old Southwest, 1778–1838* [Louisville: John Knox Press, 1952]); Dorothy Bass, "Gideon Blackburn's Mission to the Cherokees," *Journal of Presbyterian History* [Fall 1974]: 219; V. M. Queener, "Gideon Blackburn, East Tennessee Historical Society, *Publications,* no. 6 [1934]: 23). "But if they were so successful," asks McLoughlin, "why did not the Presbyterians find someone else to carry on the schools?" While, according to McLoughlin, "there was nothing odd about a parson's selling whiskey in pre-prohibition days," it was against federal law to sell it among Indians. Basing his study on extensive primary sources in federal archives and Moravian mission records, McLoughlin persuasively argues that the matter of Blackburn's guilt was hushed up by the federal Indian agent who had supported Blackburn's mission, as well as by the federal government, the Presbyterian Church, and others from whom he had obtained financial support ("Parson Blackburn's Whiskey

and the Cherokee Indian Schools, 1809–1810," *Journal of Presbyterian History* 57.4 (Winter 1979): 427–45).

3. See, for example, Adams, *Education for Extinction* (291–98); Hill (198–209); McLoughlin, *The Cherokees and Christianity* (109–26); and Phillips and Phillips (foreword).

4. McLoughlin cites several instances of conflict between the missionaries and the Cherokee people they hoped to evangelize. For example, the missionaries preached about Christ's command to feed the hungry, house the homeless, and clothe the naked—teachings consistent with the hospitality ethic of the Cherokees; yet when a poor Cherokee asked for assistance, he was called a "lazy beggar" and turned away. Also, the missionaries forbade church members to participate in tribal ceremonies, including athletic contests, rainmaking ceremonies, and traditional medical practices. When members secretly resorted to traditional healing methods, etc., the missionaries called them before the church and publicly censured or expelled them. According to mission statistics, as many as 50 percent of those Cherokees who converted were either expelled or voluntarily abandoned Christianity (see *The Cherokees and Christianity* 10–33).

5. Recommended readings include William Anderson, *Cherokee Removal: Before and After* (Athens: Univ. of Georgia Press, 1991); Charles Hudson, *The Southeastern Indians* (Univ. of Tennessee Press, 1976); Theda Perdue and Michael D. Green, eds., *The Cherokee Removal: A Brief History with Documents* (Boston: St. Martin's Press, 1995); and Grace Steele Woodward, *The Cherokees* (Norman: Univ. of Oklahoma Press, 1963).

6. In a series of letters written in 1838, missionary Daniel Butrick reports numerous incidents of military torture, including murder, of the Cherokees who were "collected" for removal. The following are only a fraction of the abuses recorded: a Cherokee mother, whose two small children had fled to the woods when soldiers advanced toward their house, was denied permission to wait for the children and was driven away without them to one of the stockades; a Cherokee, "deaf and dumb," began running when he saw the soldiers coming, and the soldiers, "because he did not obey their commands [to stop], shot him dead on the spot"; one man attempted to defend his children when the soldiers, "as if driving swine," goaded the children with the points of their bayonets; for this offense he was handcuffed, punished on his arrival at the fort, and, "on leaving the fort, was again whipped a hundred lashes"; a young woman, "seized with the pangs of childbirth," requested a little time to rest—this was denied, and after being thrown in a wagon and "driven over mountains and rocks till she could endure no more," she died (Butrick, "Antiquities of the Cherokee Indian," Ayer MS 689).

7. Will Thomas, who had lived among the Cherokees for some twenty years, became their agent and used his influence to purchase land for them. When his adoptive father, Yonaguska, died in 1839, Thomas became the de

facto chief of the Eastern Cherokees, handling all official relations with their white neighbors, as well as with state and federal officials (see Finger, *Cherokee Removal* 96–111).

8. Jane's father, Rev. Jesse Bushyhead, was part of a delegation appointed by Chief John Ross to travel to St. Augustine, Florida, to serve as mediators between the United States and the Seminoles, who had been at war since 1835. Ross hoped that by negotiating a peace treaty with the Seminoles, removal of the Cherokees could be avoided (Jacqueline Fiorato elaborates on these meetings in "The Cherokee Mediation in Florida," *JCS* 3.2 (1978): 111–19). The fact that federal troops had intercepted a letter from her father to Stephen Foreman (a Cherokee preacher), therefore, was understandably of great concern to the young girl.

9. Founded near Jamestown, Virginia, in 1868, Hampton Institute was a normal school, established primarily for the industrial education of blacks.

10. Armstrong's motives for accepting Indian students at Hampton were not altogether altruistic, it seems. In a letter written April 19, 1878, to his wife, the general noted some of the benefits of such a venture: "They are a new step ahead & make the school very strong, and really, Kitty, they are a big card for the school & will diminish my grey hairs. There's money in them I tell you" (Hultgren and Molin 18).

11. Many Cherokees attended more than one boarding school, including Carlisle, Chilocco, Hampton, and Haskell. As Sarah Hill points out, not all these students went willingly. During the 1890s, for example, Betty Welch was "dragged out" of the Cherokee Boarding School (in Qualla) by former school superintendent H. W. Spray and taken by force on the train to Carlisle. Agent Thomas Potter reported to the commissioner of Indian Affairs that "the girl cried unmercifully," but in spite of the bitter protests of Betty's aunt and demands that her niece be returned home, the child remained at Carlisle (Hill 204).

12. According to Fournier and Crey (52), "It was their powerful cultural and spiritual traditions, founded on seemingly immutable bonds between children and extended families that enabled aboriginal nations to hold their ground in early encounters with Europeans. . . . Aboriginal children, regarded as the very future of their societies, were considered integral members of the family who learned by listening, watching and carrying out tasks suited to their age, sex, and social standing. While diverse in language as well as cultural and spiritual practices, [Indian people] across North America shared a remarkable commonality in their approaches to child rearing. Invariably they placed their children at the heart of a belief system closely aligned with the natural world . . . [and] the survival of indigenous societies depended on the transmission of a vast amount of spiritual and practical knowledge from elders to the young, through an exclusively oral tradition."

13. Maureen Konkle suggests that one of the effects of U.S. colonialism is that many critics still understand sympathy for Indians as "a kind of terminal response to American history"—that nothing further needs to be said on the matter. "Sympathy for Indians is seldom if ever examined carefully to understand who exactly it benefits, under what circumstances, and for what reasons," Konkle adds (482).

14. Paulette Fairbanks Molin, former director of the American Indian program at Hampton, points out that some Native language use occurred at the institute, especially in the early years before federal requirements mandated English-only policies and practices. Also, some of the Hampton students, including the EBC girls, used their tribal languages during various fund-raising events for the school and in public performances of songs, plays, and speeches (personal correspondence, Oct. 16, 2003).

15. According to school records, only eleven of the sixty EBC students who attended Hampton ever graduated. One student died while at school; others left for various reasons, including poor health, "unsatisfactory conduct," "expiration of time" (i.e., the term set by the federal government and the school—normally three or four years), illness in the family, and running away from school (Makofsky 40). EBC females seemed happier at Hampton than at Carlisle, where, according to Genevieve Bell, at least 1,850 Indian students ran away from school (210). Although they were not as prone as males to run away from school, Indian girls found other means of expressing their unhappiness. In 1905, Nannie Saunooke (CIIS 2279, EBC) was suspected of setting fire to the New Jersey "outing" home to which she had been assigned, and she returned home to North Carolina the following summer (for an interesting discussion of other acts of arson, as well as further details pertaining to Nannie's case, see Bell, 250–53; also, *Indian Helper*, Nov. 19, 1897, 3).

16. While white men were seemingly free to marry Indian women without compunction, social restrictions against the marriage of white women to Indian men persisted. The Cherokees, who had always known that white frontier people considered them an innately inferior race, expected the views of whites of New England to be more enlightened. Between 1821 and 1827, however, the Cherokees discovered that "their friends at the North" shared the same racial prejudices as the whites of the South and West. The proposed marriages of two highly educated and pious young Cherokee men (John Ridge and Elias Boudinot) resulted in their being burned in effigy near the Cornwall Academy in Connecticut, where they were students. Both young men had fallen in love with white girls in the town who reciprocated their affection, but local newspapers and ministers— including the most famous clergyman in New England, Lyman Beecher— joined the townspeople in repudiating the marriages. John Ridge was married to Sarah Bird Northrup, daughter of the school's white steward, in

Cornwall in 1824; Elias Boudinot and Harriet Ruggles Gold, daughter of a Cornwall physician, were united in marriage there in 1826. By 1827, public outrage was so great that the ABCFM decided to close the Cornwall Academy (McLoughlin, *Cherokees and Missionaries* 187).

17. Sioux scholar Elizabeth Cook-Lynn disagrees with these views, arguing that from the perspective of many Plains Indians, "the destruction of culture caused by the killing of the buffalo was no more and no less devastating than the destruction of culture caused by the dismissal of marriage patterns deriving from and supportive of the extended family, so long protected by the tribes." To claim that a society produced through mixed marriages could be considered a buffer, contends Cook-Lynn, is "to look at it from a purely European point of view, not from the vantage point of the [Indian] value system" (*Why I Can't* 36).

18. A Lottie Smith (CIIS 2282) from Cherokee, North Carolina, also attended the Carlisle Indian School in Pennsylvania (1896–1901). The Lottie who attended Carlisle, however, was registered as a fifteen-year-old orphan and a "full-blood." The Lottie Smith at Hampton, on the other hand, was registered as three-eighths Cherokee, the daughter of Chief N. J. Smith, and nineteen years old at the time of her enrollment in 1889.

19. The 1891 annual report for the Indian School at Hampton declared writing to be "a branch in which Indians are apt to excel, their powers of close observation and imitation standing them in good stead" (*SW,* June 1892, 90). *Talks and Thoughts* provided a literary forum for Indians at Hampton from 1886 to 1907. Indian students "contributed all the material, edited and printed it, and held themselves responsible for its finances" (Hultgren and Molin 32).

20. While the term "civilization program" usually refers to George Washington's Indian policy, a marked resurgence of Washington's ideas and attitudes occurred during the boarding school era. The term "civilization," therefore, is ubiquitous in the literature of that period, and federal money set aside for educating Indians at Carlisle was called the "Civilization Fund."

21. Since Lottie refers to the kindness extended her by other school children and teachers, it is reasonable to assume that the sentence in her letter, "Today I began my school," is her way of saying, "Today I began teaching." Just before he was ousted as Principal Chief, Lottie's father, Nimrod Jarrett Smith, vetoed a resolution by the Tribal Council for the continued operation of the Cherokee Boarding School by the Society of Friends. After Quaker control ended, the federal government took over the school under the direction of the Bureau of Indian Affairs (French and Hornbuckle 44).

22. Dancing posed a serious moral question for nineteenth-century Christians and was banned at Hampton. Students were not blind, however, to the double standard of certain Hampton faculty and staff members. For example, teacher Cora Folsom recalled that General Armstrong himself was

"very fond of dancing and often gave little hops in the two big parlors here, a student orchestra furnishing the music," for the staff. Indian students pointed out to Miss Folsom that "Indians dance all alone, White man and woman dance together, no good" (Lindsey 167).

23. This is a reference to students who have attended Hampton Institute but are now living back on the reservation.

24. Lottie's father, after serving twelve years as Principal Chief of the Eastern Band Cherokees, was soundly rejected by his people in the election of 1891 (shortly after Lottie's wedding), due to charges of scandalous circumstances in his personal life. Chief Smith is said to have died two years afterward as "a disgraced, lonely figure" (Hoig 267–68). In 1902, Lottie's sister, Rosa, was forced to drop out of classes at Hampton and return home to Cherokee to care for their mother (a white woman), who was dying of tuberculosis. In one of her letters to Hampton, Rosa wrote, "I have five sisters and two brothers, but they all have homes of their own now. So that left my mother and I all alone" (R. Smith, SF, HUA). Given the unfortunate circumstances of her father's death and her mother's critical illness, one can only conjecture concerning Lottie's infrequent mention of her family after moving to South Dakota.

25. For an extensive list of these characteristics and a discussion of the Cherokee ethos, see French and Hornbuckle, *The Cherokee Perspective* 11–14.

26. For a more detailed study of Hampton Indians and issues confronting them in various work environments, see Wilbert H. Ahern's "The Returned Indians: Hampton Institute and Its Indian Alumni, 1879–1893," *Journal of Ethnic Studies* 10 (Winter 1983): 101–24.

27. Estelle Reel was the federal Superintendent of Indian Schools from 1898 to 1910.

28. This is a reference to Arizona Swayney, Lottie's Cherokee friend and former classmate at Hampton.

29. Fred, who was about nine years old at the time, grew up and became a devoted son; Lottie's later letters refer frequently to how well he was doing in school, his willingness to help his mother with gardening, etc. The young man even attended Hampton Institute briefly during his adolescent years; however, in 1911, school officials learned that a young Oneida student, Rachel Somers, was pregnant and that Fred was the father. The young couple planned to marry, but Rachel's mother put a stop to their plans, saying that Fred had ruined her daughter's reputation (Brudvig 218–20). In October 1917, Lottie wrote to a friend at Hampton that Fred had been drafted into military service and "passed a good physical examination and does not claim exemption on any grounds." In an undated letter to Miss Folsom, Lottie's daughter Cora writes, "You ask about Fred—he and his family are at present in Detroit, Mich. I think he is living there temporarily as work was scarce in Syracuse" (L. Smith, SF, HUA).

30. The concept that children—especially boys—raised by single mothers are more likely to contribute to the social ills plaguing America remains as popular today as it was at the turn of the twentieth century. For example, in an editorial published April 24, 1999, in the *Chattanooga Free Press,* the writer indicts "one-parent homes" as the major cause of the "deplorable poverty" in the United States. Lottie Smith was particularly vulnerable as a young widow to the guilt American society attempts to place on mothers struggling to raise their sons without the assistance of a father.

31. Perhaps it was too difficult for Lottie to return to the place where she had begun married life with John, or maybe the Dakotas simply held too many bad memories of poverty and heartache. Several historians, moreover, have noted that Crow Creek was "altogether unsuitable for human habitation" (see especially Roy W. Meyer, *History of the Santee Sioux* 142–49). In his 1864 *Annual Report,* the Commissioner of Indian Affairs described the reservation as "a drought-stricken desolation, a land with no lakes, almost no timber—the whole country being one wilderness of dry prairie for hundreds of miles around" (411). Lottie's letters never mention Crow Creek or the Dakotas again.

32. The "bunch" to which Lottie refers is probably a goiter, one of the classic symptoms of a form of hyperthyroidism known as Graves' disease. It is now known to be a hereditary disease, and without treatment it can cause critical illness or even death.

33. Whatcom, located on the Canadian border in Washington, is now known as Bellingham. In 1902, the Clarks moved to Sumas, Washington, where Dr. Clark established a practice as a surgeon, with railroad workers comprising most of his clientele. On March 24, 1911, the *Sumas News* printed a full-page article featuring Dr. Clark and the proposed opening of his new hospital and sanitarium on July 1.

34. In Armstrong's summer outing program Indian students spent three to four months earning money by performing various farm and household chores for white families in New England. Rigorous rules and regulations were imposed on the outing students, and careful records were kept documenting the responses of both the students and their employers to this experience. Like their male counterparts, female students, who began participating in the outing program in 1883, were expected to learn fluent English and the basics of establishing a "well-ordered home" from their daily association with white Christian families (Hultgren and Molin 31). Black students, on the other hand, did not participate in the program. Instead, they were allowed to use their summer breaks to find jobs and earn money to pay their tuition for the following school term (Ludlow 9).

35. Richard Pratt, who claimed the African American experience of slavery as his model, believed that just as blacks had learned the domestic and industrial habits of "civilized" Christianity during slavery, so could

American Indians be civilized under the system of outing (Lindsey 37). As Arizona's complaint suggests, outing students were often treated in the same demeaning manner that household slaves had experienced prior to emancipation.

36. The philosophy that industrial training is an essential component of true education permeates the speeches and sermons of Hampton faculty members. For example, in an address at the Mohonk Indian Conference in 1890, Gen. Samuel Armstrong declared, "In all men, education is conditioned, not alone on an enlightened head and a changed heart, but very largely on a routine of industrious habits, which is to character what the foundation is to the pyramid . . . Morality and industry generally go together . . . Labor, next to the grace of God in the heart, is the greatest promoter of morality, the greatest power for civilization" (*Education for Life* 18–19).

37. By 1800, more than 300,000 whites had moved into the states of Kentucky and Tennessee, originally Cherokee country. By the 1900s, the majority of Cherokees educated in missionary schools had white parentage. Such Cherokees, notes Sarah Hill, "diverged from clan systems by race, language, and residence, and increasingly by education, wealth, and subsistence" (94).

38. Arizona's Returned Student Record at Hampton simply notes that she married "Blankenship" in 1908, with a parenthetical addendum beside his name: (Poor white trash). An additional comment is penciled in: "Not a legal marriage according to laws of state which forbids intermarriage between negro, Indians & white if of more than 1/16 blood. See Zona's history on back of biography card." The "history" referred to here reads as follows: "Mr. Harris—superintendent at Cherokee—says he had occasion to look up family history very carefully in making out tribal rolls. Zona's grandmother was a negro—a slave belonging to a family named Gibbs. She lived with an Indian named Nickojack. After the war closed, an order was issued for all persons who had not been legally married to appear before a magistrate & the marriage would be considered legal & the children legitimate. Lucy Gibbs quickly persuaded Nickojack to appear. They had two children: Zona's mother, who married a white man, & one other. Zona is therefore 1/2 white, 1/4 negro, 1/4 Cherokee." In spite of the value judgments placed on her husband/marriage by Hampton officials, Zona herself was reported to have excellent deportment and character, excelling in "amiability & conscientiousness."

39. Dr. Mooney, the famous Smithsonian ethnologist and author of the popular *Myths of the Cherokee and Sacred Formulas of the Cherokees,* was a frequent guest in the home of the Blankenships, often bringing his wife and five children along. Mooney also provided funding for a library at the Swayney School, placing Zona in charge of the facility.

40. It was customary for the letters of former Hampton students to be read aloud in CES meetings, and often alumni would request that a special scripture be read or a specific hymn be sung when their names were announced during roll call. These rituals are clearly outlined in the pledge of the Indian Christian Endeavor Society at Hampton:

> Trusting in the Lord Jesus Christ for strength, I promise Him that I will strive to do whatever He would like to have me do; that I will make it the rule of my life to pray, and to read the Bible every day, and to support my own church in every way, especially by attending all our regular Sunday and mid-week services unless prevented by some reason which I can conscientiously give to my Saviour; and that, just as far as I know how, throughout my whole life, I will endeavor to lead a Christian life.
>
> As an active member I promise to be true to all my duties, to be present at, and to take some part, aside from singing, in every Christian Endeavor prayer meeting unless hindered by some reason which I can conscientiously give to my Lord and Master. If obliged to be absent from the monthly consecration-meeting of the society, I will, if possible, send at least a verse of Scripture to be read on the response to my name at the roll-call. ("Model Constitution")

41. Lack of government funding, combined with escalating racial tensions between blacks and Indians, led to the resignation in 1922 of Caroline Andrus, Hampton's last teacher of Indian students, and to the ultimate demise of the school's Indian Program.

42. Lula's assertion that "the children of white mothers and Indian fathers are not enrolled as Cherokees" did not always hold true, either, for Lottie Smith, whose mother is listed as "white" on school enrollment forms and census records, was tribally enrolled, as were her siblings.

43. In the 1880s, neighboring whites began threatening the Mormon elders working among the Catawbas, and eventually an angry mob killed two of the missionaries. As Lula Owl points out, however, their murderous actions had an antithetical effect, for "Indians are great worshipers of brave men, so the death of their brave and beloved elders only caused them to become firmer believers in the Mormon faith" ("Life among the Catawba Indians," *SW,* Sept. 1914, 485).

44. According to a notice dated June 15, 1913, "Lula Owl, who furnished an excellent paper in telling how the word of God is being carried among her people, the Cherokees in North Carolina, was awarded a five-dollar gold piece for first place in the [essay] contest" (SF, HUA).

45. The annual Hampton Librarian's Report for 1892 stated that "books on oratory or debate, and books of famous orations are eagerly sought for by the [students]" (*SW,* June 1892, 104). The *Columbian Orator*—a text that convinced the ex-slave Frederick Douglass that if he could persuade men with his rhetoric he could move the universe—was taught in mission schools and reservation day schools throughout the United States. Furthermore, the Cherokee people had a long history of eloquent speakers,

so both her cultural training and her formal education had taught Lula Owl that if she could speak words beautifully and correctly she could make a difference in her world.

46. Lula tells Miss Andrus that she would love to play tennis every day and "can when I get my regular two hours off again." As things are, however, the young nurse has been "off the grounds" only twice in several weeks— once to go to church and once "for a long walk"—but, she adds, "I get four hours off duty on the Sundays Mrs. Hall feels well."

47. In a later letter, Lula explains that winning the obstetrical prize would enable her to pay for her brother George's tuition at Hampton (five of her brothers and a younger sister attended the school). Much to her surprise, she was awarded the coveted prize.

48. Lula enlisted in the U.S. Army's medical corps as a second lieutenant, serving as the only Eastern Cherokee officer in World War I (Finger, *Cherokee Americans* 36). For additional information on Lula's military career, see Brenda Finnicum, "The Role of Native Women in the Military," at http://www.nativeculture.com/features/finnicum/default.htm.

49. Cherokee people have never wholly trusted white doctors, and after hearing of the atrocities suffered by their people at the hands of government physicians—from removal to the present—many are still understandably wary of hospitals and non-Native "healers."

50. Child observes that many Indian girls, introduced to "the dazzling design known as the Star of Bethlehem among Anglo quilters" at Carlisle Indian School, took back the art of quilting to their individual tribes when they left boarding school. American Indian women have since become "renowned for their skill, and their decorative quilts are the most highly prized item at give-aways during tribal celebrations." Like the star quilt, states Child, boarding schools have become part of a collective, pan-Indian identity (4).

51. Theda Perdue points out that by the end of the nineteenth century, some white Americans had come to view the traditional status of Indian women far more favorably. One example of this change in attitudes/perceptions is reflected in an 1892 article in the *Albany Law Review,* in which the author praised the revision of U.S. property laws to protect the rights of married women, noting that "such a progressive practice" had long existed among the southeastern Indians ("Southern Indians" 48). Glenda Riley finds reports in the diaries of frontierswomen of white and Native women trading "bits of female knowledge, lore, and folk medicine with each other" (176). As early as 1850, Frederika Bremer wrote in her travel letters that, in comparison to the Indian woman's life, she found the "hard, gray, domestic life in the civilized world" unbearably rigid and confining. After visiting in the homes of American Indian women in St. Paul, she declared, "I thought that the wigwam of an Indian was better and a happier world than that of the drawing room" (Riley 80).

Chapter 4

1. According to Cherokee census records, Nancy's father, Harrison A. Coleman, was the son of a full-blood Cherokee and a white mother; her mother's parents are simply listed as "Negro and Indian." Nancy was born in Birdtown on the Qualla Boundary, attended Cherokee schools, and, for the first twenty-four years of her life, identified as Cherokee. More important, she was considered Indian by her friends and neighbors on the reservation. The insistence of Superintendent Henderson, and subsequently Hampton officials, that Nancy be identified as black is even more puzzling in light of the fact that Arizona Swayney, who was also identified in school records as "¼ negro," was hired by Hampton Institute as a Cherokee teacher and was allowed to remain on EBCI tribal rolls.

2. A series of slave rebellions and conspiracies during the early 1800s (Gabriel Prosser, 1800; Denmark Vesey, 1822; Nat Turner, 1831) had resulted in increased legislation aimed at controlling African Americans and in widespread racial prejudice throughout the United States (Zinn 167). Also, social theories of racial determinism helped to legitimize white fears and opposition to social equality.

3. In this "separate-but-equal" decision, the U.S. Supreme Court ruled that railway companies could segregate black and white passengers if equal facilities were provided for both groups.

4. The Friends of the Indian were several hundred white Americans who, through a network of local and national organizations, sought to influence public opinion and change policies pertaining to American Indians. From 1883 to 1916, they officially met with the Board of Indian Commissioners at the Lake Mohonk Resort in New York.

5. In *Indians Are Us?* (221–26), Ward Churchill (Creek/Cherokee) takes to task several Indian people he identifies as "hucksters." He also condemns Indians who run sweats, hold vision quests, and teach the medicine wheel ceremony to non-Indians.

6. In the census notes of David W. Siler, special agent of the Department of Indian Affairs in 1851, we learn that enrollment procedures were often left to the discretion of the individual census taker. For example, Siler notes that since one family could produce no proof of their Indian blood, he "came to the conclusion that they were mixed with some other race." Upon consulting with a local physician, however, Siler was informed that the family was indeed Cherokee. Based upon the recommendation of the physician, therefore, he included them in the Indian census (96–97). In another notation, Siler remarks, "Indeed these people [Cherokees] are so scattered since the breaking up of the nation that I do not flatter myself with the belief that with all the pains I have taken, their names [have all been recorded] in the course of four months (122).

7. In a surprise announcement, head of the Bureau of Indian Affairs, Kevin Gover (Pawnee), informed the Senate Committee on Indian Affairs on May 24, 2000, that the BIA "no longer wishes to be the entity that grants federal recognition to Indian tribes" ("Native American Agency Wants to Give Up Key Role," *The Record* [Bergen County, NJ], May 25, 2000: A13). Earlier, Senator Ben Nighthorse Campbell (Northern Cheyenne) introduced a bill—the Indian Federal Recognition Administrative Procedures Act of 1999—that would appoint a three-member commission on Indian recognition to oversee the business of federal recognition of Indian tribes.

8. Testifying before the Senate Committee on Indian Affairs, May 24, 2000, Principal Chief Leon Jones listed twenty-eight tribes claiming Cherokee heritage and petitioning for federal recognition. As Principal Chief of the Cherokee Nation of Oklahoma, Wilma Mankiller compiled a list of some two hundred tribes claiming Cherokee affiliation. Although tribal officials of the EBCI do not make a point of disputing individual claims of "Cherokee ancestry," they are adamant about who is "Eastern Band Cherokee." In general, only those individuals who are tribally enrolled and who live on the Qualla Boundary (or who maintain active ties with the community) are recognized as Eastern Band Cherokees.

9. For a description of the plot of *The Cherokees* plot, which "almost defies comprehension," see Fiske 529–32.

10. In 1829, Thomas Dartmouth Rice, a white man, blackened his face and jumped "Jim Crow" for the first time, setting in motion black minstrelsy, one of the most popular entertainment forms of the nineteenth century. These shows portrayed blacks as simpleminded, lazy, fun-loving, and foolish and have been roundly condemned by most African Americans (see Willis 188–91).

11. Chief Ross and other Cherokee leaders were in Washington to protest the government's plan to remove their people to the West.

12. Edward L. Wheeler points out that among African Americans education was viewed as having the greatest potential for uplift. Religious education was of particular importance; therefore, reformers focused on uplifting the black ministerial elite so that they could, in turn, uplift the race (128–29).

13. According to Patricia Swan, Maggie Wachacha and her husband, Jarrett, initially walked the fifty miles from Snowbird to Cherokee—a journey of several days—for Council meetings, never missing a single meeting in all her years as clerk. When Maggie Wachacha first became clerk, the Council meetings lasted two weeks and were held once a year in the fall (Calonehuskie 48).

14. On March 9, 2002, Louise Bigmeat Maney, master potter, former teacher, and renowned storyteller/poet, was posthumously endowed with the title of "Beloved Woman"—only the third woman in 225 years to receive this honor.

15. See Ong 14–15.

16. Anthropologist Jack Goody also insists on the superiority of writing to orality, arguing that "verbatim memory" can only flourish in literate societies, for oral cultures have "neither the developed techniques nor the developed requirements for rote learning" (189). For a persuasive rebuttal to the literacy-orality theory espoused by such scholars as Goody, Ong, and Eric Havelock, see Beth Daniell's "Narratives of Literacy: Connecting Composition to Culture."

17. U.S. English, a pressure group designed to promote English as "the lone official language of the country," was founded in 1986 by Senator S. I. Hayakawa. This group quickly gained 350,000 members, including such distinguished "advisory supporters" as Saul Bellow, Alistair Cooke, and Norman Cousins, and received annual donations of $7.5 million. By late 1988, Hayakawa's organization had managed to have English made the official language of seventeen states; since 2002, another seven states have joined them. Official English legislation is also being considered in additional states.

18. Robert Bushyhead, the "Voice of Kituhwa," died on July 28, 2001. He was eighty-six years old.

19. One of the projects to which Marie Junaluska has devoted considerable time is the translation, from Cherokee into English, of original articles from the *Cherokee Phoenix,* an early-nineteenth-century newspaper. She also has a Cherokee language sampler—a book of Cherokee words and phrases, accompanied by an audiotape—which is available for purchase to those wishing to learn more about the Kituwah dialect.

20. *Smoke Signals,* written by Sherman Alexie, directed by Chris Eyre, and distributed by Miramax Films, was widely acclaimed as the first major film written and produced by Native Americans.

21. The Cherokee plaque is expected to be viewed by more than a million people each year, and Junaluska is hopeful that some of that number will be Cherokees who can read the plaque and rejoice in finding the Lord's Prayer, written in their Native language, in such an unexpected place.

22. The Cultural Resources Division of the EBCI was founded in 1996 and is charged with overseeing the Repatriation Program, the Tribal Linguist Program, the Kituwah Language Project, the Cherokee Ceremonial Grounds, and the Historic Preservation for the Eastern Band Cherokees. The Cultural Resources Division also consults with a number of other community, state, and national groups about the importance of historic preservation and its impact on Eastern Cherokees.

23. Chief Junaluska, who is credited with saving the life of Andrew Jackson in the Battle of Horseshoe Bend (1814) against the Creek Indians, is reported to have been so unwilling to leave his Appalachian homeland that he escaped the soldiers on the Trail of Tears. He and several other deserters

were soon captured near Knoxville, Tennessee, and Junaluska was taken west in chains, under heavy guard. Even so, the Chief eventually managed to walk back home to the hills of North Carolina (Rozema 170–71).

24. The American Indian Ritual Objects Repatriation Foundation is a non–federally funded intercultural partnership committed to assisting in the return of sacred ritual material to American Indian nations and to educating the public of the importance of repatriation (see *AIRORF News and Notes,* Spring/Summer 1997).

25. In the film *Mask,* based on the true story of Rocky Dennis, a teenager born with craniofacial disfiguration, Rocky (Eric Stoltz) attempts to gain his mother's attention by reading aloud a poem for which he had received an "A" in his high school English class. The poem reads in part:

> These things are *good* . . .
> The rain on my tongue
> And the sun shining on my face.
> These things are *a drag* . . .
> No money in my pockets
> And the sun shining on my face.

26. In light of the profound social changes taking place in the United States during the 1960s—Vietnam War protests, the Civil Rights movement, the Free Speech movement, the Equal Rights movement, and the Gay Pride movement—American Indians drew little attention. Not until 1973, when American Indian movement leaders clashed with FBI agents at Wounded Knee on the Pine Ridge Reservation in South Dakota, did the news media turn their attention to Indians.

27. Some scholars maintain that "squaw" is merely an Anglicization of *xkwa* (the Lenape word for "woman") or of Massachusett *squa,* meaning "younger woman" (Cutler 202). Historian Marge Bruchac (Abenaki) argues that "squaw" is an Algonkian word and that any insult from the word is "in the usage, not in the original word." Bruchac suggests that Indians "reclaim our language rather than let it be taken over" (see "Thoughts on Indian Images"). In many Indian languages, however, the word for "female" bears no resemblance to the word "squaw." In the Cherokee language, for example, the word for "girl" is *agehyuja,* and "woman" is *agehya*; most Cherokees consider "squaw" a disparaging term, referring to the female genitalia. Lynne Harlan told NPR's Elizabeth Blair: "When Europeans came, of course, we couldn't communicate with them, and they didn't travel with women, so they were wanting companionship. They would hold their groin area and say 'squaw.' That's how the word *squaw* became used as woman; it basically meant 'whore' or 'prostitute'" (*Morning Edition,* Aug. 21, 1998).

28. An example of racial "numbness" was demonstrated by one of the Erwin High School basketball players in an interview with National Public

Radio reporter Elizabeth Blair, who traveled to Asheville, North Carolina, in 1998 to cover the mascot controversy. Introduced as a senior who voted to keep the mascot, Lauren Christiansen maintained that being a Squaw is a source of family pride. Citing three generations of family members who had graduated from Erwin High School, the student declared, "When my mother played, Squaw was pride, it was traditional, that's what it was. So it's just like my roots are down into this school and it's like, if it's not the Squaws, then it's not Erwin to me" (*Morning Edition,* Aug. 21, 1998).

29. According to Marita Matray, news reporter for the public television program *North Carolina Now,* documenting the North Carolina section of the Trail of Tears for National Park Service will take about two years and will cost more than $100,000.

30. Dugan was the 1965 valedictorian of Vashti High School, a Methodist boarding school in Thomasville, Georgia, where she lived in a dormitory housing 150 girls, ranging in age from twelve to eighteen.

31. On October 26, 1996, Western Carolina University bestowed the 1996 Distinguished Alumnus Award upon Chief Dugan, praising "her accomplishments as an educator and leader of the Cherokee people" and citing her as an individual "with a special sense of responsibility to the tribe's school children" (*COF,* Nov. 6, 1996).

32. After Jonathan "Ed" Taylor was impeached in 1995 on charges of misappropriating tribal funds, CPA Thomas Mahoney found multiple financial inequities involving Qualla Housing Authority. An itemized list of these deficits was published on the front page of the *Cherokee One Feather* on February 19, 1997. In April 1997, Chief Dugan announced that, for the first time since 1992, the tribe had received a clean audit.

33. Dugan's mother, a product of government boarding schools, was not allowed to speak her native language or practice her culture as a child; thus, she was fearful of teaching her daughter about Cherokee culture (personal interview, May 25, 1997).

34. Sovereignty does not render Native Americans immune to the laws of the United States. Rather, tribal sovereignty grants Indian tribes "the right to be free from state control, while they remain subordinate to the will of Congress." On reservations, tribal police can arrest tribal members for minor crimes but have no jurisdiction over non-Indians. Major crimes such as murder, racketeering, or armed robbery are prosecuted by the federal authorities. Senator Gorton, however, persisted in his campaign against Indian sovereignty, contending, "Making a case out of what happened to your grandfather is not the best way to decide public policy" (Egan, "Backlash" 3–4). In September 1997, Gorton, under pressure from the Senate, withdrew a motion that would have required any tribe receiving federal funding to waive sovereign immunity as a condition for receiving those funds. Gorton was defeated in 2000 by Democratic candidate Maria Cantwell.

35. At issue was whether Alaska tribes are part of Indian Country, a designation used on Lower 48 reservations where tribes have jurisdiction and the state does not. Commenting on the Supreme Court ruling, *Anchorage Daily News* reporter Tom Kizzia wrote:

> The ruling is a defeat for Alaska tribes . . . and it could open the door to further challenges of tribal efforts under way in rural villages, from airport alcohol searches to local misdemeanor courts. ("Indian Country" 1).

36. According to an August 2004 report from the National Indian Gaming Association, twenty-eight states now have Indian casinos (*Indian Gaming: Final Impact Analysis,* 4). The most successful of these casinos is Foxwoods in Connecticut. It is also the world's largest casino and generates about $2 million a day in profits on its slot machines.

37. Several gift shops in Cherokee, many of them white-owned or leased, still feature caged bears as tourist attractions. On July 19, 1997, Honey Bear, a black bear which had been living outside the Raindancer Gift Shop for twenty-five years, was shot and killed inside her cage, angering local residents, as well as animal rights activists. Tim Smith, the bear's owner, surmised that poachers or someone trying to remove the bear's gall bladder (gall bladders sell for a high price on the black market) committed this atrocity (*COF,* July 30, 1997).

38. In 1999, the Supreme Court of Canada passed a law providing for more lenient sentencing for aboriginals because of the dysfunctional backgrounds of many First Nations offenders. This ruling has understandably caused an outcry from white Canadians, as well as from other Natives, and is not at all the same "justice" for which Chief Dugan was pleading in the Locust case.

39. After consulting with the family of the victim, and taking into consideration testimony and evidence presented during Locust's trial, U.S. Attorney Mark Calloway issued a statement indicating that his office "believed the right thing to do was withdraw [the death penalty request]" and urge all those involved to "allow for closure in this case" (see *COF,* Sept. 1, 1999, for full report).

40. This is an allusion to the tumultuous days of investigation, criminal charges, and, finally, the impeachment of her predecessor, Principal Chief Ed Taylor.

41. When the U.S. government compelled the Cherokees to cede their land along the Tuckaseegee River in 1819, Indian families were given the right to claim a 640-acre reservation within the ceded area. Yonaguska, a leader of Kituwah, claimed Governor's Island, and the reserve families, known as Citizen Cherokees, took refuge under his leadership. According to archaeologist Brett Riggs, these Citizen Cherokees formed the nucleus of what later became the EBCI; hence, Kituwah is viewed as the actual

political birthplace of the Eastern Band, as well as the symbolic birthplace of the Cherokee people. The reacquisition of Kituwah after 173 years, therefore, was a "monumental step in the Cherokees' reclamation of their cultural heritage" (*COF*, Oct. 15, 1997).

42. In August 1997, the Tribal Council also voted to purchase the Smoky Mountain Raceway—property located adjacent to the tribe's proposed softball complex—for a price of $462,500. This transaction led one council representative to complain, "We bought a graveyard. Now we have bought a swamp and a rock yard. We've got to look at what we're buying first." Chief Dugan stood firmly by her decision to buy both sites.

43. Chief Dugan was referring to the fact that future gaming compacts must be negotiated with North Carolina Gov. James B. Hunt Jr., who "is categorically opposed to casinos." However, according to a *Sylva Herald* report (Nov. 16, 2000), Gov. Hunt did agree to a thirty-year extension of the state-tribal gaming compact before leaving office.

44. President Clinton also appointed Chief Dugan to the fifteen-member, congressionally established Diabetes Research Working Group (DRWG), a committee charged with developing a road map to cure diabetes.

45. Cf. Nancy Ward's oratorical boldness in confronting British and American military leaders, as well as Katteuha's forthright letters to Benjamin Franklin during the late 1700s and early 1800s (chapter 1).

46. The Dialysis Center eliminated the need for dialysis patients to travel from thirty to fifty miles from home for treatment; the Wellness Center will focus on prevention of diabetes, with special educational programs directed at Cherokee children.

47. Two fine collections of essays addressing the ethical issues of contemporary ethnographic inquiry are Caroline Brettell, *When They Read What We Write* (Westport, CT: Bergin & Garvey, 1993), and Peter Mortensen and Gesa Kirsch, eds., *Ethics and Representation in Qualitative Studies of Literacy* (Urbana, IL: NCTE, 1996).

48. This is a line from Hill's poem "Lines for Marking Time" (Green 280–81).

Conclusion

1. In a letter to the editor of the *Seattle Times,* a Washington woman took the Makahs to task for "need[ing] to kill something to restore their culture." She concluded her letter by observing, "The white man used to kill Indians and give them smallpox-infected blankets. Is this a tradition we should return to?" (see Steilacoom B5).

2. According to historical accounts, Nancy Ward exercised her power as Beloved Woman to save the life of Lydia Bean, a white woman whom Cherokee warriors were prepared to burn at the stake. She took Bean home with her and asked her to teach the Ward family how to process cow's milk to make butter and cheese. Eventually, Ward started her own herd of cattle, and she encouraged the Cherokees to learn "more of the white man's ways and style of living in order to deal with them as equals" (see Alderman 44). She remained a "traditional" Cherokee, however, until her death, believing in the power of a string of beads, Black Drink (a concoction made from winterberry leaves and used in purification rituals), tobacco, and strong words.

3. Ramon Gutierrez, author of the controversial *When Jesus Came, the Corn-Mothers Went Away,* has been accused by Pueblo scholars such as Simon Ortiz and Ted Jojola of failing to balance Franciscan records with oral and written histories of the Pueblo people themselves. In her essay, "Licensed Trafficking and Ethnogenetic Engineering" (*Natives and Academics* 100–110), Susan Miller (Seminole), professor of history and Native American Studies at the University of Nebraska–Lincoln, also takes Gutierrez to task for his "mauling of Native history." Gutierrez's conclusion concerning the missionaries' doctrine of male supremacy, however, is one with which few Native scholars would disagree.

4. Hugh Blair (1718–1800), best known for his *Lectures on Rhetoric and Belles Lettres,* is often referred to as "the Quintilian of his time" and was especially revered by theorists of the eighteenth and nineteenth centuries.

5. Not until Superintendent of Indian Schools Estelle Reel urged her to put her children in boarding schools did Lottie Smith Pattee protest, but eventually she expressed (in a letter) her contempt for Mr. Potter, the white superintendent at the Chemawa Indian School in Salem, Oregon, calling him her "bitter enemy." Lula Owl was perhaps the most outspoken of the Cherokee girls who attended either Carlisle or Hampton, but even she was reticent, for to speak too boldly was to risk losing her job or not graduating from college.

6. The boarding schools even found ways of enforcing military *posture* among their students. A note in Carlisle's newspaper, the *Indian Helper* (June 25, 1897, 4), warns, "According to science the growing boy or girl who will not sit erect and stand erect will very likely die of consumption before he or she is thirty."

7. These young women had to contend with hegemonic forces not only while enrolled in boarding school but also during their careers as teachers and nurses. Such agencies as the Bureau of Indian Affairs, which until the early 1990s was in control of Cherokee education, and Indian Health Services, which continues to operate health facilities on the reservation, have often been at odds with the values of Cherokees. In spite of conflicts with these

agencies, however, Lottie Smith and Arizona Swayney persisted in using Cherokee cultural traditions as a basis for educating Indian children, and Lula Owl became the first Cherokee to hold a responsible health-care position on Qualla Boundary.

8. Among those praised by the editor for their accomplishments were Senator Robert L. Owen (Cherokee), D-OK; Rep. Charles D. Carter (Choctaw), D-OK; Senator Charles Curtis (Kaw), R-KS; Rev. S. A. Brigham (Ojibwe), an ordained Episcopal priest; Rev. Frank Wright (Choctaw), an evangelist in the West; Dr. Charles Eastman (Sioux), a noted author and lecturer; Arthur C. Parker (Seneca), official archaeologist of the state of New York; James Thorpe (Sac/Fox), Olympic champion and all-round athlete; and Lewis Tewanima (Hopi), world-famous distance runner.

9. According to Census Bureau figures, released during American Indian Heritage Month (Nov. 1–30) in 1999, the nation's American Indian and Alaska Native resident population grew by more than 300,000 between April 1, 1990, and July 1, 1999, to a total of 2.4 million.

10. One of the positive effects of integrating the Cherokee language and cultural traditions into the curriculum of schools on the Qualla Boundary has been a renewed sense of pride in acquiring an education. Cherokees have always placed a great deal of emphasis on education, as is reflected in Article IV of the *Cherokee Constitution*:

> Religion, morality, and knowledge being necessary to good government, the preservation of liberty and the happiness of mankind, schools and the means of education shall forever be encouraged in this nation.

11. The AAUW, which has since 1881 promoted education and equity for women and girls in the United States, is open to all graduates—regardless of race or gender—who hold the baccalaureate or higher degree from a regionally accredited college or university.

12. Also, local churches, in some cases, made an issue of her gender, insisting that God never intended a woman to "have dominion over males" (personal interview, May 25, 1997).

13. Gonzalez and Cook-Lynn note that it was during Abraham Lincoln's presidency that the dialogue on race relations in the United States was framed as black versus white, "relegating the indigenous people's struggle to the back burner, where it has been ever since" (145). On December 6, 1862—just days before signing the Proclamation of Emancipation for black slaves—Lincoln signed an executive order that thirty-eight Santee Indians be publicly hanged in Minnesota for their participation in defending their own homes against invading whites in Eastern Dakota Territory. The Sioux have not forgotten that act of racism.

14. Like other Americans, Eastern Cherokees do pay taxes; one of the nineteenth-century treaty rights they received from the U.S. government,

however, was an exemption from paying property taxes on tribally owned lands. Many banks cite the property tax issue in refusing to loan money to EBCI members.

15. Supporters argued that the proposed constitution, which would have replaced three different governing documents, would strengthen tribal sovereignty and provide for a better system of checks and balances through a stronger Grand Council and voter recall. Opponents charged that the new constitution would allow less participation from enrolled members living off the reservation and would further politicize the judicial system. The proposed constitution was overwhelmingly rejected by voters in October 1999.

16. In a primary election held Thursday, June 5, 2003, Principal Chief Leon Jones was defeated in his bid for a second term.

17. *Tsa-la-gi* is the Cherokee word for "Cherokee."

Works Cited

Manuscript Collections

Ayer Collection, Newberry Library, Chicago
> Butrick, Daniel S. Antiquities of the Cherokee Indians.
> Longe, Alexander. "A Small Postscript of the Ways and Maners of the Indians Called Charikees." Copy of Ms.
> Payne, John Howard. Papers. 14 vols.

Hampton (VA) School Student Records Collection, 1878–1923
Museum of the Cherokee Indian Archives
National Archives, Washington, DC
> Record Group 75. Records of the Bureau of Indian Affairs.
> Enrollment Records of Students at the Carlisle Indian Industrial School. Series 1330.

Newspapers and Periodicals

Anchorage Daily News
Albuquerque Journal
Asheville (NC) Citizen-Times
Bartlesville (Indian Territory) Magnet, Sept. 20, 1900
Cherokee One Feather, 1993–99
Connecticut Courant, Jan. 7, 1793
Gazette of the United States, July 25, 1789
Indian Helper (Carlisle Indian School)
Journal of Cherokee Studies, vols. 1–20
Missionary Herald, Mar. 1821–Oct. 1822
New York Times
Panoplist, 1808
Polk County (TN) News, 1938–99
Raleigh (NC) Register, 1818
Red Man (Carlisle Indian School)

Smoky Mountain Indian Trail

Southern Workman

Talks and Thoughts (Hampton student newspaper)

(Washington) Daily National Intelligencer, Aug. 28, 1838

Printed Primary Sources

Adair, James. *History of the American Indian.* 1775. Ed. Samuel Cole Williams. Johnson City, TN: Watauga Press, 1930.

American Indian Correspondence: The Presbyterian Historical Society Collection of Missionaries' Letter, 1833–1893. Westport, CT: Greenwood Press, n.d.

American State Papers, Documents Relating to Indian Affairs. Vol. 2. Washington: Gales and Seaton, 1832–34.

Anderson, Rufus. *Memoir of Catharine Brown.* Boston: Crocker and Brewster, 1825.

Annual Report of the ABCFM. Boston: Crocker and Brewster, 1823.

Annual Report of the Board of Indian Commissioners. Washington: GPO, 1871.

Aristotle. *The Art of Rhetoric.* Trans. J. H. Freese. Cambridge: Harvard Univ. Press, 1926.

Bradford, William. *History of Plymouth Plantation.* Ed. Samuel Eliot Morison. New York: Modern Library, 1967.

Harriot, Thomas. *A Brief and True Report of the New Found Land of Virginia.* London, 1588.

Hawkins, Benjamin. *Letters of Benjamin Hawkins, 1796–1806.* Savannah: Georgia Historical Society, 1916.

Hilderbrand, Jack. "Some Recollections of Jack Hilderbrand as Dictated to Jack Williams, Esq., and M.O. Cate, at the Home of Hilderbrand, in the Summer of 1903." Cleveland Public Library, Cleveland, TN.

Jones, Calvin. "Account of the Cherokee Schools." *Raleigh Register,* Nov. 13, 1818, 118–23.

Laws of the Cherokee Nation: Adopted by the Council at Various Periods. Tahlequah: Cherokee Advocate Office, 1852.

Marrant, John. *A Narrative of the Lord's Wonderful Dealings with John Marrant, A Black.* London: Gilbert and Plummer, 1785.

Memorial Volume of the First Fifty Years of the American Board of Commissioner for Foreign Missions. 4th ed. Boston: ABCFM, 1861.

Menzies, David. *Account of the Sufferings of Doctor Menzies amongst the Cherokee Indians.* London: J. Bailey, n.d.

Mooney, James. *Myths of the Cherokee and Sacred Formulas of the Cherokees: From 19th and 7th Annual Reports B.A.E., 1900 and 1891.* Nashville: Charles and Randy Elder Booksellers, 1982.

Morgan, Thomas J. "A Plea for the Papoose." *Southern Workman and Hampton School Record* (Apr. 1892): 58–61.

Occom, Samson. "A Short Narrative of My Life." 1768. *The Heath Anthology of American Literature*. Ed. Paul Lauter. Lexington, MA: D.C. Heath and Co., 1994. 942–47.

Papers of Andrew Jackson. Ed. Harold D. Moser, David R. Hoth, and George Hoemann. Knoxville: Univ. of Tennessee Press, 1994.

Pennsylvania Archives. Vol. 11, series 1. Philadelphia: Joseph Severns & Co., 1855.

Phillips, Joyce B., and Paul Gary Phillips, eds. *The Brainerd Journal: A Mission to the Cherokees, 1817–1823*. Lincoln: Univ. of Nebraska Press, 1998.

Pratt, Richard H. "The Advantages of Mingling Indians with Whites." *Proceedings and Addresses of the National Education Association, 1895.*

———. *American Indians, Chained and Unchained, Being an Address before the Pennsylvania Commandery of the Military Order of the Loyal Legion*. Columbus, Ohio. Oct. 23, 1912.

Presidential Papers Microfilm: Andrew Jackson. Washington, 1961. Series 1, reel 22.

Records of the Cherokee Indian Agency in Tennessee, 1801–1835. National Archives Microfilm Publications no. 208, roll 14.

Royall, Anne Newport. *Letters from Alabama, 1817–1822*. 1830. Introduction by Lucille Griffith. Tuscaloosa: Univ. of Alabama Press, 1969.

Schurz, Carl. "Present Aspects of the Indian Problem." *North American Review* 133 (July 1881): 16–17.

Smith, J. M., Jr. *The American Indian Girl*. New York: Dubois & Bacon, 1835.

Timberlake, Henry. *Memoirs, 1756–1765*. 1765. Ed. Samuel Cole Williams. Marietta, GA: Continental Book Co., 1948.

Books and Articles

Adams, David W. *Education for Extinction: American Indians and the Boarding School Experience, 1875–1928*. Lawrence: Univ. Press of Kansas, 1995.

Alcoff, Linda Martin. "The Problem of Speaking for Others." *Who Can Speak? Authority and Critical Identity*. Eds. Judith Roof and Robyn Wiegman. Urbana: Univ. of Illinois Press, 1995. 97–119.

Alden, John Richard. "The Eighteenth-Century Cherokee Archives." *American Archivist* 5.4 (1942): 240–42.

Alderman, Pat. *Nancy Ward: Cherokee Chieftainess and Dragging Canoe: Cherokee-Chickamauga War Chief*. Johnson City, TN: Overmountain Press, 1978.

Allen, Paula Gunn. *The Sacred Hoop*. Boston: Beacon Press, 1986.

Anderson, Benedict. *Imagined Communities: Reflections on the Origin and Spread of Nationalism*. New York: Verso, 1983.

Anderson, Karen. *Changing Woman: A History of Racial Ethnic Women in Modern America*. New York: Oxford Univ. Press, 1996.

Anderson, William L., ed. *Cherokee Removal: Before and After*. Athens: Univ. of Georgia Press, 1991.

Andrew, John A. *From Revivals to Removal: Jeremiah Evarts, The Cherokee Nation, and the Search for the Soul of America.* Athens: Univ. of Georgia Press, 1992.

Appiah, K. Anthony, and Amy Gutmann. *Color Conscious: The Political Morality of Race.* Princeton, NJ: Princeton Univ. Press, 1996.

Armstrong, Jeannette C. "Land Speaking." *Speaking for the Generations: Native Writers on Writing.* Ed. Simon J. Ortiz. Tucson: Univ. of Arizona Press, 1998. 174–94.

Awiakta, Marilou. *Abiding Appalachia: Where Mountain and Atom Meet.* Bell Buckle, TN: Iris Press, 1995.

———. *Selu: Seeking the Corn-Mother's Wisdom.* Golden, CO: Fulcrum Publishing, 1993.

Benke, Richard. "American Indians Fight for Language." *Albuquerque Tribune Online.* http://www.abqtrib.com/archives/news01/041201_native.shtml.

Bercovitch, Sacvan, ed. *The Cambridge History of American Literature.* New York: Cambridge Univ. Press, 1994.

Berkhofer, Robert. *The White Man's Indian: Images of the American Indian from Columbus to the Present.* New York: Vintage Books, 1979.

Berlin, James A. *Rhetoric and Reality: Writing Instruction in American Colleges, 1900–1985.* Carbondale: Southern Illinois Univ. Press, 1987.

Bernhard, Virginia, David Burner, and Elizabeth Fox-Genovese, eds. *Firsthand America: A History of the United States.* 2nd ed. St. James, NY: Brandywine Press, 1992.

Bird, Elizabeth, ed. *Dressing in Feathers: The Construction of the Indian in American Popular Culture.* Boulder, CO: Westview Press, 1996.

Bird, Gloria. "Breaking the Silence: Writing As 'Witness.'" *Speaking for the Generations: Native Writers on Writing.* Ed. Simon J. Ortiz. Tucson: Univ. of Arizona Press, 1998. 27–48.

———. *The River of History.* Portland: Trask House, 1997.

Bizzell, Patricia, and Bruce Herzberg. *The Rhetorical Tradition: Readings from Classical Times to the Present.* Boston: St. Martin's Press, 1990.

Brackenridge, Hugh Henry. *Modern Chivalry.* 1792–1815. Ed. Claude M. Newlin. New York: American Book Co., 1937.

Brant, Beth. *Writing as Witness: Essay and Talk.* Toronto: Women's Press, 1994.

Brown, Penelope, and Stephen Levinson. *Politeness: Some Universals in Language Usage.* Cambridge, UK: Cambridge Univ. Press, 1987.

Bruchac, Marge. "Thoughts on Indian Images, Names, and Respect." Dec. 1999. http://genweb.net/~massasoit/bruchac.htm.

Calhoun, Craig. *Critical Social Theory: Culture, History, and the Challenge of Difference.* Cambridge, MA: Blackwell, 1995.

CallingThunder, Debra. "Voices of the Invisible." *A Circle of Nations: Voices and Visions of American Indians.* Ed. John Gattuso. Hillsboro, OR: Beyond Words Publishing, 1993.

Calonehuskie, Lois. "Maggie Wachacha Interview." *JCS* 4 (1989): 46–50.

Carney, Ginny. "Native American Loanwords in American English." *Wicazō Sa Review* (Spring 1997): 189–203.

Carolina Preserves. Videocassette. UNC-TV. Asheville, NC, 1994.

Carroll, Andrew, ed. *Letters of a Nation*. New York: Kodansha International, 1997.

Chaffee, Steven H., and Godwin Chu. "Communication and Cultural Change in China." *Comparatively Speaking: Communication and Culture across Space and Time.* Ed. Jay G. Blumler, Jack McLeod, and Karl E. Rosengren. London: Sage Publications, 1992. 209–37.

Cherokee, "The Principal People": The History and Culture of the Eastern Band of the Cherokee Nation. Narr. Wes Studi. Dir. Ron Ruehl. Videocassette. UNC-TV. Asheville, NC, 1998.

Child, Brenda J. *Boarding School Seasons: American Indian Families, 1900–1940.* Lincoln: Univ. of Nebraska Press, 1998.

Churchill, Ward. *Indians Are Us? Culture and Genocide in Native North America.* Monroe, ME: Common Courage Press, 1994.

Cobb, Amanda. *Listening to Our Grandmothers' Stories: The Bloomfield Academy for Chickasaw Females, 1852–1949.* Lincoln: Univ. of Nebraska Press, 2000.

Coleman, Michael C. *American Indian Children at School, 1850–1930.* Jackson: Univ. Press of Mississippi, 1993.

———. "American Indian School Pupils As Cultural Brokers: Cherokee Girls at Brainerd Mission, 1828–1829." *Between Indian and White Worlds: The Cultural Broker.* Ed. Margaret Connell Szasz. Norman: Univ. of Oklahoma Press, 1994. 122–35.

Comaroff, Jean, and John Comaroff. *Of Revelation and Revolution: Christianity, Colonialism, and Consciousness in South Africa.* Chicago: Univ. of Chicago Press, 1991.

Conley, Robert J. *War Woman.* New York: St. Martin's Press, 1997.

Connors, Robert J. *Composition-Rhetoric: Backgrounds, Theory, and Pedagogy.* Pittsburgh: Univ. of Pittsburgh Press, 1997.

Cook-Lynn, Elizabeth. "American Indian Intellectualism and the New Indian Story." *Natives and Academics: Researching and Writing about American Indians.* Ed. Devon A. Mihesuah. Lincoln: Univ. of Nebraska Press, 1998.

———. "The Radical Conscience in Native American Studies." *Wicazō Sa Review* (Spring 1986): 38–40.

———. *Why I Can't Read Wallace Stegner and Other Essays: A Tribal Voice.* Madison: Univ. of Wisconsin Press, 1996.

Corkran, D. H. "The Nature of the Cherokee Supreme Being." *Southern Indian Studies* (Oct. 1956): 27–35.

Crater, Michael. "Whaling Debate Deserves More Adult Voice Than This." *Lewiston Morning Tribune,* May 20, 1999, 10A.

Cutler, Charles L. *O Brave New Words! Native American Loanwords in Current English.* Norman: Univ. of Oklahoma Press, 1994.

Daniell, Beth. "Narratives of Literacy: Connecting Composition to Culture." *CCC* (Feb. 1999): 393–410.

Dauenhauer, Nora Marks. *The Droning Shaman*. Haines, AK: Black Current Press, 1988.

———. *Life Woven with Song*. Tucson: Univ. of Arizona Press, 2000.

Decker, William M. *Epistolary Practices: Letter Writing in America before Telecommunications*. Chapel Hill: Univ. of North Carolina Press, 1998.

DeJong, David H. *Promises of the Past: A History of Indian Education in the United States*. Golden, CO: North American Press, 1993.

Deloria, Philip J. *Playing Indian*. New Haven: Yale Univ. Press, 1998.

Deloria, Vine, Jr. "Comfortable Fictions and the Struggle for Turf: An Essay Review of *The Invented Indian: Cultural Fictions and Government Policies*." *Natives and Academics: Researching and Writing about American Indians*. Ed. Devon A. Mihesuah. Lincoln: Univ. of Nebraska Press, 1998.

———. *Custer Died for Your Sins: An Indian Manifesto*. 1969. Norman: Univ. of Oklahoma Press, 1988.

———. *Red Earth, White Lies: Native Americans and the Myth of Scientific Fact*. New York: Scribner, 1995.

Derrick, Christopher W. "Trouble Is What's Coming 'Round the Mountain." *Asheville Citizen-Times,* Nov. 18, 1997, A5.

"Different Voter Expectations of Male and Female California State Senators and Members of the California Congressional Delegation: Educational, Occupational, and Political Backgrounds." California Association for the National Organization for Women, 2001. www.canow.org/politics/nographs.PDF.

Donovan, Kathleen M. *Feminist Readings of Native American Literature*. Tucson: Univ. of Arizona Press, 1998.

Dugan, Joyce C. "Critics Ignore Evidence of Casino Benefits." *Asheville Citizen-Times,* Dec. 13, 1997, A9.

Dunaway, Wilma A. "Rethinking Cherokee Acculturation: Women's Resistance to Agrarian Capitalism and Cultural Change, 1800–1838." *American Indian Culture and Research Journal* (Spring 1997): 155–92.

Duncan, Barbara, ed. *Living Stories of the Cherokee*. Chapel Hill: Univ. of North Carolina Press, 1998.

Eastman, Charles. *The Soul of the Indian*. 1911. Lincoln: Univ. of Nebraska Press, 1980.

Egan, Timothy. "Backlash Growing as Indians Make Stand for Sovereignty." *New York Times,* Mar. 9, 1998, B1.

———. "New Prosperity Brings New Conflict to Indian Country." *New York Times,* Mar. 8, 1998, B1.

Ehle, John. *Trail of Tears: The Rise and Fall of the Cherokee Nation*. New York: Anchor Books, 1988.

Ellison, Quentin, and Jon Ostendorff. "Churches to Offer Apology to Cherokee." *Asheville Citizen-Times*. July 22, 2002. http://www.citizen-times.com/news/index.shtml.

Finger, John R. *Cherokee Americans: The Eastern Band of Cherokees in the Twentieth Century*. Lincoln: Univ. of Nebraska Press, 1991.

———. *The Eastern Band of Cherokees, 1819–1900*. Knoxville: Univ. of Tennessee Press, 1984.

Fiske, Roger. *English Theatre Music in the Eighteenth Century*. London: Oxford Univ. Press, 1973.

Fixico, Donald L. *The Invasion of Indian Country in the Twentieth Century*. Niwot: Univ. Press of Colorado, 1998.

Foreman, Carolyn Thomas. *Indians Abroad, 1493–1938*. Norman: Univ. of Oklahoma Press, 1943.

———. *Indian Women Chiefs*. Muskogee, OK: Star Printery, 1954.

Foster, George. *Literature of the Cherokees*. Ithaca: Office of *The Democrat*, 1889.

Fournier, Suzanne, and Ernie Crey. *Stolen from Our Embrace: The Abduction of First Nations Children and the Restoration of Aboriginal Communities*. Toronto: Douglas & McIntyre, 1997.

Fox-Genovese, Elizabeth. *Feminism without Illusions*. Chapel Hill: Univ. of North Carolina Press, 1991.

Fredrickson, George M. *The Black Image in the White Mind: The Debate on Afro-American Character and Destiny, 1817–1914*. Hanover, NH: Wesleyan Univ. Press, 1971.

French, Laurence, and Jim Hornbuckle, eds. *The Cherokee Perspective*. Boone, NC: Appalachian Consortium Press, 1981.

Friday, Sarah. "Saving Grace: Father-Daughter Team Work to Preserve Cherokee Dialect." *Southern Living* (Mar. 1998): 14–17.

Frye, Marilyn. "Oppression." *Race, Class, and Gender*. Eds. Margaret L. Anderson and Patricia Hill Collins. Belmont, CA: Wadsworth Publishing Co., 1992. 37–42.

Fuss, Diana. *Essentially Speaking: Feminism, Nature, and Difference*. New York: Routledge, 1989.

Gates, Henry Louis, Jr., ed. *"Race," Writing, and Difference*. Chicago: Univ. of Chicago Press, 1986.

———. *The Signifying Monkey: A Theory of African-American Literary Criticism*. New York: Oxford Univ. Press, 1988.

Gilmore-Lehne, William. "Early American History and Culture, 1500s–1865." Feb. 2, 2000. http://www.stockton.edu/~gilmorew/Ocolhis/c2wkshop.htm.

Gonzalez, Mario, and Elizabeth Cook-Lynn. *The Politics of Hallowed Ground: Wounded Knee and the Struggle for Indian Sovereignty*. Urbana: Univ. of Illinois Press, 1999.

Gould, Janice. *Beneath My Heart*. Ithaca, NY: Firebrand Books, 1990.

Green, Rayna, ed. *That's What She Said: Contemporary Poetry and Fiction by Native American Women*. Bloomington: Indiana Univ. Press, 1984.

Gutierrez, Ramon. *When Jesus Came, the Corn Mothers Went Away: Marriage, Sexuality and Power in New Mexico, 1500–1846*. Stanford: Stanford Univ. Press, 1990.

Hand, Dawn M. "Native Americans Honored." June 10, 2003.
    http://www.wnccumc.org/2003nativeamerican.html.

Harjo, Joy. *In Mad Love and War.* Middletown, CT: Wesleyan Univ. Press, 1990.

———. *A Map to the Next World.* New York: W.W. Norton & Co., 2000.

———. "Metamorphosis." *A Circle of Nations: Voices and Visions of American Indians.*
    Ed. John Gattuso. Hillsboro, OR: Beyond Words Publishing, 1993. 14–20.

———. *Secrets from the Center of the World.* Tucson: Univ. of Arizona Press, 1989.

Harjo, Joy, and Gloria Bird, eds. *Reinventing the Enemy's Language: Contemporary
    Native Women's Writings of North America.* New York: W. W. Norton & Co.,
    1997.

Harmon, Alexandra. "When Is an Indian Not an Indian? The 'Friends of the Indian' and
    the Problems of Indian Identity." *Journal of Ethnic Studies* 18.2 (Summer
    1990): 95–123.

Hill, Sarah H. *Weaving New Worlds: Southeastern Cherokee Women and Their Basketry.*
    Chapel Hill: Univ. of North Carolina Press, 1997.

Hobson, Geary, ed. *The Remembered Earth: An Anthology of Contemporary Native
    American Literature.* Albuquerque: Univ. of New Mexico Press, 1980.

Hoig, Stanley W. *The Cherokees and Their Chiefs.* Fayetteville: Univ. of Arkansas Press, 1998.

hooks, bell. "Racism and Feminism." *The Gender Reader.* Ed. Evelyn Ashton-Jones et. al.
    Boston: Allyn and Bacon, 2000. 275–84.

Hoxie, Frederick E., ed. *Encyclopedia of North American Indians.* Boston: Houghton
    Mifflin Co., 1996.

———. *The Indians Versus the Textbooks: Is There Any Way Out?* Chicago: Newberry
    Library, 1984.

Hultgren, Mary Lou, and Paulette Fairbanks Molin. *To Lead and to Serve: American
    Indian Education at Hampton Institute, 1878–1923.* Virginia Beach: Virginia
    Foundation for the Humanities, 1989.

Indian Gaming: Final Impact Analysis. Washington, DC: National Indian Gaming
    Association, 2004.

"Indian Race, Perishing, Gives Nation Men of Influence." *Red Man* (Mar. 1913): 277–78,
    283–84.

Jacobs, Laverne. "The Native Church: A Search for an Authentic Spirituality." *Native
    and Christian: Indigenous Voices on Religious Identity in the United States and
    Canada.* Ed. James Treat. New York: Routledge, 1995.

Jaimes, M. Annette, ed. *The State of Native America: Genocide, Colonization, and
    Resistance.* Boston: South End Press, 1992.

Johnson, Nan. *Nineteenth-Century Rhetoric in North America.* Carbondale: Southern
    Illinois Univ. Press, 1991.

Johnston, Carolyn. "Burning Beds, Spinning Wheels, and Calico Dresses." *JCS* 19 (1998):
    3–17.

———. *Sexual Power: Feminism and the Family in America.* Tuscaloosa: Univ. of
    Alabama Press, 1992.

Kehoe, Alice. *North American Indians: A Comprehensive Account*. Englewood Cliffs, NJ: Prentice-Hall, 1981.

Kelly, Mary. "The Sentimentalists: Promise and Betrayal in the Home." *Signs* 4 (Spring 1979): 434–46.

Kidwell, Clara Sue. "Indian Women as Cultural Mediators." *Ethnohistory* 39.2 (Spring 1992): 97–107.

———. "The Power of Women in Three American Indian Societies." *Journal of Ethnic Studies* 6.3 (1979): 113–21.

Kilpatrick, Alan. *The Night Has a Naked Soul: Witchcraft and Sorcery among the Western Cherokee*. Syracuse: Syracuse Univ. Press, 1997.

Kilpatrick, Jack Frederick, and Anna Gritts Kilpatrick. *Walk in Your Soul: Love Incantations of the Oklahoma Cherokees*. Dallas: Southern Methodist Univ. Press, 1965.

Kizzia, Tom. "Indian Country Claim Falls: Justices Rule Alaska Natives Lost Tribal Powers in Alaska Native Claims Settlement Act." *Anchorage Daily News*, Feb. 26, 1998, A2.

Kolodny, Annette. "Letting Go Our Grand Obsessions: Notes Toward a New Literary History of the American Frontier." *American Literature* (Mar. 1992): 1–18.

Konkle, Maureen. "Indian Literacy, U.S. Colonialism, and Literary Criticism." *American Literature* 69.3 (Sept. 1997): 457–86.

Krupat, Arnold. *The Voice in the Margin: Native American Literature and the Canon*. Berkeley: Univ. of California Press, 1989.

Kupferer, Harriet J. "The Isolated Eastern Cherokee." *Midcontinent American Studies Journal* 6 (Fall 1975): 128–29.

Landers, Rich. "Makahs Merely Followed a Path Long-Established." *Spokesman-Review (Spokane, WA)*, May 20, 1999, C1.

Lanham, Richard A. *A Handlist of Rhetorical Terms*. 2nd ed. Berkeley: Univ. of California Press, 1991.

Large, Jerry. "Amid Concern for a Whale, Logic Is Sunk." *Seattle Times*, May 20, 1999, D1.

Lepore, Jill. *The Name of War: King Philip's War and the Origins of American Identity*. New York: Alfred A. Knopf, 1998.

Lindsey, Donal F. *Indians at Hampton Institute, 1877–1923*. Chicago: Univ. of Illinois Press, 1995.

Linthicum, Leslie. "Queen of Two Cultures." *Albuquerque Journal*, Mar. 1, 1998, A11+.

Lomawaima, K. Tsianina. *They Called It Prairie Light: The Story of Chilocco Indian School*. Lincoln: Univ. of Nebraska Press, 1994.

Loy, Wesley. "War Woman." *Native Peoples Magazine* (Winter 1999): 36–40.

Lurie, Nancy O., ed. "Indian Women: A Legacy of Freedom." *Look to the Mountain Top*. San Jose: Gousha Publications, 1972.

Lyons, Scott Richard. "Rhetorical Sovereignty: What Do American Indians Want from Writing?" *College Composition and Communication* (Feb. 2000): 447–68.

McClary, Ben Harris. *Nancy Ward: The Last Beloved Woman of the Cherokees*. Benton, TN: Polk County Publishing, 1995.

McLoughlin, William G. "An Alternative Missionary Style: Evan Jones and John B. Jones among the Cherokees." *Between Indian and White Worlds: The Cultural Broker.* Ed. Margaret Connell Szasz. Norman: Univ. of Oklahoma Press, 1994. 98–121.

———. *The Cherokees and Christianity, 1794–1870.* Ed. Walter H. Conser, Jr. Athens: Univ. of Georgia Press, 1994.

———. *Cherokees and Missionaries, 1789–1839.* New Haven: Yale Univ. Press, 1984.

———. *Cherokee Renascence in the New Republic.* Princeton: Princeton Univ. Press, 1986.

———. "Parson Blackburn's Whiskey and the Cherokee Indian Schools, 1809–1810." *Journal of Presbyterian History* (Winter 1979): 427–45.

Maddox, Lucy. *Removals: Nineteenth-Century American Literature and the Politics of Indian Affairs.* New York: Oxford Univ. Press, 1991.

Makofsky, Abraham. "Experience of Native Americans at a Black College: Indian Students at Hampton Institute, 1878–1923." *Journal of Ethnic Studies* (Fall 1989): 31–46.

Mankiller, Wilma. *Mankiller: A Chief and Her People.* New York: St. Martin's Press, 1993.

Maracle, Lee. *I Am Woman: A Native Perspective on Sociology and Feminism.* Vancouver: Press Gang Publishers, 1996.

Martin, Joel W. "'My Grandmother Was a Cherokee Princess': Representations of Indians in Southern History." *Dressing in Feathers: The Construction of the Indian in American Popular Culture.* Ed. S. Elizabeth Bird. Boulder: Westview Press, 1996. 129–47.

Medicine, Bea. "Native Americans and Anthropology." *Native Heritage: Personal Accounts by American Indians, 1790 to the Present.* Ed. Arlene Hirschfelder. New York: Macmillan, 1995. 254–55.

Meyer, Roy W. *History of the Santee Sioux: United States Indian Policy on Trial.* Lincoln: Univ. of Nebraska Press, 1967.

Mihesuah, Devon A. *American Indians: Stereotypes and Realities.* Atlanta: Clarity Press, 1996.

———. *Natives and Academics: Researching and Writing about American Indians.* Lincoln: Univ. of Nebraska Press, 1998.

Miller, Susan. *Assuming the Positions: Cultural Pedagogy and the Politics of Commonplace Writing.* Pittsburgh: Univ. of Pittsburgh Press, 1998.

Momaday, N. Scott. *The Man Made of Words.* New York: St. Martin's Press, 1997.

Moquin, Wayne, and Charles Van Doren, eds. *Great Documents in American Indian History.* New York: Da Capo Press, 1995.

Morales, Aurora Levins. "The Historian as Curandera." JSRI Working Paper #40. East Lansing, MI: Julian Samora Research Institute, 1997.

"Native American Agency Wants to Give Up Key Role." *The Record* [Bergen County, NJ], May 25, 2000, A13.

Neely, Sharlotte. *Snowbird Cherokees: People of Persistence.* Athens: Univ. of Georgia Press, 1991.

Niethammer, Carolyn. *Daughters of the Earth*. New York: Macmillan, 1977.

Noble, Ray. "Cherokee." *The Big Bands Songbook*. Comp. George T. Simon. New York: Barnes & Noble Books, 1975.

Ong, Walter. *Orality and Literacy*. Boston: Methuen & Co., 1982.

Orwell, George. "Marrakech." *The Essay Connection*. Ed. Lynn Z. Bloom. Toronto: D. C. Heath and Co., 1991. 650–56.

Paredes, J. Anthony, ed. *Indians of the Southeastern United States in the Late 20th Century*. Tuscaloosa: Univ. of Alabama Press, 1992.

Pearce, Roy Harvey. *A Study of the Indian and the American Mind*. Berkeley: Univ. of California Press, 1988.

Pease, Donald. "Mary Rowlandson's Sanctification of Violence." *United States Literary History: The Colonial through the Early Modern Period*. Audiocassette. Chantilly, VA: Teaching Co., 1996.

Perdue, Theda. *The Cherokee*. New York: Chelsea House Publishers, 1989.

——. *Cherokee Women: Gender and Culture Change, 1700–1835*. Lincoln: Univ. of Nebraska Press, 1998.

——. "Nancy Ward." *Portraits of American Women*. Ed. G. J. Barker-Benfield and Catherine Clinton. New York: St. Martin's Press, 1995.

——. *Slavery and the Evolution of Cherokee Society*. Knoxville: Univ. of Tennessee Press, 1979.

——. "Southern Indians and the Cult of True Womanhood." *The Web of Southern Social Relations: Women, Family, and Education*. Ed. Walter J. Fraser Jr., Frank Saunders Jr., and Jon L. Wakelyn. Athens: Univ. of Georgia Press, 1985.

Perdue, Theda, and Michael D. Green, eds. *The Cherokee Removal: A Brief History with Documents*. Boston: St. Martin's Press, 1995.

Pewewardy, Cornel. "Why Educators Can't Ignore Indian Mascots." Sept. 16, 1999. http://members.tripod.com/earnestman/full_text_version_.htm.

Phillips, Joyce B., and Paul Gary Phillips, eds. *The Brainerd Journal: A Mission to the Cherokees, 1817–1823*. Lincoln: Univ. of Nebraska Press, 1998.

Pratt, Mary Louise. "Arts of the Contact Zone." *Profession* (1991): 33–40.

Prucha, Francis Paul. *The Great Father: The United States Government and the American Indian*. Lincoln: Univ. of Nebraska Press, 1984.

Rains, Frances V. "Indigenous Knowledge, Historical Amnesia and Intellectual Authority: Deconstructing Hegemony and the Social and Political Implications of the Curricular 'Other.'" *What Is Indigenous Knowledge? Voices from the Academy*. Ed. Ladislaus M. Semali and Joe L. Kincheloe. New York: Falmer Press, 1999. 317–31.

Reid, John Phillip. *A Law of Blood*. New York: New York Univ. Press, 1970.

Remini, Robert V. *Andrew Jackson*. 3 vols. New York: Harper and Row, 1977–84.

Rendleman, Julie. "Back to Her People." *Daily Egyptian*, Mar. 5, 1997, 1–2.

Riley, Glenda. *Women and Indians on the Frontier, 1825–1915*. Albuquerque: Univ. of New Mexico Press, 1984.

Robinson, Jennifer. "Some Traditions, Like Makah Whale Hunting, Should Die." *Montreal Gazette,* May 20, 1999, B2.

Rogin, Michael P. *Fathers and Children: Andrew Jackson and the Subjugation of the American Indian.* New York: Alfred A. Knopf, 1975.

Ronda, James P., and James Axtell. *Indian Missions: A Critical Bibliography.* Bloomington: Indiana Univ. Press, 1978.

Roosevelt, Theodore. *The Winning of the West.* Vols. 1–2. New York: G. Putnam's Sons, 1900.

Rosaldo, Renato. *Culture and Truth: The Remaking of Social Analysis.* Boston: Beacon Press, 1989.

Rosteck, Thomas, ed. *At the Intersection: Cultural Studies and Rhetorical Studies.* New York: Guilford Press, 1999.

Rozema, Vicki. *Voices from the Trail of Tears.* Winston-Salem, NC: John F. Blair, 2003.

Ruffo, Armand Garnet. "Why Native Literature?" *Native North America: Critical and Cultural Perspectives.* Ed. Renee Hulan. Toronto: ECW Press, 1999. 109–21.

Ruoff, A. LaVonne Brown. *American Indian Literatures.* New York: MLA, 1990.

Satz, Ronald N. "Rhetoric Versus Reality: The Indian Policy of Andrew Jackson." *Cherokee Removal: Before and After.* Ed. William L. Anderson. Athens: Univ. of Georgia Press, 1991.

Scheckel, Susan. *The Insistence of the Indian: Race and Nationalism in Nineteenth-Century American Culture.* Princeton: Princeton Univ. Press, 1998.

Schreiner, Olive. *Woman and Labor.* 7th ed. New York: Frederick A. Stokes Co., 1911.

Schultz, Lucille M. *The Young Composers: Composition's Beginnings in Nineteenth-Century Schools.* Carbondale: Southern Illinois Univ. Press, 1999.

Semali, Ladislaus M., and Joe L. Kincheloe, eds. *What Is Indigenous Knowledge?* New York: Falmer Press, 1999.

Shanley, Kate. "Thoughts on Indian Feminism." *A Gathering of Spirit: A Collection by North American Indian Women.* Ed. Beth Brant. Ithaca, NY: Firebrand Books, 1988. 213–15.

Sheard, Cynthia Miecznikowski. "The Public Value of Epideictic Rhetoric." *College English* (Nov. 1996): 765–94.

Shoemaker, Nancy, ed. *Negotiators of Change: Historical Perspectives on Native American Women.* New York: Routledge, 1995.

Silko, Leslie Marmon. *Storyteller.* New York: Arcade Publishing, 1981.

Simon, George T. *The Big Bands Songbook.* New York: Barnes & Noble Books, 1975.

Simpson, David. *The Politics of American English, 1776–1850.* New York: Oxford Univ. Press, 1986.

Skolnick, Sharon. *Where Courage Is Like a Wild Horse.* Lincoln: Univ. of Nebraska Press, 1997.

Smith, Linda Tuhiwai. *Decolonizing Methodologies: Research and Indigenous Peoples.* New York: Zed Books, 2002.

Solomon, Chris. "Makahs Continue Getting Threats As They Plan Feast." *Seattle Times,* May 20, 1999, A20.

Speck, Frank G., and Leonard Broom. *Cherokee Dance and Drama.* Norman: Univ. of Oklahoma Press, 1983.

Stannard, David E. *American Holocaust: Columbus and the Conquest of the New World.* New York: Oxford Univ. Press, 1992.

Starr, Emmet. *History of the Cherokee Indians and Their Legends and Folk Lore.* 1921. Tulsa: Oklahoma Yesterday Publications, 1993.

Steilacoom, Mary McGovern. "[Letter to the Editor]: Makah Whale Hunt." *Seattle Times,* May 20, 1999, B5.

Strickland, Rennard. *Fire and the Spirits.* Norman: Univ. of Oklahoma Press, 1975.

Sunstein, Bonnie. "Culture on the Page: Experience, Rhetoric, and Aesthetics in Ethnographic Writing." *Ethics and Representation in Qualitative Studies of Literacy.* Ed. Peter Mortensen and Gesa E. Kirsch. Urbana, IL: National Council of Teachers of English, 1996. 177–201.

Swan, Patricia A. "Maggie Axe Wachacha: Beloved Woman of the Cherokees." *Now and Then* (Fall 1986): 14.

Takaki, Ronald. *Iron Cages: Race and Culture in Nineteenth-Century America.* New York: Alfred A. Knopf, 1979.

Tall Mountain, Mary. *There Is No Word for Goodbye.* 1981. Oakland: Red Star Black Rose Printing, 1990.

"Team Nickname Controversy." Narr. Elizabeth Blair. *NPR Morning Edition.* National Public Radio, WEKU, Richmond, KY. Aug. 21, 1998. Transcript.

Treat, James, ed. *Native and Christian: Indigenous Voices on Religious Identity in the United States and Canada.* New York: Routledge, 1995.

Trennert, Robert A. "Educating Indian Girls at Nonreservation Boarding Schools, 1878–1920." *Western Historical Quarterly* 13 (1982): 271–90.

Tsosie, Rebecca. "Changing Women: The Cross-Currents of American Indian Feminine Identity." *American Indian Culture and Research Journal* 12.1 (1988): 1–37.

Van Doren, Carl. *Letters and Papers of Benjamin Franklin and Richard Jackson, 1753–1785.* Philadelphia: American Philosophical Society, 1947.

Vizenor, Gerald. *Manifest Manners: Postindian Warriors of Survivance.* Hanover, NH: Wesleyan Univ. Press, 1994.

Walker, Robert Sparks. *Torchlights to the Cherokees.* New York: Macmillan, 1931. Johnson City, TN: Overmountain Press, 1993.

Warrior, Robert. *Tribal Secrets: Recovering American Indian Intellectual Traditions.* Minneapolis: Univ. of Minnesota Press, 1995.

Washburn, Wilcomb E. *The Assault on Tribalism: The General Allotment Law (Dawes Act) of 1887.* Philadelphia: J. B. Lippincott Co., 1975.

Weatherford, Jack. *Indian Givers: How the Indians of the Americas Transformed the World.* New York: Ballantine Books, 1988.

Weaver, Jace. "Ethnic Cleansing, Homestyle." *Wicazō Sa Review* (Spring 1994): 27–39.

————. *That the People Might Live*. New York: Oxford Univ. Press, 1997.

Welter, Barbara. "The Cult of True Womanhood: 1820–1860." *American Quarterly* (Summer 1966): 151–74.

"We're Turning Red." *Bartlesville Magnet* (Sept. 20, 1900): n.p.

Wexler, Laura. "Tender Violence: Literary Eavesdropping, Domestic Fiction, and Educational Reform." *Yale Journal of Criticism* 5.1 (1991): 151–87.

Wheeler, Edward L. *Uplifting the Race: The Black Minister in the New South, 1865–1902*. Lanham, MD: Univ. Press of America, 1986.

White, Richard. *The Middle Ground: Indians, Empires, and Republics in the Great Lakes Region, 1650–1815*. New York: Cambridge Univ. Press, 1991.

Wicasa, Wambdi. "Covenant Versus Contract." 1974. Feb. 1, 2000. http.//www.bluecloud.org/dakota.html.

Wiget, Andrew, ed. *Dictionary of Native American Literature*. New York: Garland Publishing, 1994.

Wilkins, David E. "The Cloaking of Justice: The Supreme Court's Role in the Application of Western Law to America's Indigenous Peoples." *Wicazō Sa Review* (Spring 1994): 1–13.

Willis, Susan. "I Shop Therefore I Am: Is There a Place for Afro-American Culture in Commodity Culture?" *Changing Our Own Words: Essays on Criticism, Theory, and Writing by Black Women*. Ed. Cheryl A. Wall. New Brunswick: Rutgers Univ. Press, 1989. 173–95.

Woloch, Nancy. *Women and the American Experience*. New York: Alfred A. Knopf, 1984.

Womack, Craig S. *Red on Red: Native American Literary Separatism*. Minneapolis: Univ. of Minnesota Press, 1999.

"Women of Hope." *Study Guide for the Native American/Hawaiian Women of Hope*. Poster series of the Bread and Roses Culture Project, 1997. Jan. 12, 2000. http://www.rodenter.com/nativeam/nativewom/htm.

"Women's Issues." *The Wind River Rendezvous*. July 15, 1998. http://www.bluecloud.org/dakota.html.

Woodward, Grace Steele. *The Cherokees*. Norman: Univ. of Oklahoma Press, 1963.

Woody, Thomas. *A History of Women's Education in the United States*. Vol. 1. New York: Science Press, 1929.

Wright, Ronald. *Stolen Continents: The "New World" Through Indian Eyes Since 1492*. Toronto: Viking Penguin Press, 1991.

Young, Mary. "The Cherokee Nation: Mirror of the Republic." *American Quarterly* 33 (Winter 1981): 501–23.

Zinn, Howard. *A People's History of the United States*. New York: HarperCollins Publishers, 1990.

Unpublished Works

Adams, David W. "The Federal Indian Boarding School: A Study of Environment and Response, 1879–1918." Diss. Indiana Univ., 1975. Bell, Genevieve. "Telling Stories out of School: Remembering the Carlisle Indian Industrial School, 1879–1918." Diss. Stanford Univ., 1998.

Brudvig, Jon L. "Bridging the Cultural Divide: American Indians at Hampton Institute, 1878–1923." Diss. College of William and Mary, 1996.

Bullock, Kathy. "Worship and the Black Church Experience." Unpublished essay, 1999.

DiNova, Joanne. "Spiralling Webs of Relation: Movements towards an Indigenist Criticism."Diss. Univ. of Waterloo (Ontario), 2003.

Duggan, Betty J. Being Cherokee in a White World: The Ethnic Persistence of a Post-Removal American Indian Enclave. Diss. Univ. of Tennessee, 1998.

Justice, Daniel Heath. "Our Fire Survives the Storm: Removal, Rebellion, and Tribal Nationalism in the Cherokee Literary Tradition." Diss. Univ. of Nebraska, Lincoln, 2002.

Monteith, Carmaleta Littlejohn. "The Role of the Scribe in Eastern Cherokee Society, 1821–1985." Diss. Emory Univ., 1985.

Parker, Sara Gwenyth. "The Transformation of Cherokee Appalachia." Diss. Univ. of California, Berkeley, 1991. 9228802.

Tingey, Joseph Willard. "Indians and Blacks Together: An Experiment in Biracial Education at Hampton Institute, 1878–1923." Diss. Columbia Univ., 1978.

Index